A River
in the
Desert

A River in the Desert

12 Retreats for Women's Groups

ELLEN SHEPARD

Abingdon Press
Nashville

A RIVER IN THE DESERT
12 Retreats for Women's Groups

Copyright © 2001 by Abingdon Press

This book is printed on recycled, acid-free, elemental-chlorine–free paper.

Library of Congress Cataloging-in-Publication Data

Shepard, Ellen, 1954-
    A river in the desert : 12 retreats for women's groups / Ellen Shepard.
       p. cm.
    Includes bibliographical references.
    ISBN 0-687-05090-1 (alk. paper)
    1. Christian women—Religious life. 2. Retreats for women—Methodist Church. I. Title.

BV4844 .S532 2001
269'.643—dc21

00-067649

01 02 03 04 05 06 07 08 09 10—10 9 8 7 6 5 4 3 2 1
MANUFACTURED IN THE UNITED STATES OF AMERICA

For Kelly, my best friend and soul mate;
for my children: Travis, Martin, and Meg;
and for Mama, who calls me her "shining star"

*If you ever begin looking for the God
that is all around you, every moment becomes a prayer.*
—Frank Bianco

Contents

Acknowledgments

First and foremost, I would like to thank the women of St. Luke's United Methodist Church, Houston, Texas. You are the most loving, encouraging, willing, creative, and dedicated women with whom I have worked. You have allowed me to follow my heart and explore the spiritual world through our retreats together. I thank God for you!

This book never would have been written if it were not for a wonderful retreat center in Round Top, Texas, whose owners have followed God's call and provided a bit of heaven on earth. Thanks, Euphanel and Nick!

I also would like to thank those who regularly assist with our retreats. Your talents add a great dimension to our work: Nancy, who knows me better than I know myself; Colleen, my dear friend and "songbird"; Marlys, our "enhancer"; and Laura, Chris, Annie, L. V., and Mary Jane, who kept things sane and organized at our office.

I also want to thank my wonderfully patient family, who have allowed me the privilege of going on many retreats and who have endured the writing and rewriting of this manuscript. I love you all!

In addition, my new church family at Roswell United Methodist Church has added an increased depth of spiritual insight and Christlike love. I praise God that we are in ministry together!

Foreword

Drinking Deeply from the River in the Desert

It has been said that the three major killers in today's culture are calendars, telephones, and clocks—the tyranny of an accelerated life. What can we do about these adversaries? How do we cope? How do we celebrate life and not just endure or survive it? Is there life after stress? How do we withstand the onslaught, the pressures, the demands? Let me make three suggestions.

1. Travel light. Decide what is really important to you and focus your energy on those things. We can't do everything, so we have to decide what really matters and weed out all the rest. A short time before his death, Dr. William Barclay made this amazing statement: "I'm an old man. I have lived a long time, and over the years I have learned that there are very few things in life that really matter. But those things matter intensely." Isn't that a great quotation?

So often we get uptight and stressed out over things that do not really matter that much. Well, what *are* the things that matter intensely? Love, honesty, integrity, fairness, truth, compassion, commitment, loyalty, forgiveness—these are the things that really matter. Now, wait a minute. Where have we heard these words before? At church! Perhaps we've heard them at home as well, but even then their origins probably can be traced back to the church. The church, or faith community, by the grace of God, shows us how to center in and focus and travel light. God, through the presence and power of the Holy Spirit and through the witness of the Scriptures, shows us over and over the things that really matter. When we make those things our priorities, we can travel light.

2. Take one step at a time. Do one thing at a time. Love one day at a time. In an old elementary reader there was a story about a clock that had stopped. The clock figured out that it would have to tick more than thirty-one million times in one year. Overwhelmed by that thought, the clock just "up and quit" until someone reminded the clock that it wouldn't have to tick them all at once—just one tick at a time.

Jesus talked about this concept in the Sermon on the Mount when he told us not to worry about health, food, or the future (Matthew 6:25-34). We need to take one day at a time, one thing at a time, one step at a time. By the way, did you know that the phrase *do not fear* appears in the Bible 365 times? That's one *fear not* for each day of the year!

3. Relax your soul in God. Jesus' parable of the seed speaks to this concept (Mark 4:1-9). The idea is to sow the seed the best you can and trust God to bring the harvest. It does not matter if the odds are against you. It does not matter if things may seem hopeless. It does not matter how bleak the outlook may be. Don't worry about that. Just sow the seed. Do your best and trust God for the rest.

These three ideas are what this book is about: traveling light, taking one step at a time, and relaxing your soul in God. The author, Ellen Shepard, is my good friend. We worked together for many years and I had the unique privilege of watching her live her faith daily in her relationships with family, friends, and colleagues. She has many remarkable abilities, but one of her finest is leading retreats for women. As God's instrument of love and grace, she can lead people to slow down and focus in and drink deeply from the "river in the desert."

Jim Moore
St. Luke's United Methodist Church
Houston, Texas

Preface

◆

Retreat—the very word takes me to a wonderful place called Epworth by the Sea, a retreat center on St. Simons Island, Georgia . . . or to a holy place in Round Top, Texas . . . or to the mountains of North Carolina . . . or to the beach . . . or to the lake . . . or to my home.

Retreat. As I sit in "Annie's Room," located in a retreat center in Round Top, Texas, and contemplate the ministry of retreats and retreating, I can hardly begin to fathom the changes that I have experienced and witnessed for myself and others during retreats. A retreat is a time set apart to explore, deepen, unclutter, and set straight one's spiritual path. It is a time for deepening and strengthening the relationships that we have with others through Christ. It is a time and a place for new beginnings, farewells, and renewal. A retreat is a process that gives rhythm to the life cycle of the journey of God's people.

As women, we are seekers. We seek the Word as it relates to our lives. We seek God's presence and God's guidance. We seek to understand ourselves and those with whom we are in relationship. We seek time and space and the ability to order our world. We seek experiences that we can share with other "pilgrims" on the journey of becoming women of God. We seek an understanding of the wholeness that exploring our spirituality brings. We seek "spiritual mothers" who lead and guide and question us into faith.

Why "a river in the desert"? It comes from Isaiah 43:19. Our lives are filled with babies and briefcases, dishes and duties. We need to punctuate our lives with moments of authenticity, surround ourselves with the love of God, and grow into that love in deeper and more meaningful ways. Sometimes those ways are as likely as a river in the desert! A retreat is an opportunity for all of these things—and many others—to happen. May God bless you richly as you experience the retreats in this book.

Ellen Shepard
Annie's Room
Round Top, Texas

How to Use This Book

◆

Planning and Preparing for Retreats

Welcome to your journey into the "river in the desert." This book is designed for women who seek spiritual growth—women of all ages, stages, and interests; women who have experienced retreats before and women who do not know what retreats can be; women who lead retreats and women who attend retreats; women who go away on retreat and women who stay home to retreat; women who seek intentional growth and who journey to become the women God intends them to be. This book is for you—the extraordinary woman God made.

This very book has been a journey in itself. It began in the fall of 1989 with a small group of women in a church in Houston, Texas, who wanted to go on a retreat. Since that time, hundreds of women in that church have been shaped and molded by God's seeking Spirit while on retreat. This book is a compilation of the many retreats that I have been a part of since that first fall afternoon. Before you begin thumbing through the retreats, let me answer some of the questions you may have about retreats in general as well as the particular retreats in this book.

What exactly is a retreat?
• It is time set apart to explore and deepen one's spiritual path.
• It can be an opportunity to develop and strengthen community with others.
• It can be a place of beginnings or renewal or struggle.
• It is a process that gives rhythm to the life of a journeying Christian.

The key word for me is *process*. A retreat is part of the spiritual life process of becoming the women God intends us to be. Can this spiritual life process happen without a retreat? Certainly. However, within the circle of a retreat, there seems to be a time and space away from the distractions of daily life that often inhibit spiritual growth. A retreat provides the opportunity for life, experience, and purpose to come together. This coming together is *retreat*.

As retreat leader, where do I begin?
Begin by selecting a retreat/topic. Let it pull at your heart strings. Mull it over. Pray about it. Let it evolve. When you have decided on your retreat/topic, invite four or five women of different ages and life experiences to be your design team. This team will provide the framework for the retreat. Together you will choose a time, select a site, publicize the retreat, recruit participants, make nametags, plan meals, prepare any necessary materials such as journals or retreat bags, and evaluate your experience. I have always found it helpful to include someone on the design team who has never attended a retreat. Her fresh eyes will enhance the retreat for everyone.

When and where should the retreat take place?
Your retreat can take place in a retreat center (check your denominational headquarters for retreat locations), in your church, in a hotel, in a community center, or in any other number of locations—including your own home! Are you planning a half-day or one-day retreat, a weekend retreat, or a retreat that takes place over a series of weeks? Do you prefer rustic and primitive settings? Would you like to camp? Do you prefer to be in a lovely home or hotel? Is it impossible for you to get away now? Can you turn your phone off for several hours at a time? There is not a definitive answer. The length and location of your retreat should meet the needs, schedules, and interests of your particular group. The right time and place are what you want them to be!

How many people can participate?
Any number of people can retreat—from one to one hundred or more. It has been my experience that a good number for a weekend retreat is forty to forty-seven. This number provides a lot of diversity yet allows for plenty of intimacy. Let me say, however, that there have been many successful retreats with hundreds of women

attending. You can better determine the number of desired participants after setting the goals for your retreat. Always remember that community is the heart of any retreat. We share the responsibility of accompanying and guiding one another on our spiritual journeys.

Are the retreats in this book easy to lead?

Yes! The retreats in this book have been designed to be "leader friendly"—from suggested schedules to easy-to-follow leader cues and instructions. For starters, all notes to the leader—which are not meant to be spoken aloud—appear in italics. All words to be spoken aloud by the leader appear in regular type.

The leader cue **Talk** identifies segments of material to be presented by the leader; these words are meant to be guidelines, not scripts. The leader should become very familiar with the words in these sections prior to the retreat so that she may rephrase them in her own words.

Another helpful leader cue is the clock icon, 🕐, which is used throughout the book to represent a pause—a time for one individual or all gathered to take whatever action is indicated, whether it is reading a Bible passage aloud, journaling, discussing a question or thought with a partner or the full group, reflecting, or engaging in some other activity. The clef icon, 𝄞, is also a helpful clue that is used to indicate a time for singing or listening to a song. If a time limit is given, remember that it is only a suggestion; the leader should monitor the participants and be prepared to allow more time or cut time as necessary. When it comes to schedules and time-keeping, I have found it helpful to ask participants to leave their watches at home and trust the leader and/or design team to lead them during their time together.

What format will we follow?

The format and specific components of any retreat should support the goals and objectives of the those planning the retreat. In other words, there are no hard-and-fast rules. Flexibility and creativity are essential to successful retreat planning. There are, however, some core components included in most spiritual retreat formats, such as discussion, reflective exercises, Bible study, and worship. The retreats in this book follow a similar format, which you may revise as necessary to meet the needs and desires of your particular group. Basic components for both one-day and weekend retreats include the following:

Get-to-know-you games—games or activities that help break the ice so that participants can get to know one another for a first time or, if already acquainted, on a different level. It is a good practice to do one of these activities before each of the first two or three sessions. A few suggestions follow. You will think of others. There are also many resource books, written for this very purpose, available at your local library or bookstore.

- Divide into small groups according to:

  shoe size
  zip code
  neighborhood, community, or geographic area
  eye color
  hair color
  birth month
  favorite season
  favorite day of the week
  number of suitcases or items you brought
  number of pairs of shoes you brought
  and so forth

- Discuss any of the following in pairs or small groups:

  Who was the tower of strength in your family when you were growing up?
  What room in your home was your favorite as a child?
  Name a Christmas present you remember from your childhood.
  A time I got into trouble was when . . .
  My favorite childhood book was . . .
  When I was a child, I wanted to be . . .

A fun thing my family did was . . .
You'd be surprised to know that I . . .
The chore I hate doing most is . . .
My favorite season is . . . because . . .
and so forth

Remember, the purpose of icebreakers is to get people talking and sharing. This is only surface-level sharing, but it can lead to a greater depth of sharing later. Let it be fun and relaxed.

Session—a block of time dedicated to a chosen subject matter or topic, usually lasting from one to one-and-a-half hours. Generally, there are three sessions in a one-day retreat and four sessions in a weekend retreat.
Leaders need to be intentional about opening and closing each session. Clear beginnings and endings are especially helpful with large groups. Specific suggestions for using music, quotations, poetry, or questions to open and close each session appear under the headings **Open** and **Close**.
What happens between **Open** and **Close** will vary from session to session and retreat to retreat. During this time, any combination of the following may take place:

- *Talk*—a presentation time when the leader shares information and material with the group. As stated previously, the leader should become very familiar with the words in these sections prior to the retreat so that she may rephrase them in her own words.
- *Scripture Surf*—a time set apart for reading and discussing numerous Bible verses related to the chosen topic. This usually takes place in small groups during a session, but it also can be an individual activity. Do not skip this part of the retreat, for this is the biblical foundation for growth.
- *Journaling*—reflective writing in response to a particular subject, question, theme, situation, or experience. The value, purpose, and details of journaling are discussed at length in several of the retreat models. Journaling helps provide a chronicle of time, questions, struggles, and growth. As a retreat leader, it has been my custom to provide a special journal for each participant. Journals of all kinds can be bought and embellished, hand made from scratch, or creatively put together with the use of a computer program. The desired intent is for the participants to continue using their journals as spiritual tools once the retreat is over. If you are expecting a large group, you may ask each participant to bring a blank journal with her.
- *Explore*—an activity that takes the retreat experience to a deeper, more personal level with other participants—either in a small group or the full group.

Morning Watch—a block of time during a weekend retreat, ranging from thirty to sixty minutes, set apart for individual quiet time. It can be as simple and unstructured as a gentle invitation to "go and watch the morning with your Lord." Or it can be a guided meditation that includes scripture and directed reading. This is often the most important part of the retreat and the one component that many participants choose to weave into their daily lives. Morning Watch takes place first thing each day.

Worship—an intentional, short celebration of our faith and life in Christ together that includes music, scripture, message, and wonder. Worship can take place outside or inside; in a barn or by a lake; on the ground or in chairs. This part of the retreat is simply time set aside to worship and praise God. For one-day retreats, worship usually takes place at the close of the retreat; for weekend retreats, worship generally takes place at the close of each day.

When should we divide into small groups?
If your group is larger than fifty, you may want to think about dividing into groups of eight to ten women during the sessions to develop community. Prior to the retreat, recruit certain participants to be small-group leaders, who will work with their groups after the session material has been presented to the full group. You will want to conduct a training session before the retreat, providing clear goals and objectives for the small-group leaders. The design team can float through each of the small groups during the retreat to see how things are going and provide assistance as necessary.

Should we include free time?
We live such scheduled, busy lives. A retreat is the perfect opportunity to let your schedule be flexible and

free-flowing. Try to provide a good balance in terms of free time. This may be the only opportunity someone has to be alone, to take a nap, to write, or to walk in the woods. Free time works better after the second session, when relationships are forming and natural conversation is beginning to take place among the participants.

What about doing a craft or art project during the retreat?

I have found that participants often share with one another in even greater degrees during some sort of creative expression exercise. You may choose to allocate a block of time to a craft or art project, but the project should not be mandatory for the group. Some ideas include making a wreath from dried flowers (perhaps from plants that are included in the Bible), making a Christmas ornament or other seasonal remembrance, making bookmarks, decorating T-shirts, having someone teach watercolor, and so forth. The list is absolutely endless, and many participants will enjoy the creativity. Those who do not wish to participate should have the option of free time or quiet time.

What kind of supplies will we need?

Although the specific supplies required vary from retreat to retreat (see the supplies and materials list provided for each retreat), here is a list of general supplies you will need:

To be brought by the leader

- nametags—Make them special and relevant to your theme.
- cassettes/CDs—Music is a must on retreats. If you are not fortunate enough to have a musician in your group, a simple CD or cassette can add a depth of dimension to your time together. Make sure the music you choose includes meditative as well as high-energy selections. Browse through your favorite Christian bookstore for favorites. Ask friends for their favorites. Remember that it is helpful to include some instrumental selections only—perhaps unfamiliar tunes—so that the words are not a distraction to the participants.
- cassette/CD player—Are your batteries fresh? An extension cord may be necessary.
- newsprint and marker, chalkboard and chalk, or dry erase board and marker—Many retreat centers, churches, and other locations have these on hand. Check in advance.
- hymnals or other songbooks—See the suggested songs and hymns referenced throughout each retreat.
- white pillar candle and matches or lighter—Wonderful for a worship table.
- books and/or other resources required for the retreat—See the supplies and materials list provided for each retreat.
- paper, stationery, envelopes, pens, pencils—Consider the particular needs of the retreat you have chosen. Although each participant should bring a pen or pencil (see below), it is always a good idea to keep an ample supply of these on hand.
- medium-size basket—This can be handy for holding any number of things, such as pens, pencils, nametags, and so forth.

To be brought by each participant

- Bible—for study and worship. (The leader/design team may want to bring some extras.)
- Quilt or blanket—for sitting or resting or setting a mood.
- Pen or pencil—for taking notes!

What about food?

Most churches and retreat centers have full kitchen facilities. Some have only "bare bones" kitchens. Research where you are going. What are your options? Can you have meals catered? Do you have a design team member who can plan the meals and direct teams to implement them? Could your church kitchen staff or volunteers prepare the food? What about inviting men (husbands, fathers, brothers, friends) to come along and serve as chefs? Be creative, and remember that great community happens in the kitchen!

It also is a good idea to invite participants to bring snacks to place on a "sharing table." Then, during breaks, there will always be something good to discover and enjoy together. *Note:* You may want to invite the women to bring their own coffee mugs—or provide a mug for each of them as a special retreat remembrance. This will help you be good stewards by reducing the amount of trash.

What about music?

Music speaks to the heart as nothing else can. It clarifies, moves, and leads us into new places. Second only to Morning Watch, music is a key ingredient of all retreats. Is there someone in your group who plays the guitar? How about the piano or keyboard? Is there someone who could lead singing? Someone who could sing a solo? Look around, ask questions, and recruit individuals to help. You will want to prepare song sheets or bring hymnals or songbooks to use for group singing. If you use song sheets, be sure that the church's music license number is recorded on each sheet.

There is a CD available with original music written and performed by Colleen Haley specifically for use with the retreats in this book. You will find it quite wonderful and helpful.

From the Heart
Colleen Haley
608 Post Oak Road
Fredericksburg, Texas 78628
830-997-7679

What should happen after the retreat?

It is sometimes valuable to gather the participants together for a postretreat event. You might want to sing any special retreat songs and, in small groups, discuss what elements of the retreat participants have woven into their personal lives, what difference the retreat experience has made in their lives, and how they have felt closer to God because of this experience. This becomes a time to reaffirm any and all of the life-work that happened on the retreat. It also is a good time to reconnect friendships that were started on the retreat. If a postretreat gathering is not an option for your group, you might consider sending a letter that reminds the women of the retreat experience and encourages them in their walk of faith. The letter also might include a special prayer or the words to a favorite retreat song.

Retreat Overviews

◆

One-Day Retreats

Seeking Growth
Women of all ages will grow spiritually through an inventory of their current spiritual habits and experiences, leading to the identification of five holy habits that will enrich the journey of faith.

The Tapestry
We all come into God's presence through different life situations and experiences. This model for growth identifies our need for one another and develops our sense of wonder through the presence of God.

Discovering My Spiritual Gifts
"But I don't have any spiritual gifts!" Perhaps this is one of the most common statements made by persons when asked about their spiritual gifts. As they define and explore spiritual gifts together, individuals are led through a process of naming, claiming, and using the gifts God has given each of them.

Sacred Listening
Holy silence—listening for God's guidance in wonder, faith, hope, pain, and adoration. Participants' "quiet eyes" are turned to the Holy One as they learn the habit of holy listening through methods that include the use of the Bible, journaling, music, and spiritual friends. This retreat is intended for those whose prayer life is just beginning to broaden.

Weekend Retreats

Retreats Based on Themes

Getting First Things First—and Keeping Them There! (Priorities)
One of the hardest things about life today is the busyness in which we all are caught. This model helps women simplify their daily lives as they learn how to put what is truly important first in their lives. Participants will explore holy habits and healthy balance that will help them keep God first in their lives.

Come to the Well (God Meets Our Needs)
The story of the woman at the well, found in the fourth chapter of John, is the foundation of this study. We all come to God's well—whether it is to take something or to bring something. Whichever it is, God will and does provide.

Windows of Prayer (Prayer)
After a historical presentation of the spiritual discipline of prayer, participants explore various personalities and prayer styles and their meaning for our lives. Prayer as process, method, and journey are considered, and the powerful benefits of personal transformation are brought into focus.

Becoming: A Journey of Spirituality for Women (Spirituality)
"I'm not finished yet!" we often explain. We all know that we are never quite finished. The women who journey through this retreat will outline their past and current spirituality to identify trends and styles that can enhance and develop their future spiritual growth.

Retreats Based on Books

God's Simple Path
This retreat is based on Mother Teresa's book *A Simple Path*, and Macrina Wiederkehr's *Song of the Seed: A*

Monastic Way of Tending the Soul. Participants work through the parable of the sower, found in Matthew 13, and search to find places of fertile soil in which to tend a deep yearning for God and nurture their own spirituality.

Power for Living

This retreat is based on the book *Do What You Have the Power to Do* by Helen Bruch Pearson. Participants study several biblical women face-to-face and heart-to-heart. The inner strength of the individual is identified as a tool for nurturing personal spiritual growth.

If Only I Had More Time!

This retreat model is a compilation of reflections and journal writings after reading *Ordering Your Private World* by Gordon MacDonald. Participants will find it helpful to read the book either before or after this retreat. Methods of prioritizing one's own life in order to find deeper meaning and a closer walk with God are outlined.

Joyful Heart—Dancing Spirit

This can be an intergenerational women's retreat. Based on Maria Harris's book *Dance of the Spirit,* the retreat helps participants step back and take a deep, penetrating look at their spiritual lives. At its conclusion, every woman will learn to embrace her own unique spirituality.

One-Day

Retreats

The One-Day Retreat Model

E ach of the retreats in this section is intended to be used as a one-day retreat for women. Although the retreats are designed and written for *groups* of women, individuals also may use them as personal one-day retreats, making adjustments in the schedule and instructions as appropriate. Whether alone or in a group, each participant will be challenged in much the same way as one is challenged on a weekend retreat. This model works well for those who find it difficult to get away overnight. These retreats may also be adapted for use as "mini" weekend retreats—an evening and half day. Find the time model that works well for you and adjust the schedule accordingly.

Preparing for a one-day retreat is as important and essential as preparing for a weekend retreat. You will want to read "How to Use This Book: Planning and Preparing for Retreats" thoroughly. Nametags and journals are especially important during a one-day retreat. Providing nametags helps participants get to know one another and fosters name recognition. Journals help the women capture the stirrings that move within so that their questions and thoughts may be saved for other days. Journaling is also a wonderful way to keep the spirit of the day alive for another time. The entire event needs to be "framed"—remembered and revisited as a whole experience.

Before the retreat, prepare nametags, journals, and song sheets; gather the necessary supplies and materials; and consider any special needs of participants. See that the retreat space is cozy, appropriately arranged, and ready for you to begin as soon as the participants arrive. A member of the design team may want to arrive the night before to have ample time for setting up. Here are some questions to ask yourself:

- Will you be sitting on the floor or on couches, or will you be using tables and chairs or back jacks?
- Where will your worship space be? Do you need to create an altar? Will you need candles, flowers, a Bible, a special cloth? (I sometimes have used an altar cloth that participants can write their names on with a permanent ink pen. This can become a permanent worship cloth for future retreats.)
- What will the participants see, hear, and experience the moment they arrive?

The following one-day retreat schedule will help you plan your retreat; feel free to make revisions and additions to the schedule to meet your needs. Remember that the time allotments are estimates and are offered as suggestions.

9:00 Arrival and Welcome. Personally greet each participant as she arrives and direct her toward the nametag table. Make sure that the members of the design team visit with every person upon arrival as well. All should feel welcome. Be especially eager to help those who come without a special friend to feel welcome and part of the activities. Remember that participants will want to know where restrooms and telephones are located. They also will want to know that there is a procedure for emergency notification. Begin the get-acquainted game as soon as most of the participants have arrived.

9:30 Session 1. Begin on time! Start with a warm welcome and a powerful opening.

11:00 Break. Allow time for a restroom break and for stretching and talking.

11:15 Session 2. Begin on time!

12:15 Lunch and Free Time. Make sure everyone is aware of the procedure and time frame for lunch. What else may participants do during this time? How will you make sure that "newcomers" are sitting with "old timers"?

1:30 Session 3. Begin on time!

3:00 Closing Worship. Timing is critical. Be sure that you "take the pulse" of your group. Is there some element that you may need to add or delete as a result of the day? Be aware of what is going on with the participants.

4:00 Return Home. Thank each person for her participation and make any necessary closing remarks. After the retreat, the design team will need to clean, pack up, and evaluate the day.

Seeking Growth

◆

OVERVIEW
Women of all ages will grow spiritually through an inventory of their current spiritual habits and experiences, leading to the identification of five holy habits that will enrich the journey of faith.

PREPARING FOR THE RETREAT
- Review "How to Use This Book: Planning and Preparing for Retreats" (pp. 11-15).
- Assemble the design team.
- Read through the retreat; make revisions and additions as appropriate for your group or situation.
- Pray for the retreat.
- Advertise; invite and recruit participants.
- Send correspondence noting details of the retreat. (Be sure to let participants know what items they are to bring.)
- Gather the supplies.

SUPPLIES AND MATERIALS
To be brought by the leader
- nametags
- cassette/CD player
- cassettes/CDs, including meditative music
- hymnals or other songbooks (see suggested hymns and songs throughout the retreat)
- newsprint and marker, chalkboard and chalk, or dry erase board and marker
- white pillar candle and matches or lighter
- paper, pens, pencils
- a journal for each participant (Note: For large groups, ask participants to bring their own.)
- medium-size basket
- *Opening to God,* by Carolyn Stahl (optional, see Session 2)
- words to the hymn "Take My Life, and Let It Be" (see Session 3)
- stationery and envelopes (see Closing Worship)

To be brought by each participant
- Bible
- quilt or blanket
- pen or pencil

The Retreat

ARRIVAL AND WELCOME   (9:00–9:30)

See pages 12-13 for arrival and welcome suggestions. Once everyone has arrived and received a nametag, begin a get-acquainted game or activity. 🕐

SESSION 1   (9:30–11:00)

Open   (15 minutes)

Sing together "This Is the Day" and "Swing Low, Sweet Chariot" (add motions if you like). 𝄞

If possible, play the selection "The Lord Will Provide," included on Colleen Haley's CD From the Heart *(see p. 15), or choose another appropriate song. Invite the participants to reflect on the words as they listen.* 𝄞

Read aloud the following scripture verses:

Hear, O Israel: The LORD our God, the LORD is one. Love the LORD your God with all your heart and with all your soul and with all your strength. These commandments I give you today are to be upon your hearts. (Deuteronomy 6:4-6)

Talk   (5 minutes)

Read this section several times until you can paraphrase and present it in your own speaking style.

It's been said that life is made up of tiny moments. That's a profound statement; you see, when we remember, we think of moments in time, suspended in days and months and years. The moments might be happy, sad, ordinary, or fleeting; of great significance or of little interest to anyone but you. These are some of the heartwarming moments shared by the author of this retreat *(feel free to replace the author's memories with your own fond memories):*

- riding in my friend Becky's VW Bug on a beautiful spring day
- holding my babies for the first time
- having a kitten fall asleep on my lap
- being with my father and father-in-law when they died
- marching in the processional on the day of my graduation from seminary
- meeting the eye of a friend and trying to stifle the giggles
- lying in the back of a red pickup truck with my daughter Meg in the springtime, watching the clouds and talking about remembering that very moment all of our lives
- watching a glorious summer sunset on the bay of South Padre Island with my husband
- going to the beach in February with a friend and being wrapped up in blankets, freezing cold and still not wanting to leave

Do you get my drift? It's the moments of our lives that we hold so close. Life is made up of tiny moments.

Journal   (30–35 minutes)

Let's take time to journal. Write about your happiest moment in the last three or four weeks. What made it your happiest moment? Who was involved? What kind of day was it? Was there anything spiritual about that moment? We'll pause for about ten minutes. 🕐 Now write about your saddest or most anxious moment in the last three or four weeks. What made it your saddest/most anxious moment? Who was involved? What kind of day was it? Was there anything spiritual about that moment? We'll pause for another ten minutes. 🕐

Listen to the truth in these quotations:

There can be no happiness if the things we belive in are different from the things we do.
—Freya Stark

In a society that judges self-worth on productivity, it's no wonder we fall prey to the misconception that the more we do, the more we're worth. —Ellen Sue Stern

Now spend another ten minutes journaling about where you find yourself in your spiritual journey. What do you need in order to "jump-start" your spirituality? 🕐

Talk   (5 minutes)

Read this section several times until you can paraphrase and present it in your own speaking style—with the exception of the scripture passage, which is to be read aloud.

Listen to these words of wisdom:

Look at the birds of the air; they do not sow or reap or store away in barns, and yet your heavenly Father feeds them. Are you not much more valuable than they? Who of you by worrying can add a single hour to his life?

And why do you worry about clothes? See how the lilies of the fields grow. They do not labor or spin. Yet I tell you that not even Solomon in all his splendor was dressed like one of these. If that is how God clothes the grass of the field, which is here today and tomorrow is thrown into the fire, will he not much more clothe you, O you of little faith? So do not worry saying, "What shall we eat?" or "What shall we drink?" or "What shall we wear?" For the pagans run after all these things, and your heavenly Father knows that you need them. But seek first his kingdom and his righteousness, and all these things will be given to you as well. Therefore do not worry about tomorrow, for tomorrow will worry about itself. Each day has enough trouble of its own. (Matthew 6:26-34)

In other words, if you pray, why worry? And if you worry, why pray? We must immerse ourselves into the silence that leads us into the presence of God. It is in the silence that we can begin to pray.

Scripture Surf   (30 minutes)

Write the following scripture references and the statement below on newsprint, a chalkboard, or a dry erase board; or instruct participants to write them in their journals as you read the references and statement aloud.

In silence, "scripture surf" the following verses:

Luke 15:1-32	The Parable of the Loving Father
Ephesians 1:3-14	Spiritual Blessing in Christ
Colossians 1:9-23	Prayer
Mark 8:1-21	Jesus Feeds the Four Thousand

Read each passage silently. Meditate on the words. Then journal as God's Great Spirit leads you. As you do this, reflect on this statement and its meaning for you:

In losing, we find, we rejoice, and we are filled with joy.

You may record your reflections on this statement in your journal as well, if you wish. We'll come back together in twenty-five minutes. 🕐

Close   (5 minutes)

Sing together the hymn "Spirit of the Living God." 🎼

BREAK   (11:00–11:15)

SESSION 2   (11:15–12:15)

Open   (10 minutes)

As you regroup for your second session, play the selection "Put Your Life in His Hands," included on Colleen Haley's CD From the Heart, *or choose another appropriate song.*

Welcome back. Take a minute to break into pairs. 🕐 Now, take turns sharing with each other some of the images that came to mind as you relived a recent happy and sad or anxious moment of your life. We'll allow three to five minutes for this, and then we'll come back together. 🕐

Talk   (20 minutes)

Read this section several times until you can paraphrase and present it in your own speaking style.

We call ourselves Christians. As Christians, followers of Christ, we need to grow. Just as babies grow, so also we must grow. If we aren't growing, we aren't living our faith. Yet it is acceptable—in fact, it is normal—in most of our communities that we "get comfortable." When we are comfortable, we don't grow spiritually. We don't put ourselves in the places where God may gently—or not so gently—stretch us. We know that in order to grow physically, we need to eat, exercise, rest, learn, socialize, and love. But what do we need to grow spiritually? We need some of the same things to grow in our spiritual life; we must eat, love, rest, and learn. But we also must incorporate a new way of thinking into our everyday living. We must trust God completely for all things. Spiritual growth comes at a great cost; we must sacrifice every-thing so that we do not become distracted or have any false gods.

Here are a few misconceptions about spiritual growth:

- Growth in the Spirit has nothing to do with who you are; rather, it has to do with how you act. (The truth is, spiritual growth has everything to do with who you are!)
- We need more money or time or relationships or a bigger house in order to grow spiritually. (Colossians 2:9-19 tells us that we are complete in Christ.)
- Growth in the Spirit earns us more love. (God already loves each of us fully. Spiritual growth doesn't help God love us more. Romans 5:8 tells us, "While we were still sinners, Christ died for us.")
- Spiritual growth comes with time. (Actually, spiritual growth has nothing to do with time. It is possible to be a Christian for a long time and still be a spiritual infant. Age has nothing to do with it.)
- Spiritual growth requires volunteer work. (As we learn from Matthew 7:21-23, you can over-dose on Christian activity and still be lost.)

Spiritual growth changes our behavior. Did you get that? Let me say it again: Spiritual growth changes our behavior! It is an obedience issue. In 2 Peter 3:18 we read, "Grow in the grace and knowledge of our Lord and Savior Jesus Christ." What is the goal of this spiritual growth? The glory of God. In fact, the goal of everything we do should be the glory of God. If we fail to glo-rify God, we fail to grow spiritually.

Read 1 Peter 2:4-12 silently as I read it aloud. *Read the passage aloud now.* 🕐 Peter was writ-ing to people who were without direction. Are you without direction? We all are at times. One woman keeps a smooth black stone on her desk to remind her to strive to be a living stone, chosen and precious to God, glorifying God.

Why were we created? We were created to glorify God in our families, our jobs, our schools, our marriages, our friendships, our exercise, and in all areas of our lives. Read 1 Corinthians 10:31 silently as I read it aloud. *Read the verse aloud now.* 🕐 Can you attach that statement to everything that you do? Can you develop a passion for God's glory? Let's pray the Lord's Prayer aloud right now. Be conscious of the words *thy will* as you say them. Ask yourself, "Do I really mean that?" 🕐

If time permits, ask a volunteer to read aloud the scripture verse enclosed in parentheses after you read each of the following points; otherwise, suggest that participants record the references for later study.

Why is spiritual growth absolutely necessary?

- It is the only way to have real stability—to know who we are, where we are going, and who we belong to. (James 1:5; Ephesians 4:13)
- Spiritual growth is guaranteed, but it is not automatic. (Romans 11:36)

- Spiritual growth allows us to perceive God correctly. (1 Corinthians 2:15)
- Spiritual growth brings peace—no matter what the circumstances. (Think of Mother Teresa, Dietrich Bonhoffer, Henri Nouwen, Corrie Ten Boom, Anne Frank, Dorothy Day, and others.)

The world offers bandages for spiritual growth. In other words, we cover ourselves with things that distract us from focusing on our spiritual growth. There are many. Can you think of some? *Pause for at least twenty seconds; then continue.* ⏱

Did your mental list include television, shopping, food, money, cars, hobbies, friends, magazines, books? None of these things is bad in and of itself. However, if we allow any one of them to control who we are and what we do, we have lost our focus on God.

Someone once gave this analogy: Is it OK for you to cheat on your spouse or boyfriend? Of course not. Similarly, we can't "cheat" on God either! As growing women on spiritual journeys, we need to spend quality time devoted to our Christian formation—time with God, Creator of all.

Journal   (10 minutes)

Read John 15:1-17. Then paraphrase it—rewrite it in your own words. Make it personal and meaningful. You will not share this with anyone. We'll allow about five to seven minutes. ⏱

Close   (15–20 minutes)

Close with a guided imagery excerise from Carolyn Stahl's book Opening to God *(Nashville: Upper Room Books, 1977), pp. 100-102. If you cannot find a copy of the book, try writing your own guided meditation. For our purposes, a guided meditation is simply an imaginary story that requires participants to picture themselves in a place where they may come into contact with God. Using a lot of descriptive words, describe a beach or mountain scene; then ask a "wondering" question, such as, "What/Where is God calling you to do? . . . to be? . . . to go?" Afterward, instruct participants to write about the experience in their journals. Allow fifteen to twenty minutes for the entire exercise.* ⏱

LUNCH AND FREE TIME   (12:15–1:30)

SESSION 3   (1:30–3:00)

Note: More material is provided for this session than you may have time to include. If you choose to use everything as written, you will need to allow an extra twenty-five minutes, extending the session to 3:25 P.M. Otherwise, you may make adjustments as necessary to meet your particular group's needs and time constraints.

Open   (5 minutes)

Play the selection "Come Remember," included on Colleen Haley's CD From the Heart, *or choose another appropriate song.* 🎼

Read aloud Psalm 8. ⏱

Talk   (15 minutes)

Read this section several times until you can paraphrase and present it in your own speaking style—with the exception of the author's story, which is to be read aloud.

So how do we seek growth? I would like to offer five holy habits.

- Scripture
- Prayer
- Self-control
- Silence or solitude
- Service

An entire retreat could be spent on each one of these holy habits, but today we'll take a brief look at each one, pausing periodically to journal or scripture surf.

Holy Habit #1: Scripture

We are a culture rich in Bibles. That is, we have more Bibles in our homes than the generations before us. We can acquire Bibles easily—in any language, any version, any translation. Why, we even can have the Bible on computer disk or cassette tape. It is the most frequently sold book, yet it is the least read book. What does that say about us? Listen to this story, told by the author of this retreat.

My paternal grandmother, Gran (or Annie Laurie), lived with us for a short time in Eastman, Georgia, when I was eight years old. She had a little apartment on the far side of the carport. I remember spending a lot of time sitting with her. We would sit in her kitchen; she had a stool there that I just loved. The seat and back were covered with yellow plastic. Underneath the seat, there were two steps that could be pulled down to make a step ladder. It was perfect for an eight-year-old's short legs. It was on that stool, in Gran's kitchen, that I memorized my first scripture. During that summer, Gran taught me Psalm 100. To this day, I cannot read, sing, recite, or pray that psalm without thinking of that summer, sitting on that stool with my Gran.

What are your favorite Bible verses? Have you asked that question of your grandparents, parents, children, spiritual mothers, friends? Some people keep a list inside the back cover of their Bibles, noting the specific verses and the dates they learned them—as well as the favorite verses of other family members. (Gasp! Yes, some people write in their Bibles!) When one woman's relative died, everyone was trying to remember the man's favorite Bible verse. The woman knew because she had recorded it in her Bible. Gran's Bible was a part of her—recorded in her heart. Where is your Bible? Is it in your heart? Is it something you can share easily? If not, start today to change that. Choose a verse that is meaningful for you and spend a week memorizing it and "getting it into your heart."

Scripture Surf   (10 minutes)

Write the following scripture references on an easel board, chalkboard, or dry erase board; or instruct participants to write them in their journals as you read the references aloud.

In silence "scripture surf" two of the following verses.

Romans 5:1
John 3:16
John 10:10
Romans 11:26
Ecclesiastes 3

Read each passage silently. Meditate on the words. Then journal as God's Great Spirit leads you. You have approximately ten minutes to do this. 🕐

Journal   (10 minutes)

In advance, write the following questions on newsprint, a chalkboard, or a dry erase board.
For the next ten minutes record your responses to these questions in your journal:

- Do you read your Bible daily? If so, how does this daily discipline influence your life? If not, why not, and what would it take for you to begin this habit?
- How can you increase the time you currently spend with God's Word?
- Do you "pray the scriptures"? In other words, do you spend time meditating on the words of a specific verse? Do you let the verses settle into your soul? If so, how has this helped you grow spiritually? If not, why not try it this week! 🕐

Talk   (10 minutes)

Read this section several times until you can paraphrase and present it in your own speaking style—with the exception of the author's story, which is to be read aloud.

Holy Habit #2: Prayer

Prayer: spending time in communion with God, communicating with God, listening, talking, writing, resting in God's presence, reading the prayers of others. We pray in all of these ways and more. Actually, it is our hearts that pray. Our hearts are moved to prayer by many things, such as music, nature, silence, and scripture. What other things have moved your heart to prayer? *Allow participants to comment briefly, and acknowledge their responses.* 🕐

Listen to this story, told by the author of this retreat.

By the time my son Martin was three years old, he had learned the Lord's Prayer. He usually spent the Sunday morning worship service playing with his friends in the nursery. On one particular Sunday, however, he was sitting with us in "big church." It came time for the Lord's Prayer, and as he heard the congregation say the words, he said, "Mommy, they know our prayer." The quiet time in "big church" was disrupted by the voice of a child. Everyone laughed, and they were blessed by his presence and honesty. Yes, that is our prayer.

We often pray in our faith communities and in our lives without thinking about the prayers we are saying. We pray automatically, routinely. Martin was present to the prayer. When was the last time you were present with a simple prayer?

Scripture Surf   (15 minutes)

Write the following scripture references and questions on newsprint, a chalkboard, or a dry erase board; or instruct participants to write them in their journals as you read the questions and references aloud.

Now, let's break into small groups of *(state a number appropriate for your group)*. Each group is to read together James 5:7-8, Mark 4:1-9, and Matthew 13:1-23. Then discuss the following questions:

• What does each passage have to do with prayer?
• What are your obstacles to prayer?
• In what ways do you lack depth in your prayers or prayer life?

We'll come back together in about twelve minutes. 🕐

Talk   (10 minutes)

Read this section several times until you can paraphrase and present it in your own speaking style—with the exception of the author's story, which is to be read aloud.

Holy Habit #3: Self-Control

Have someone read aloud 2 Peter 3:18. 🕐

In William Bennett's *The Book of Virtues*, self-control is the theme of the very first chapter—all 104 pages of it! Self-control certainly is an important habit of the Christian life. Self-control is a strange thing; by practicing self-control, we can help others grow spiritually while we are growing spiritually ourselves. Self-control implies an action that we can do for ourselves—with God's help. It helps us live out God's commandments for ourselves. Self-control should be at the heart of everyday behavior. It helps give order to our souls. With self-control comes tremendous freedom.

In his book *My Utmost for His Highest*, Oswald Chambers writes:

Many of us are all right in the main, but there are some domains in which we are slovenly. It is not a question of sin, but of the remnants of the carnal life which are apt to make us slovenly. Slovenliness is an insult to the Holy Ghost. There should be nothing slovenly, whether it be in the way we eat and drink, or in the way we worship God.[1]

Not only must our relationship with God be right, but also the outward expression of that relationship must be right. Ultimately, God will allow nothing to escape; every detail of our lives is under his scrutiny. God will bring us back to the same point over and over again in countless ways. And God never tires of bringing us back to that one point until we learn the lesson, because his purpose is to produce the finished product!

Beware of becoming careless over the small details of life, saying, "Oh, that will do for now." Whatever it may be, God will point it out with persistence until we become entirely his.

Have someone read aloud the words to the hymn "Take My Life, and Let It Be." 🕐

Scripture Surf   (10 minutes)

Write the following scripture references on newsprint, a chalkboard, or a dry erase board; or instruct participants to write them in their journals as you read the references aloud.

In silence, "scripture surf" the following verses.

2 Corinthians 2:5
James 4:1-2

Read each passage silently. Meditate on the words. Then journal as God's Great Spirit leads you. You have about seven minutes to do this. 🕐

Talk   (5 minutes)

Read this section several times until you can paraphrase and present it in your own speaking style.

Holy Habit #4: Silence/Solitude

Silence helps us break barriers. Silence makes us humble. Silence makes us focused. Guard it. Treasure it. There are some who design their worship around it. Jesus showed us the way to silence in his own life.

- He spent forty days in the wilderness to prepare for his ministry (Matthew 4:1-11).
- He spent the night alone before he chose the twelve (Luke 6:12).
- He sought the lonely mountain with three disciples for the transfiguration (Matthew 17:1-2).
- He prepared for the crucifixion in prayer at Gethsemane (Matthew 26:36-44).
- He connected other significant acts of ministry with solitude. After the feeding of the five thousand, he went alone to pray (Matthew 14:23).
- He told the twelve, "Come away by yourselves to pray" (Mark 6:31).
- He withdrew after healing the leper (Luke 5:12-16).

Solitude was a regular practice with Jesus. He calls us to silence and solitude because they are essential for prayer and listening to God. It's been said that there are few persons who are still enough to hear God speak.

Mother Teresa said of silence: "Silence is God's language." God speaks to us in the silence of the heart. In silence, we allow the Spirit of God to pray in us. What is essential is not what we say, but what God says to us.

Journal   (5 minutes)

What is silence? Write a word or phrase in your journal to complete this sentence: "Silence is . . ." Then reflect on the ways God has used silence to speak to you. Record your thoughts in your journal. We'll come back together in three to five minutes. 🕐

Talk   (5 minutes)

Read this section several times until you can paraphrase and present it in your own speaking style.

Holy Habit #5: Service

Demonstrate your love and concern for the people of God, and growth is guaranteed. A word of caution: Do not let your service be automatic. Hear these words from Richard Foster's book *Prayer: Finding the Heart's True Home:*

Each activity of daily life in which we stretch ourselves on behalf of others is a prayer of action—the times when we scrimp and save in order to get the children something special; the times when we share our car with others on rainy mornings, leaving early to get them to work on time; the times when we keep up correspondence with friends or answer one last telephone call when we are dead tired at night. These times and many more like them are lived prayer.[2]

Prayer in action is love. Love in action is service. Service yields the freedom to do something—but not everything.

The work of God is constant. Our problems continue and change; the important thing is that we do something. What can *you* do? Can you read stories to children, mentor someone, bake for a neighbor, take someone to the doctor, take an elderly person shopping? Each of us is called to do something.

What are the attributes of true service? True service is motivated by the heart, is patient, is not looking for anything in return, and is not concerned with a projected goal. Have you ever known anyone who lived this way?

Scripture Surf   (10 minutes)

Write the following scripture references on newsprint, a chalkboard, or dry erase board; or instruct participants to write them in their journals as you read the references aloud.

In silence, "scripture surf" three of the following passages.

Philippians 1:3-30
2 Timothy 2:1-13
Mark 10:1-30
Acts 10:1-48
John 15:12-17
Romans 1:1-17
Luke 5:1-11

Read each passage silently. Meditate on the words. Then journal as God's Great Spirit leads you. You have approximately ten minutes to do this. 🕐

Close   (5 minutes)

Be yourself. Be authentic. Trust God to see you through. Don't live for the future. Today is a gift. Live in the present moment. Treasure the moment.

The following reading is taken from *The Meaning of Salvation*, written by Charles Ewing Brown. The book has long been out of print, but it is a treasure.

The Awakening of Love

Into our home five children were born. One died at the age of four. There is no sweeter memory than the experience of waking one of these babies when it became necessary to do so. As I bent over the sweet little innocent face, I knew that there was nothing but love for me in that heart, but it was latent, or sleeping, love. Then I would awaken the child and she would open her little eyes, look up into my face, see who it was, smile, and then put her arms around my neck and hug me tightly. The love which had been sleeping in her heart had wakened and had become active, and through that activity it grew with the passing years and became stronger. If I had been forced to go away while that little child was asleep and had not returned for fifteen or twenty years, when I came back I would have found that that love had slept so long it had died away entirely. And to me this is a parable of prayer. Our heavenly Father bends over us, as it were, each morning, and as we awaken we look into his face and gaze into his eyes; our love awakens and manifests itself in prayer, communion, and praising the beauty of holiness and exalting the love that redeemed us. . . .

The love is always in our hearts but it grows stronger as it awakens from time to time and expresses itself in fruitful, refreshing, and passionate communion with God.[3]

CLOSING WORSHIP   (3:00–4:00)

Opening Ritual

If possible, gather together in an outdoor location. Give each of the women a pretty piece of stationery, an envelope, and a pen. Invite each woman to write herself a letter about her spiritual life, responding to these questions: What difference has today made in your life? Which holy habit(s) do you intend to take back and weave into the fabric of your life? What changes do you need to make? 🕐

Instruct each woman to place her letter in the envelope, seal it, and address it to herself. Then, one at a time, have the women place their letters silently in a basket. * 🕐

Lighting of the Candle

As you light a white pillar candle, representing Christ's presence, say: We light this candle knowing that God is with us.

Worship Song

Sing together "Amazing Grace." 🎵

Special Music (Optional)

Ask one of the women in advance to sing a solo that deals in some way with the theme of spiritual growth. 🎵

Scripture Reading

Have someone read aloud Deuteronomy 6:4-6. 🕐

A Special "Offering"

Pose this question to the group: What have we left unsaid? *Assure the group that there are no right or wrong answers. Wait silently for the reponses. Listen, rephrase, and accept the women's offerings.* 🕐

Closing Prayer

Gracious God, we gather and lift our day to you. We thank you for the lives of the women in our midst. Call us into action as we seek growth—as we become the women you would have us become. Amen.

* Mail the letters to the women about four to six weeks after the retreat. It will bring back the joy and depth of the day.

RETURN HOME   (4:00)

Thank each person for her participation and make any necessary closing remarks. 🕐 *Now it is time for the design team to clean, pack up, and evaluate the day.*

The Tapestry

OVERVIEW

We all come into God's presence through different life situations and experiences. This model for growth identifies our need for one another and develops our sense of wonder through the presence of God.

PREPARING FOR THE RETREAT

- Review "How to Use This Book: Planning and Preparing for Retreats" (pp. 11-15).
- Assemble the design team.
- Read through the retreat; make revisions and additions as appropriate for your group or situation.
- Pray for the retreat.
- Advertise; invite and recruit participants.
- Send correspondence noting details of the retreat. (Be sure to let participants know what items they are to bring.)
- Gather the supplies.

SUPPLIES AND MATERIALS

To be brought by the leader

- nametags
- cassette/CD player
- cassettes/CDs, including meditative music
- hymnals or other songbooks (see suggested hymns and songs throughout the retreat)
- newsprint and marker, chalkboard and chalk, or dry erase board and marker
- white pillar candle and matches or lighter
- paper, pens, pencils
- a journal for each participant (Note: For large groups, ask participants to bring their own.)
- medium-size basket
- handout of 1 Corinthians 13 (same translation), one for each participant (see Session 2)
- words to the hymn "We Meet You, O Christ" (see Session 3)

To be brought by each participant

- Bible
- quilt or blanket
- pen or pencil

The Retreat

ARRIVAL AND WELCOME   (9:00–9:30)

See pages 12-13 for arrival and welcome suggestions. Once everyone has arrived and received a nametag, begin a get-acquainted game or activity. 🕐

SESSION 1: TAKING INVENTORY (9:30–11:00)

Open   (5 minutes)

If possible, play the selection "Put Your Life in His Hands," included on Colleen Haley's CD From the Heart *(see p. 15), **or choose** another appropriate song to play for the group or sing together.* 🎼

Talk   (10 minutes)

Read this section several times until you can paraphrase and present it in your own speaking style.
Carole King sings a famous song about a tapestry: "My life has been a tapestry of rich and royal hue. . . . a tapestry to feel and see, impossible to hold."[1] This retreat is about this very thing! We come into God's presence through different situations and experiences. This one-day retreat for growth identifies our need for one another and develops our sense of wonder through the presence of God.

Listen to the words of Anne Morrow Lindbergh—wife, working woman, and mother of five:

I mean to lead a simple life . . . But I do not. I find that my frame of life does not foster simplicity. My husband and five children must make their way in the world. The life I have chosen as wife and mother entrains a whole caravan of complications. It involves a house in the suburbs and either household drudgery or household help which wavers between scarcity and non-existence for most of us. It involves food and shelter; meals, planning, marketing, bills, and making the ends meet in a thousand ways. It involves not only the butcher, the baker, the candlestickmaker but countless other experts to keep my modern house with its modern "simplifications" (electricity, plumbing, refrigerator, gas-stove, oil-burner, dish-washer, radios, car, and numerous other labor-saving devices) functioning properly. It involves health; doctors, dentists, appointments, medicine. . . . It involves education, spiritual, intellectual, physical, schools, school conferences, car pools, extra trips for basketball or orchestra practice; tutoring, camps, camp equipment and transportation. It involves clothes, shopping, laundry, cleaning, mending, letting skirts down and sewing buttons on, or finding someone else to do it. It involves friends, my husband's, my children's, my own, and endless arrangements to get together; letters, invitations, telephone calls and transportation hither and yon.

For life today in America is based on the premise of ever-widening circles of contact and communication. It involves not only family demands, but community demands, national demands, international demands on the good citizen, through social and cultural pressures, through newspapers, magazines, radio programs, political drives, charitable appeals, and so on. My mind reels with it. What a circus act we women perform every day of our lives. It puts the trapeze artist to shame. . . .

This is not the life of simplicity but the life of multiplicity that the wise men warn us of. It leads not to unification but to fragmentation. It does not bring grace; it destroys the soul. And this is not only true of my life, I am forced to conclude; it is the life of millions of women in America. I stress America, because today, the American woman more than any other has the privilege of choosing such a life. . . .

Yet, the problem is particularly and essentially woman's. Distraction is, always has been, and probably always will be, inherent in woman's life.[2]

Did you find yourself anywhere in this dramatic description? I certainly did! We have no corner on the market: This was written by a woman who was born in 1906! What amazes me is how far we *haven't* come! We struggle endlessly for peace and simplicity. This realization, I believe, calls us to reshape our lives, to look anew at the tapestry of our lives and choose the people, activities, and disciplines that can make our life-tapestry something beautiful to see and hold.

Journal   (20 minutes)

In a moment, you are going to map your life story in your journal. You'll begin by making a horizontal line across the page. Then, on the left end of the line, you will write the actual or approximate date of your birth, your baptism, or the first realization you had that you are a child of God. As you move across the line, you will chart the highs and lows and the significant people and events of your life. After you've done this, pause to reflect on your experience and acknowledge the ways God has been at work in your life. I hope that you will find this an ongoing process, for we must continually take the time to step back and take a look at our lives. We'll allow about fifteen minutes for this exercise. 🕐

Talk   (10 minutes)

Read this section several times until you can paraphrase and present it in your own speaking style. Listen to these words from the author of this retreat:

My husband's Grandfather Jess, who is ninety-three years old, has a wagon in his barn that he bought the summer he turned twelve. His father thought that Jess was old enough to raise a crop of cotton on one hundred acres, pick it, bale it, sell it, and use the profits to begin his adult life. Each time we return home and I get the privilege of seeing that wagon, I am amazed at the sturdiness of its construction. Perhaps the strongest part of the wagon continues to be the wheels—huge, round, wooden, balanced wheels with strong crossties.

I believe that God wants our lives to be similar to those huge, balanced wheels. The balance of life includes the physical, social, mental, spiritual, financial, and personal elements of our lives. Sometimes the elements are beyond our own control—such as physical or mental challenges of ourselves or family members—yet we still can achieve balance. Your life's "balance" may not look like that of anyone else, and that's as it should be. Remember, God created us as individuals with different needs and abilities.

Let's consider what a balanced life might look like versus an out-of-balance life.

A well-balanced life might look like: An out-of-balance life might look like:

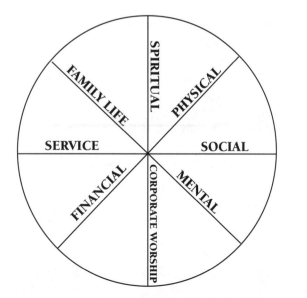 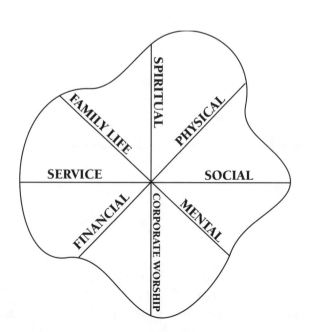

Which wagon wheel does your own life most resemble? Quickly sketch your own wagon wheel on a page in your journal. We'll take just a couple of minutes for this. Go with your first impulses. 🕐

Journal   (10 minutes)

One of the many paradoxes in life is this: We must have change in order to change, and growth produces change. Think about that for a moment. In your journal, write about a time in your own life when you found this paradox to be true. We'll take about ten minutes for this. 🕐

Talk   (15 minutes)

Read this section several times until you can paraphrase and present it in your own speaking style. Some of the growth-producing changes that we can claim are known as spiritual disciplines. They include meditation, fasting, contemplation, prayer, study, solitude, submission, and service. When we do not have discipline in our lives, we are disobedient and full of anxiety. We read in Isaiah 26:3 about perfect peace: "Those of steadfast mind you keep in peace—in peace because they trust in you" (NRSV).

Do you live for the weekend? Are you trying to just get through each day? Do you just need to finish this one project? There is a better way. As children of God, we need to live in the present; to be fully present; to enjoy the moment and not simply "get through the day." How are you living your life now? Philippians 3:12-14 reads:

Not that I have already obtained all this, or have already been made perfect, but I press on to take hold of that for which Christ Jesus took hold of me. Brothers [and Sisters], I do not consider myself yet to have taken hold of it. But one thing I do: Forgetting what is behind and straining toward what is ahead, I press on toward the goal to win the prize for which God has called me heavenward in Christ Jesus.

We are called to live each moment abundantly with Christ. To do that, we must let go of the past and not worry about the future, choosing instead to live fully present in this day.

I have been told that when a sculptor molds the face of a person, he or she begins with the eyes. Likewise, we begin abundant life by making our eyes those of God. In other words, we must make God our first priority! We are so many things: wives, mothers, employees, sisters, daughters, aunts, friends. But one day, we will stand in front of God *by ourselves.* So we had better put first things first in our tapestries!

Are you tired? Do you need a vacation? Well, as often happens, once we have taken a vacation and have rested, we return to the grind of our daily routines. We haven't changed anything—we simply hit the pause button! To receive true rest, we simply have to abide in God. How do we do this?

- Practice the presence of God: "I keep the LORD always before me; because he is at my right hand, I shall not be moved" (Psalm 16:8 NRSV).
- Guard your daily quiet time, whether it is in the morning, during a walk, after dinner, or before bedtime; the key is to find the time that *regularly* works for you.
- Occasionally seek God in longer chunks of time—occasional mornings or afternoons; a one-day retreat such as this one; a weekend away; be creative.
- Be diligent about worship just as Jesus was. In Luke 4:16 (NRSV) we read: "[Jesus] went to the synagogue on the sabbath day, as was his custom."
- Hold a positive self-image—a positive mental picture of yourself. Gain self-confidence by setting new goals and taking new action.

It's been said that if you do what you always did, you get what you always got. This makes sense. Most of us just choose to feel comfortable and therefore use only one-third of our true potential. We can increase that number with relatively little effort. Our self-image comes from how much of our potential we choose to use. It's true that self-image begins early and is formed through our environment. But you can—yes, you *can*—change your self-image. We must learn to stretch—to place ourselves in environments that encourage change to take place. Just as an athlete faces the next race and a weaver faces the next tapestry, so also we must face fear, anxiety, and discomfort. As we face these things, we gain maturity, independence, and security. We must remember, however, that it is impossible to win the approval of *all* the people who are important in our lives; we simply must be happy with ourselves. We also must remember this: Our reach should exceed our grasp.

Journal   (15 minutes)

Create your own dream list in your journal. List your tangible goals (those things that can be quantified or measured) and your intangible goals (such as personality changes). Make it a list of all that you want to do, be, and accomplish during your life. Put anything on it. Brainstorm. Then star the five "burning" items on your list. We'll take about fifteen minutes for this. 🕐

Close   (5 minutes)

Play a selection of meditative music and read the following aloud: As you are listening to the music, imagine that you are having a conversation with God. What is the Holy One asking of you? Telling you? Can you picture yourself as the woman God wants you to be? What does she look like? How does she act? How is she spending her time? *Pause until the music has ended.* 🎵

Close this session with the following quotation. In *Disciplines of the Beautiful Woman,* Anne Ortlund writes, "In recent years we have been obsessed with figuring out what a woman should be allowed to do. God says in his Word a woman can do anything; the point is not what she *does* but what she *is.*"[3]

BREAK   (11:00–11:15)

SESSION 2: GOAL SETTING   (11:15–12:15)

Open   (3 minutes)

Read aloud the following:

- "She can laugh at the days to come" (Proverbs 31:25b).
- I have a dream: it is precious; it carries me forward; it keeps me on the right track; it gives me purpose and power; it gives me enthusiasm and momentum.
- Imagine yourself on a cruise. Each day you wake in a new place. The captain of the ship is constantly refocusing and redirecting and recentering so that each planned destination can be reached. Do you live your life this way? It has been said that you can't step into the same river twice; that the water is always moving, and the very place you stand will be different the next moment. So it is with life.

Talk   (3 minutes)

Read this section several times until you can paraphrase and present it in your own speaking style.

In order to avoid letting the tapestries of our lives run out of control, we must do some life planning. God gives us direction and purpose. Are we listening? God speaks to us, and we need to be listening, waiting for instruction, for it will surely come. When we listen, we feel the nudges of the Holy Spirit that help us determine our direction. Life goals are the things we hope to do. For instance, you might hope to complete a major project, to raise children who love God with their entire being, to travel to a certain city or country, and so on. These goals work together to accomplish a larger purpose—our life's mission.

Mission statements have become popular these days. Many companies prominently display their mission statements for all to see; one company has even carved its mission statement into the stone of the building. Anyone who enters the building knows what the company is aiming to accomplish and how they will take action.

Do *you* have a mission statement for your life—a purpose? Can you state it? Do those who are closest to you know it? As a rudder directs a ship, so a statement of purpose gives direction for your life. A woman we'll call "Vicky" wrote this personal mission statement: *I want my life to leave a mark on others by pointing them toward God.* What do you want your mission statement to say about you?

Journal (10 minutes)

Take a moment now to write a rough draft of your own personal mission statement. Begin by revisiting the list of dreams you created in Session 1—all you hope to do or be or accomplish in life. Look closely at the five dreams you placed a star beside—the dreams that are burning within you. What do these dreams have in common? What purpose or calling might you fulfill by pursuing these and similar dreams? In your high moments—your moments of inspiration and vision—what has God said to you regarding these dreams? Jot down some thoughts now. Be brief, yet be specific and courageous. We'll pause for about eight minutes as you think about these questions and write a one-sentence mission statement for your life. Remember, this is a rough draft; it doesn't have to be perfect. You can revise it later. Just try to get the general idea down on paper. 🕐

Talk (2 minutes)

Read this section several times until you can paraphrase and present it in your own speaking style.
Each of us has been given a unique purpose or calling in life. Each of us also has been given an unlimited capacity to dream. In order for each of us to fulfill our God-given purpose—and make the changes in our life necessary for accomplishing that purpose—we must dream and set personal goals. To do this, we first need to be honest with ourselves, because our personal goals are just between us and God. Second, we need to set realistic goals that allow us to have the courage to stretch our comfort levels. Are we content with being mediocre? Stretching takes us out of the realm of the mediocre to higher levels. Third, we must have determination and believe in our own God-given abilities. Fourth, we must take action. Setting and pursuing personal goals not only will enable you to fulfill your life's calling, but will also increase your confidence and provide many stimulating and rewarding experiences.

Journal (35–38 minutes)

Return again to your list of dreams from Session 1, looking closely at the five dreams you drew a star beside. Now, from these five dreams, identify *three* priorities you will focus on. (Why three? Because it's the sacred number, of course!) You may find it helpful to return to your wagon wheel from the first session. The places where you are out of balance could be a good place to focus your attention. Is one of these places financial matters? Time with family? Time for God? Daily devotional time? Another approach would be to consider the three priorities most crucial to your life's purpose or personal mission. Remember our hypothetical friend Vicky, whose mission statement is "to leave a mark on others by pointing them toward God"? Her three priorities might be to bring as many people to Christ as she can, to focus on her own spiritual growth, and to stay involved in Christian service. Regardless of the approach you take, the object is to establish your own personal priorities. Remember, you can't attain everything at once. What's first? Only you can decide! We'll allow about eight minutes for this. 🕐

Next, write a one-year goal for each priority. Here are some helpful guidelines:

- Be sure that each goal is measurable; that is, it should be something you can accomplish in the next twelve months.
- State each goal specifically. Define it clearly. How will you know when you have achieved it?
- What are the conditions of your goal—the who, what, when, where, and why?
- What is the benefit or benefits of achieving each goal? Is it financial? Self-satisfaction? Community service?
- Identify the roadblocks for each goal. Do you have concerns about family, friends, time, money?

- How will you overcome the obstacles? Training? Time management? Remember: Commitment is the key. Begin by acknowledging your commitment to act—it saves a lot of time in the long run.
- What is your target date for completing or achieving each goal?

Let's consider Vicky again. Her three priorities are to bring as many people to Christ as she can, to focus on her own spiritual growth, and to stay involved in Christian service. Her three goals, then, might be to bring two people to Christ this year, to read through a one-year Bible, and to participate in four service or outreach projects during the year. Let's pause now for about eight minutes as you write your own three goals. ⏰

Now that you have set your three goals, the next step is to break them into smaller pieces—perhaps monthly or weekly action steps. Action steps are the logical and practical bite-sized tasks necessary for accomplishing a larger goal. One of Vicky's goals is to bring two people to Christ this year. Her action steps for that goal might be to identify four friends or acquaintances who are "searching for something"; to pray for them; to invite them to attend church and/or a spiritual retreat; to stay in touch with them; and to share her faith with them. Breaking goals into smaller pieces helps keep things in perspective. After all, Mother Teresa didn't start out to help 42,000 people—she started out to help only one.

We'll pause for another eight minutes as you write action steps for one of your three goals. In the interest of time, you can write action steps for your other two goals during free time or after the retreat is over. Try to be brief; you can refine your action steps later, if you like. ⏰

Take one minute now to visualize the future in light of your new mission statement and goals. What is it like? How is it different from the present? ⏰

Repeating this simple exercise periodically can heighten your confidence and add to your success and motivation.

Have you ever noticed that many grave markers simply state the person's name and date of birth, followed by a hyphen and the date of death? Life is really about the space between the dates. Life—just a hyphen on a grave marker. What do you want your life to stand for? When your life is over, what will it have been about? Take the next three minutes to record a few thoughts in your journal. ⏰

Let's close this part of our session by reading 1 Corinthians 13 aloud together. *Prepare and distribute a handout so that all are reading the same translation.* ⏰

Talk   (3 minutes)

Read this section several times until you can paraphrase and present it in your own speaking style.

Someone once commented to me, "Women must balance their time more than men because they don't have wives." How very true! Susan, a single mother, said one Christmas, "I need a wife! Someone to run errands and take care of the house." No doubt, hundreds of books have been written on time management. Millions of calendar systems are sold in an effort to get us organized and keep us that way. Whether we are detailed planners or we prefer to fly by the seat of our pants, we must have a system—a plan that works for us and is as unique as we are.

There's a saying: If you don't control your time, it will control you. How true! Do you routinely fill up your calendar or do you plan your time carefully? Are you held captive by your calendar? How do things get on your calendar? Do you check what goes on your calendar against your goals? Do you plan what happens each day or do you allow others to plan for you? The question is this: How are you going to control your time?

Close   (1 minute)

Read the following aloud:

> Gracious God,
> I praise you for
> your tender assurance,
> That in you I find
> my Strength and my Redeemer.

LUNCH AND FREE TIME   (12:15–1:30)

SESSION 3: SILENCE AND SOLITUDE (1:30–3:00)

Open   (5 minutes)

Read aloud the words of the hymn "We Meet You, O Christ." 🕐

Talk   (10 minutes)

Read this section several times until you can paraphrase and present it in your own speaking style. Silence—most of what has been written about it comes from the monastic life. It is, however, an essential discipline for spiritual growth. Silence is itself full of the voice of God. Silence and solitude are not total aloneness; nor are they the absence of involvement with others. Rather, they are opportunities to be still, to listen for God through the silence, to be still with creation. It has been said that religion is what one does with one's solitariness.

Jesus' ministry was a blend of living with others and living in solitude. Can you think of times when Jesus went alone to be with God? What about Matthew 26:36, where Jesus told the disciples with him, "Sit here while I go over there and pray" (NRSV); or Luke 4:42, "At day-break he departed and went into a deserted place" (NRSV); or Luke 6:12, "Now during those days he went out to the mountain to pray; and he spent the night in prayer to God" (NRSV); or Luke 9:18, "Once when Jesus was praying alone . . ." (NRSV)?

Now, if Jesus could find the time to be alone with God, don't you think that you and I can find the time? Listen to these words from the author of this retreat:

I have three busy teenagers; a wonderful husband who works far too hard; a mother who lives with us and depends on me for many things; a full-time job in ministry; a house to care for; a dog, a cat, and two goldfish; friends; neighbors . . . My list goes on and on, just as yours does. But I've managed to find time alone. It isn't an easy task. Now, I love to sleep, but I knew that the only time I could be absolutely alone was while everyone else was sleeping. So I prayed about it, and gently and lovingly God began to wake me in the mornings for an early morning walk outdoors with the Holy One. The results have been great: My prayer life is richer, my stress level is better, and I am a much happier person. And now, years since I began this early morning walk with God, I would rather get up for that time than to sleep—well, *almost* every day I would!

Do any of you have similar stories? How have you found time to be alone with God? *Allow participants to share freely for several minutes; then proceed.* 🕐

I challenge you to use your solitariness purposefully. Use your time alone to ponder who you are, what your life is about, what you are in quest of, and how you are related to others and to God.

Journal   (35–40 minutes)

For the next ten minutes, write in your journal how you spend your time on a typical day, and why. 🕐

Now that you have given it words, how do you feel about it? *Allow participants to respond freely for several minutes.* 🕐

List the number of times in the last seven days that you have had at least thirty minutes alone. How did you spend your time alone, if you had it? If you had no time to yourself, why didn't you? We'll pause for about five minutes as you make some notes in your journal. 🕐
Now recall the last time you spent an hour in silence. If you like, make notes in your journal. We'll pause for another five minutes. 🕐

What do you imagine the benefits of silence and solitude to be? Are you still enough to hear God speak? The benefits, among others, are the ability to hear God and, then, to speak to God about our deepest needs. Silence and solitude also bring us a sharpened sensitivity for people. We often are so busy that we crowd people out of our lives. An additional fruit of silence is enhanced creativity. Often, our creativity simply needs time to develop. If silence is full of the voice of God, then why don't you and I spend more time in silence? Let's take time for silence now. Lie down on the floor, take several deep breaths, exhaling slowly, and rest in God. I'll set a timer for ten minutes. ⏱

Close (1 minute)

Read the following aloud:

You are not here by accident. You are God's beloved. You are a child of God. You are God's creation. You are a gift from God. Stretch, grow, bend, prune, and renew yourself into the one God calls you to be. Live as God's beloved.

CLOSING WORSHIP (3:00–4:00)

Lighting of the Candle

As you light a white pillar candle, representing Christ's presence, say: We light this candle knowing that God is with us.

Prayers of the People of God

Invite the women to share their prayers aloud at this time. Open and close the prayer time. ⏱

Worship Songs

Sing together "There's a Sweet, Sweet Spirit in This Place" and, if possible, Colleen Haley's "Jesus Come into My Heart," included on the CD From the Heart. 🎼

Meditation

Once there was a child who lived in a loving home with well-intentioned parents, and who was surrounded by well-intentioned friends and family who wanted to tell her about God's great love—about how God created the world and everything in it, and how God loves us no matter what. They spent so much time talking that she couldn't *hear* what they were saying. Then, one morning while playing outside in God's beautiful world, she exclaimed, "Mommy, I get it: You can't see God, but we can all *feel* God!" The child had learned.

A Time of Sharing

What have *you* learned? What do you need to relearn? What do you need to remember? How will you do that? *Allow participants to respond freely; then continue.*

Closing Prayer

Creator of the world,
Creator of each of us,
Help us remember
that you have called us to belong to you;
that you have called us as tapestry makers.
Help us make our life tapestries beautiful creations in your honor.
Make us worthy weavers of our own unique tapestries. Amen.

RETURN HOME (4:00)

Thank each person for her participation and make any necessary closing remarks. 🕐 *Now it is time for the design team to clean, pack up, and evaluate the day.*

Discovering My Spiritual Gifts

◆

OVERVIEW

"But I don't have any spiritual gifts!" Perhaps this is one of the most common statements made by persons when asked about their spiritual gifts. As they define and explore spiritual gifts together, individuals are led through a process of naming, claiming, and using the gifts God has given each of them. This retreat is about a woman's call to peace, purpose, and practicality.

PREPARING FOR THE RETREAT
- Review "How to Use This Book: Planning and Preparing for Retreats" (pp. 11-15).
- Assemble the design team.
- Read through the retreat; make revisions and additions as appropriate for your group or situation.
- Pray for the retreat.
- Advertise; invite and recruit participants.
- Send correspondence noting details of the retreat. (Be sure to let participants know what items they are to bring.)
- Gather the supplies.

SUPPLIES AND MATERIALS
To be brought by the leader
- nametags
- cassette/CD player
- cassettes/CDs, including meditative music
- newsprint and marker, chalkboard and chalk, or dry erase board and marker
- hymnals or other songbooks (see suggested songs and hymns throughout the retreat)
- white pillar candle and matches or lighter
- paper, pens, pencils
- a journal for each participant (Note: For large groups, ask participants to bring their own.)
- paper bags, magazines, scissors, glue, markers (enough for all participants; see Arrival and Welcome)
- handout of spiritual gifts characteristics (optional, see Session 1)
- handout of the spiritual gifts definitions (optional, see Session 2)
- handout of "The Prayer of St. Francis" (optional, see Session 2)
- paper or poster board and tape for making signs (optional, see Session 4)
- various colors of tissue paper; adhesive paper or waxed paper and glue/spray adhesive; basket or other container (see Closing Worship)
- handout of Ephesians 4:11-16 (same translation), one for each participant (see Closing Worship)

To be brought by each participant
- Bible
- quilt or blanket
- pen or pencil

The Retreat

> Note: This retreat has four sessions, rather than three. The revised schedule looks like this.
>
> | | |
> |---|---|
> | 9:00–9:30 | Arrival and Welcome |
> | 9:30–10:20 | Session 1 |
> | 10:20–10:45 | Break |
> | 10:45–12:00 | Session 2 |
> | 12:00–12:45 | Lunch and Free Time |
> | 12:45–2:00 | Session 3 |
> | 2:00–3:00 | Session 4 |
> | 3:00–4:00 | Closing Worship |
> | 4:00 | Return Home |

ARRIVAL AND WELCOME   (9:00–9:30)

See pages 12-13 for arrival and welcome suggestions. Once everyone has arrived and received a nametag, begin the following get-acquainted activity. You will need markers, magazines, glue, and paper bags (one for each woman.)

On the outside of your paper bag, write words or paste pictures that define who you are. On the inside of the bag, write descriptive words or glue pictures that tell something about the kind of person you are—your likes, dislikes, feelings, beliefs, and so forth. When you are finished, find a partner and share your bags with each other. 🕐

SESSION 1: AN INTRODUCTION TO SPIRITUAL GIFTS (9:30–10:20)

Open   (7 minutes)

Sing "The Very Best Gift," included on Colleen Haley's CD From the Heart *(see p. 15), or choose another appropriate song or hymn.* 🎵
Read aloud the following:

The apostles gathered around Jesus, and told him all that they had done and taught. He said to them, "Come away to a deserted place all by yourselves and rest a while." For many were coming and going, and they had no leisure even to eat. And they went away in the boat to a deserted place by themselves. (Mark 6:30-32 NRSV)

When Jesus and his friends had been working hard, they took time to go on a retreat! We come on retreat to seek the opportunity to be alone with God so that we may live God's will for our lives in deeper and more meaningful ways. Congratulate yourself for making this a priority in your life.

Talk   (3 minutes)

Read this section several times until you can paraphrase and present it in your own speaking style.

Legend has it that Michelangelo once pushed a huge slab of marble down a street. A curious neighbor sitting lazily on the porch of his house called out to Michelangelo, "Why do you labor so hard on an old piece of stone?" Michelangelo answered, "Because there is an angel in that rock that wants to come out!"

We all face the task of releasing the "angels" or gifts within us. You hold the raw materials within your life. The struggle—or the journey, as I like to call it—leads to growth and becoming. It begins with self-discovery.

Journal   (4 minutes)

Let's pause for a time of reflection. For the next three to four minutes, journal in response to this unfinished statement: As I see it, the purpose of my life is . . . 🕐

Talk   (35 minutes)

Read this section several times until you can paraphrase and present it in your own speaking style. God is our Creator. We are created in God's image. We, in turn, are creators; we are the developers of the gifts that God has bestowed on us. The Holy One has lovingly looked on each of us and graced us with gifts that build up God's kingdom.

Why are you here today? You are here to:

- Learn that you are responsible for your own gifts.
- Learn that as long as you hold back your gifts, you are not complete.
- Understand that a gift is not a gift until it is defined, developed, and shared with God's people.
- Discover and develop your personal spiritual gifts and talents.

Imagine that it is Christmas and you are standing in front of the Christmas tree, waiting to open your gifts—and what magnificent gifts they are, wrapped in exquisite paper and tied with beautiful bows. What do you hope to find inside your packages? *Pause for a moment and then continue.*

Let's consider a few questions that will help us begin unwrapping our packages today. Think about these silently as I read them aloud. *Pause for a moment after reading each question.*

- How would you define *spiritual gift?*
- What kind of work or activity are you drawn to in the church?
- What is one gift you think you may possess?

Ask someone to read aloud 1 Corinthians 12. 🕐

The dictionary defines a *gift* as a natural ability or power. God gives us *spiritual gifts* in order that we may build up the Body of Christ and equip the Body for ministry. A spiritual gift is not something that we earn or strive to attain. It is designed and designated by God for the whole Christian community. The gift is energized through the Holy Spirit.

Have a different participant read each of the following passages aloud; after each passage has been read, ask the group this question: What do these verses tell us about spiritual gifts?

> 1 Corinthians 12:4-7
> Ephesians 4:11-12
> John 14:25-27*a*
> 🕐

Prepare in advance a handout presenting the following characteristics, or encourage participants to take notes as you speak.

Here are some of the defining characteristics of spiritual gifts:

1. Spiritual gifts flow naturally.
2. Spiritual gifts help others grow. These gifts, however, are not an end in and of themselves.
3. Spiritual gifts draw Christians closer together. (This means that the gifts are not motivated out of self-gratification.)
4. Spiritual gifts provide a balanced emphasis within our churches.
5. Spiritual gifts are motivated by love.

Listen to these words from 1 Corinthians 13:

If I speak in the tongues of [women] and of angels, but have not love, I am only a resounding gong or a clanging cymbal. If I have the gift of prophecy and can fathom all mysteries and all knowledge, and if I have a faith that can move mountains, but have not love, I am nothing. If I give all I possess to the poor and surrender my body to the flames, but have not love, I gain nothing.

Love is patient, love is kind. It does not envy, it does not boast, it is not proud. It is not rude, it is not self-seeking, it is not easily angered, it keeps no record of wrongs. Love does not delight in evil but rejoices with the truth. It always protects, always trusts, always hopes, always perseveres.

Love never fails. But where there are prophecies, they will cease; where there are tongues, they will be stilled; where there is knowledge, it will pass away. For we know in part and we prophesy in part, but when perfection comes, the imperfect disappears. When I was a child, I talked like a child, I thought like a child, I reasoned like a child. When I became a [woman], I put childish ways behind me. Now we see but a poor reflection as in a mirror; then we shall see face to face. Now I know in part; then I shall know fully, even as I am fully known.

And now these three remain: faith, hope and love. But the greatest of these is love.

If spiritual gifts build the body of believers, then it logically follows that the gifts flow through as a result of God's love. "Every good and perfect gift is from above" (James 1:17*a*). May you be filled with love!

Close   (1 minute)

Read the following quotation aloud:

Be patient toward all that is unsolved in your heart and try to love the questions themselves . . . do not now seek the answers which cannot be given . . . live the questions now.

—Ranier Maria Rilke

BREAK   (10:20–10:45)

SESSION 2: A BIBLICAL STUDY OF SPIRITUAL GIFTS (10:45–12:00)

Open   (3 minutes)

Read aloud the following:

When you look in the mirror, do you remind yourself: I am a gift from God, held in God's hand, shaped in God's image, *loved* by God? As Macrina Wiederkehr writes, "Remind yourself often: 'I am pure capacity for God, I can be *more.*'"[1]

All that I have seen of God teaches me to trust God for all that I have not seen.

—Ralph Waldo Emerson

Talk   (8 minutes)

Read this section several times until you can paraphrase and present it in your own speaking style. Ask someone to read aloud Romans 12:3-13. ⏲

What spoke to you in the reading of this verse? What did you hear in a new way? Did you experience an "aha" moment? Turn to your neighbor and reread the verses together. ⏲

One of the most important tasks of the church, the Body of Christ, is to help one another identify the gifts God has given us and use those gifts for the kingdom of God. There is much debate about spiritual gifts, including how many there are and how many gifts an individual may be given or cultivate. The truth is, the answers are not very important. What is important is to identify what we can do by the power of the Holy Spirit and then "just do it," as the slogan goes.

Scripture Surf   (20 minutes)

Write the following scripture references on newsprint, a chalkboard, or a dry erase board; or instruct participants to write them in their journals as you read the references aloud. Then have par-

ticipants work alone or in small groups to complete the following exercise. Choose the option that best suits the needs of your particular group.

"Surf" through as many of the following passages as you can and determine what gifts are included in them:

Ephesians 4:1-8, 11-16
1 Corinthians 12:4-11
Acts 1:1-8
John 16:5-15
Acts 2:1-18
Acts 2:37-47
1 Corinthians 3:16, 17
Acts 9:10-17
Exodus 3
Jeremiah 1:4-10
Galatians 5:22-23
1 Peter 4:7-11
Psalm 139
Luke 4:18-19
Isaiah 6:1-11
Luke 6:38
2 Corinthians 9:8

We'll come back together in twenty minutes. 🕐

Explore   (35–40 minutes)

Write the following fourteen gifts on newsprint, a chalkboard, or a dry erase board; or instruct participants to write them in their journals as you read the gifts aloud.

Largely, the agreed upon list of spiritual gifts includes, but is not limited to, the following:

preaching/prophecy
serving others
teaching
encouraging others
wisdom
working miracles
prophecy
speaking in tongues (unknown languages)
showing kindness/hospitality
faith
giving
healing
discernment
administration

With a partner, try to rank these fourteen gifts in order of their priority or importance to the kingdom. Work quickly; we'll allow only three to five minutes. 🕐

What did you learn? *Allow participants to respond freely; affirm that it is impossible to rank the gifts because all are essential for the proper functioning of the Body of Christ.* 🕐

Have someone read 1 Corinthians 12:7-11, 14-31. 🕐

Now ask a different person to read Ephesians 4:11-16. 🕐

Write the following definitions on newsprint, a chalkboard, or a dry erase board; or prepare a handout in advance and make copies for the group. Be sure to leave ample space between each gift for making revisions.

Let's define the gifts one at a time. I'll begin by reading a definition. We'll talk a moment about that gift. Then I'd like you to suggest additions or deletions that you'd like to make to the definition. *Remember to pause after reading each of the following definitions, being careful not to spend too much time on discussion; try to complete this part of the exercise in fifteen minutes.* 🕐

preaching/prophecy—the ability to give an immediate message of God to God's people

serving others—the ability to be a helper; a person-centered ministry; relieves worldly and spiritual burdens

teaching—the ability to communicate information about God in such a way that others may learn

encouraging others—the gift of instilling within others the confidence that they are children of God

wisdom—the ability to receive insight as to how knowledge should be applied

working miracles—this gift is used to draw people to commitment to God or to meet a human need; it is given as needs and occasions arise

prophecy—this gift is given to individuals so they may speak God's message (usually a specific message); it is given to someone who listens for God; some may have this gift for a short time

speaking in tongues (unknown languages)—the ability to speak in an unknown language that someone else in the room can translate

showing kindness/hospitality—the special ability to provide a warm and hospitable space for individuals

faith—the ability to see the adequacy of God and tap into it for particular situations; an extraordinary confidence in God; the person with this gift often spends long hours in prayer

giving—the ability to share a wealth of material goods for God's work

healing—the person with this gift functions as an instrument of God's healing grace in the lives of others; gifts of healing include body, emotion, and spirit

discernment—the ability to distinguish spirits—human, divine, or demonic

administration—the ability to organize and give direction; the person with this gift often provides leadership in a congregation or other organization

Of the gifts that we have discussed, what are you best at doing? Where do you find yourself wanting to serve? Willing to serve? Take a brief moment and identify your top three gifts as best you can at this point. List them in your journal. Then find a partner and discuss your list. We'll come back together in ten minutes. 🕐

Close   (4 minutes)

Read the following prayer aloud together; or, if you know the tune (there are several versions), sing it as a song. Print it on newsprint, a chalkboard, or a dry erase board; or prepare a handout in advance and make copies. 🕐

The Prayer of St. Francis

Lord, make me an instrument of your peace;
where there is hatred, let me sow love;
where there is injury, pardon;
where there is doubt, faith,

where there is despair, hope;
where there is darkness, light;
and where there is sadness, joy.

O Divine Master,
grant that I may not so much seek
to be consoled as to console;
to be understood, as to understand;
to be loved, as to love;

For it is in giving that we receive;
it is in pardoning that we are pardoned;
and it is in dying that we are born to eternal life.

LUNCH AND FREE TIME   (12:00–12:45)

SESSION 3: DISCOVERING YOUR GIFTS   (12:45–2:00)

Open   (4 minutes)

Play or sing together the song "You Are Beloved," included on Colleen Haley's CD From the Heart, *or choose another appropriate song.* ♪
Read the following quotations aloud:

A thankful heart is not only the greatest virtue, but the parent of all other virtues. —Cicero

While faith makes all things possible, it is love that makes all things easy. —Evan Hopkins

Explore   (10 minutes)

Let's review. Who has been given spiritual gifts? Why? *Allow the participants to respond; then continue.* 🕐

We're going to play a game called *Agree or Disagree.* First I'll read a statement about spiritual gifts. Those who agree with the statement are to stand. Those who disagree are to remain seated. Ready?

I'd rather work with machines than people.
We all are compelled to develop our gifts.
We all should be able to perform miracles.
My spiritual gifts are fully developed.
My favorite color is red.
I like to walk in the woods.
I like to swim laps.
I like to hold new babies.
I like to be around teenagers.
A pickup truck is my favorite vehicle.
I like to sing.
Jesus has always been my Lord and Savior.
I grew up in a church-going home.
Jesus had many gifts.

Now that was fun! We needed to move around a bit. We also needed to take some time to internalize some of our thoughts related to gifts. Sometimes we aren't aware of what we believe until we begin to "stand" for it.

Scripture Surf   (15 minutes)

Write the following scripture references on newsprint, a chalkboard, or a dry erase board; or instruct participants to write them in their journals as you read the references aloud.

Read silently 1 Peter 4:10, Luke 6:38, and 2 Corinthians 9:8. Write a prayer based on these passages. Then find a partner and share your prayer with her. We'll come back together in about twelve minutes. 🕐

Explore   (15 minutes)

What are some of the hindrances to the cultivation or growth of spiritual gifts? In other words, what things keep us from developing our gifts? *Brainstorm a list together and write them on newsprint, a chalkboard, or a dry erase board. The list may include such things as jealousy, strife, pride, low self-esteem, material things, boasting, "poor me" syndrome, busyness, and so forth.* 🕐 What can we do to overcome these hindrances? *Allow participants to share freely; make notes on newsprint, a chalkboard, or a dry erase board, if you like.* 🕐 Please know in the deepest place of your heart that we all have hindrances to overcome, and it is in the overcoming that we are strengthened.

Journal   (30 minutes)

Obtain one of the spiritual gifts inventories included in the following list and present it to the participants.

The remainder of this session will be completed individually and in silence. Find a quiet space and complete this spiritual gifts inventory. When you are finished, reflect on your findings and record your thoughts in your journal. Consider these questions: How do the results of this inventory compare with the top three gifts you identified in Session 2? Are there any surprises? Any disappointments? We'll allow twenty-five to thirty minutes for you to complete the inventory and write in your journal. I'll let you know when five minutes remain. 🕐

Spiritual Gifts Inventories

The Discovery Journal, Calvie and Associates, Chino Hills, Calif. (1-888-GOD-GIFT).

Discover Your Spiritual Gifts and Ideal Ministry, Michael and Karen Dittman; Growth Tools, Audubon, N.J. (609-310-9551).

Finding Your Spiritual Gifts, Peter Wagner, Gospel Light, Ventura, Calif. (1-800-4-GOSPEL).

Hout's Inventory of Spiritual Gifts, International Centre for Leadership Development and Evangelism, Winfield, B.C. (1-800-804-0777).

Mobilizing Spiritual Gifts, Fuller Institute, Pasadena, Calif. (1-800-235-2222).

Spirit Gifts: One Spirit, Many Gifts, Patricia D. Brown, Abingdon Press, Nashville, Tenn. (1-800-672-1789). This is a great detailed study of spiritual gifts that includes a leader's resource and participant's workbook.

Wesley Spiritual Gifts Questionnaire, Charles E. Fuller Institute of Evangelism and Church Growth (1-800-999-9578). (Note: This is the author's inventory of choice.)

Close   (1 minute)

As we close this session, consider these words of wisdom:

What lies behind us and what lies before us are tiny matters compared to what lies within us. —Oliver Wendall Holmes

Do not conform any longer to the pattern of this world, but be transformed by the renewing of your mind. Then you will be able to test and approve what God's will is—[the] good, pleasing, and perfect will. (Romans 12:2)

SESSION 4: SPIRITUAL ANALYSIS AND DEDICATION OF GIFTS (2:00–3:00)

Open (5 minutes)

Sing together the hymn "Have Thine Own Way, Lord." 🎵

Talk   (15 minutes)

Read this section several times until you can paraphrase and present it in your own speaking style.

What about the Bible characters and their gifts? Here is a "Who's Who" of several of the disciples and the spiritual qualities that contemporary writers have attributed to them as a result of the stories in the New Testament.

PETER, a prophet, of course. A good talker but poor listener. He was always talking—be it bold, courageous, foot-in-mouth, or encouraging words. Strong convictions, headstrong, natural born leader. Sometimes difficult to get along with or live with.

BARNABUS, a giver, steward. He was cause oriented. An analyst. Able to see the big picture.

MARTHA is synonymous with hospitality. She always had a place for the followers and was always cooking, cleaning, and caring for others. Remember the story of Lazarus? That was her brother.

PAUL, a preacher and writer. Always leading others to Christ, even at the cost of personal pain. A great missionary.

MARY had the gift of faith. She just wanted to sit at the feet of Jesus.

What other followers of Jesus come to mind, and what were some of their gifts? *Allow participants to respond freely. List the names and gifts of other disciples on newsprint, a chalkboard, or a dry erase board.* 🕐

Not a lot has changed in the faith arena these last two thousand years. People are people; people are different; people have a variety of gifts; all gifts are necessary. As you can see, life is very interesting when we share and use our different gifts!

Journal   (12 minutes)

Let's break now for a time of journaling. Choose a follower of Jesus—one we have or have not named—and journal about this individual's gifts as revealed to us in the New Testament. If you like, choose someone who possessed a gift that you believe you have as well. What can you learn from his or her example? We'll come back together in about ten to twelve minutes. 🕐

Explore   (20–25 minutes)

In Session 2, you looked closely at each spiritual gift and attempted to identify your top three gifts. Then, in Session 3, you completed a spiritual gifts inventory. Take a moment now to consider your gifts again and rank your top three gifts. We'll allow about four minutes. 🕐

Now you're going to visit with others who have one or more of your top three gifts. As I call out each gift, raise your hand if that is one of your top three gifts. With your hand still raised, look around the room and write in your journal all or some of the names of those who share this gift. After we've covered the last gift, mingle among yourselves; seek out one or more of the women you listed for each of your top three gifts and talk with them briefly. Ask one another questions such as: Did you already know this was your gift? Why or why not? How have you used it? How would you like to use it in the future? We'll come back together for our closing worship in about fifteen to twenty minutes. I'll let you know when five minutes remain.

Note: If you have a large group, you may want to use a more organized approach. Print each gift in large, bold letters on a piece of paper or poster board and tape the signs to the wall around the room. Instruct participants to go and stand under the sign that names their number-one gift. Allow five to seven minutes for those gathered to visit; then instruct them to move to the sign that names their second gift. Again, allow five to seven minutes for those gathered to visit; then instruct them to move to the sign that names their third gift. Once again, allow five to seven minutes for those gathered to visit. 🕐

Close   (3 minutes)

Read the following aloud:

Moments of Love

Today was a moment of love.
Have you seen it yet?
Have you felt it?
Are you looking?
I saw love today . . .

As newborn Jane awaited her baptism,
gathered into a family of love . . .
As a young boy hearing God's Word read
while snuggling against his father's worsted wool suit . . .
It was a tear I saw that dropped onto the altar rail during our prayer.

Love.
I saw it today in an elderly couple,
in the eyes of strangers,
in the words of a hymn.
Love.

I saw love today,
and I am blessed.

How about you?

CLOSING WORSHIP   (3:00–4:00)

Lighting of the Candle

As you light a white pillar candle, representing Christ's presence, say: "We light this candle remembering that God made every good thing."

Special Music

Play the selection "You Are Beloved," included on Colleen Haley's CD From the Heart, *or choose another appropriate song or hymn. Listen or sing along.* ♪

Scripture Reading

Have someone read aloud Isaiah 43:1-7 and Deuteronomy 33:12. 🕐

Dedication Ceremony

In Advance: Cut different colors of tissue paper into a variety of shapes and put them in a basket or other container. Place one large piece of clear adhesive paper on the altar or worship table—sticky side up. (Note: You may substitute waxed paper and glue or spray adhesive for the adhesive paper.)

During Worship: Dedicate your gifts in this special way. Invite individuals to choose a piece of colored tissue paper for each of their gifts. Then, while music is softly played or hymns are quietly sung, invite the women to walk silently to the altar one at a time, place their tissue pieces on the adhesive paper, and offer a silent prayer. 🕐 *When all have finished, place another piece of clear adhesive paper on top of the tissues—sticky side down. You have made a beautiful stained-glass window! After the worship service, you may frame it with black construction paper, if you like.*

Prayer of Thanksgiving—for the Gifts and for the Giver of Gifts

Lord God, Creator of every good and perfect thing in this world, Creator of each woman in this gathering—each woman fashioned after you, made in your image: you have held us in your hand; you know us as no other knows. We thank you for the gifts that you have woven throughout our very beings. We praise you that these are gifts you want us to develop. Lord, we ask that you help us find the right people and places we may share our gifts with. We ask these things in your holy name. Amen.

Scripture Reading

Read aloud together Ephesians 4:11-16. (Prepare a handout in advance and distribute now so that all are reading the same translation.) 🕐

Closing

As the stained-glass banner is displayed, create a spontaneous litany. As the leader, you will recite the opening and closing line. Invite each woman to speak one sentence as part of the litany. Note: Be sure the women know that it is OK to pass if they do not wish to speak.

Opening and Closing Line: We are indeed a beautiful people fashioned by God! 🕐

RETURN HOME   (4:00)

Thank each person for her participation and make any necessary closing remarks. 🕐 *Now it is time for the design team to clean, pack up, and evaluate the day.*

Sacred Listening

◆

OVERVIEW

Holy silence—listening for God's guidance in wonder, faith, hope, pain, and adoration. Participants' quiet eyes are turned to the Holy One as they learn the habit of holy listening through methods that include the use of the Bible, journaling, music, and spiritual friends. This retreat is intended for those whose prayer life is just beginning to broaden.

PREPARING FOR THE RETREAT
- Review "How to Use This Book: Planning and Preparing for Retreats" (pp.11-15).
- Assemble the design team.
- Read through the retreat; make revisions and additions as appropriate for your group or situation.
- Pray for the retreat.
- Advertise; invite and recruit participants.
- Send correspondence noting details of the retreat. (Be sure to let participants know what items they are to bring.)
- Gather the supplies.

SUPPLIES AND MATERIALS
To be brought by the leader
- nametags
- cassette/CD player
- cassettes/CDs, including meditative music
- hymnals or other songbooks (see suggested songs and hymns throughout the retreat)
- newsprint and marker, chalkboard and chalk, or dry erase board and marker
- white pillar candle and matches or lighter
- paper, pens, pencils
- a journal for each participant (Note: For large groups, ask participants to bring their own.)
- *Opening to God* by Carolyn Stahl (optional, see Session 1)
- *The Many Names of God* by Carolyn Sasso (optional, see Session 1)
- copy of James Weldon Johnson's poem "Creation" (optional, see Session 1)
- recording of the song "Breath of Heaven" by Amy Grant (see Session 1)
- lyrics to the song "Day by Day" (see Session 3)

To be brought by each participant
- Bible
- quilt or blanket
- pen or pencil

The Retreat

ARRIVAL AND WELCOME   (9:00–9:30)

See pages 12-13 for arrival and welcome suggestions. Once everyone has arrived and received a nametag, begin a get-acquainted game or activity. 🕐

SESSION 1   (9:30–11:00)

Open   (5 minutes)

Read aloud the following quotations:

Nothing in life is to be feared. It is only to be understood. —Marie Curie
All is a gift to me, everything is God to me. —Meister Eckhart
We water-ski over the deep issues of life. —M. T. Heffte

Play the selection "Just Ask and You Will Receive," included on Colleen Haley's CD From the Heart, *or choose another appropriate song, and sing along.* 🎵

Explore   (15–20 minutes)

Read the following aloud, pausing as appropriate so that the participants may do what you have instructed.

Let's begin this day apart with a guided imagery exercise. First, get comfortable. Lie down on the floor, if possible. *Pause.* Take several deep breaths. As you blow out each breath, be conscious of letting go of any pain and stress. *Pause.* Become totally relaxed.

Now lead the group in the guided imagery exercise "Let Your Light Shine" from Opening to God *by Carolyn Stahl (Nashville: Upper Room Books, 1977), pp. 69-72, or you may choose to write your own guided imagery exercise. For our purposes, a guided meditation is simply an imaginary story that requires participants to picture themselves in a place where they come into contact with God. Using a lot of descriptive words, describe a beach or mountain scene; then ask a "wondering" question, such as "What/Where is God calling you to do? . . . to be? . . . to go?" Afterward, instruct participants to write about the experience in their journals. Allow fifteen to twenty minutes for the entire exercise.* 🕐

Talk   (20 minutes)

Read this section several times until you can paraphrase and present it in your own speaking style. If possible, begin with a reading of The Many Names of God *by Carolyn Sasso, a children's book of profound truth. Note: Time for reading the book has been included in the suggested time of twenty minutes.*

We give many names to God, but they are all insufficient to describe God. They include Yahweh, Elohim, Creator, Sustainer, Friend, Lord, Father, Mother. The list is literally endless. Whenever we address God, using any name, we are entering into prayer.

What is prayer? It is the free flow of thought, a sense of peace, inner reflection, conversation with God, communion. In essence, prayer is a relationship with God. In prayer, we listen, talk, and spend time together. There are many kinds of prayers.

- **Private prayers.** These are the personal prayers that we pray aloud, silently, or in writing during our days. They are the prayers that often come automatically and are not meant for others to hear or read. These are the sudden spoken prayers of our daily struggles and recognition.
- **Communal prayers.** These are the group prayers that we pray aloud with friends or with others in Bible study and prayer groups. These also may include our mealtime prayers.

- **Institutional prayers.** These are the prayers of our denominations that we pray in church worship services, at funerals, or at weddings.
- **Historical prayers.** These are the prayers of the saints or other persons whose prayers have been recorded for our growth and nurture.

In which category do you find yourself spending most of your prayer time? In which category do you spend little or no time at all? Turn to someone sitting close to you and discuss this for about three to five minutes. 🕐

If time allows, have someone read the appropriate scripture aloud after you read each of the following statements. Otherwise, have participants note the scripture references in their journals, if they like.

Here are some basic truths about prayer from scripture:

- Prayer is natural; in other words, it is natural to pray. Prayer expands our concept of God and our relationship with God (Philippians 4:6).
- Prayer is complete freedom and honesty (James 5:13).
- Prayer is transformational—for us and for the world (Exodus 34:29).
- Prayer is cooperation with God (2 Corinthians 5:20).

There are many different ways to pray. Prayer is:

- Meditative. When we are immersed in the thought of God and God's majesty, scripture becomes the "wonderful words of life."
- Conversational. A word of caution: Don't talk too much; be sure you listen to God!
- Contemplation. Teresa of Avila called this the prayer of quiet. It is resting in God. No distractions. Nothing. Just communion with God. Waiting with God. There is an old story about an African chief who says he doesn't know God by the "tolds" but by the "feels."
- Singing hymns and listening to instrumental music or contemporary Christian music.
- Reading the Psalms—especially aloud.
- Participating in Holy Communion.
- Movement. Song interpretation and sacred dance are types of "body prayer."

I have named just a few of the many ways we may pray. Two great resources that will help you explore the rich diversity of prayer in greater depth are *The Workbook of Living Prayer* by Maxie Dunnam (Nashville: Upper Room Books, 1994) and the classic by Richard Foster, *Prayer: Finding the Heart's True Home* (San Francisco: HarperSanFrancisco, 1992). *Encourage participants to jot down these titles in their journals.* 🕐

Journal   (10 minutes)

Let's spend a few moments apart in silent reflection. Complete the following statement in your journal: *For me, prayer is . . .* We'll come back together in about ten minutes. 🕐

Talk   (15 minutes)

Read this section several times until you can paraphrase and present it in your own speaking style.

Think about this idea for a moment: We breathe the very breath of God. God created us, formed us in God's own image, and holds us in loving hands. We are precious to God. Listen to Isaiah 64:8 (NRSV): "Yet, O LORD, you are our Father; we are the clay, and you are our potter; we are all the work of your hand." God already knows our thoughts, feelings, desires, hopes, and dreams. By sharing these with God in prayer, we only clarify them for ourselves because God already knows them.

If possible, obtain a copy of James Weldon Johnson's poem "Creation" in advance of the retreat, and read it aloud now. 🕐

If we let ourselves hunger for God and allow our love for God to lie dormant, it *will* lie dormant. God wants us to be close to God's self. We must learn holy listening. We listen for the divine whisper amid the human clatter. When we listen, we are close to God. Harry Emerson Fosdick once said that prayer is all about becoming perfect in love.

There is an old story about a rabbi's child who used to wander in the woods. At first his father let him wander, but over time the father became more and more concerned. The woods were dark and dangerous. The boy might lose his way.

The rabbi decided to discuss the matter with his child. One day he took him aside and said, "I have noticed that you often walk in the woods. Why do you go there so often?"

The boy replied to his father, "I go to find God."

"That is a very good thing," his father said. "I am glad you are searching for God. But, my child, don't you know that God is the same everywhere?"

"Yes," said the boy, "but I am not."

God is constant and unchanging. We, however, are continually changing and growing. Our faith and our relationship with God are clarified again and again. Our life of faith is a journey of change.

Journal   (15 minutes)

Once again, let's take some time to reflect silently on the ideas we have been considering. Respond to the following questions in your journal: How is hunger for God expressed in my life? How do I experience God's presence? When have I been transformed in or by prayer? In what ways am I growing to be "perfect in love" at this time in my life? We'll come back together in about fifteen minutes. 🕐

Close   (5 minutes)

In advance, invite someone who knows American Sign Language—perhaps someone in your group—to sign the contemporary Christian song "Breath of Heaven," recorded by Amy Grant, while the song is played. If you are unable to have someone sign the song, use your own words to invite the women to listen to the song in silent meditation.

Many of you have seen individuals "signing" hymns or other songs in a worship service. To watch them is to witness a holy moment. So often they appear to be communing with God in another time and place. As observers, we are blessed by experiencing the presence of God in a new way. Today we have the privilege of being blessed in this way as we watch *(say the name of the individual)* interpret for us the song "Breath of Heaven." 🎼

BREAK   (11:00–11:15)

SESSION 2   (11:15–12:15)

Open   (8 minutes)

Play the song "Listen to the Words of Jesus," included on Colleen Haley's CD From the Heart, *or choose another appropriate song. Sing along together, if you like.* 🎼
Read aloud Matthew 24. 🕐

Explore   (15 minutes)

For the next eight to ten minutes, we're going to attempt to chart our prayer lives. First you will list ten or twelve significant events in your life, writing them across the page horizontally. Next you will draw a horizontal line above them. Then you will rank each of the events from one to ten, with *one* representing an inactive period of your prayer life and *ten* representing an active period. Write all *ones* on the line, all *twos* just above the line, all *threes* above the *twos*, and so on, to create a chart of highs and lows. I'll let you know when time is up. 🕐 When you look at your chart, are you able to locate the mountaintop and desert experiences? What have you learned from this exercise? *Allow participants to respond freely; continue when you are ready.* 🕐

Journal   (8 minutes)

Let's spend some time apart in silent reflection. What one person has influenced your prayer life most significantly? Journal about that for the next three to five minutes. 🕐 *Have someone read aloud Mark 11:22-25.* 🕐

What are the hindrances to your prayers? Take one minute now to list them in your journal. 🕐

Explore   (5 minutes)

Have someone read aloud Matthew 19:13-15. 🕐

If we are to become childlike in prayer, what will that mean? Let's begin to answer this by considering another question: What are the qualities of children?

Encourage participants to respond freely. List their responses on newsprint, a chalkboard, or a dry erase board. Your list may include the following: innocent, curious, trusting, enthusiastic, loving, believing, genuine, energetic, joyful, filled with wonder, and so forth. 🕐

Journal   (5 minutes)

Which childlike quality can you absorb into your prayer life? Name it and journal about it for the next three to five minutes. 🕐

Talk   (12–15 minutes)

Read this section several times until you can paraphrase and present it in your own speaking style. Here is a simple guide to prayer: Make your prayers ACTS. *Write the following acrostic on newsprint, a chalkboard, or a dry erase board as you present each point.*

A = Adoration
C = Confession
T = Thanksgiving
S = Supplication

Adoration: Simply adore God. God is great. God is loving. God is omnipotent. God is ever creating you. God is destroying barriers. God is searching you out. God is the creator of the sea and of mosquitoes. As someone once said, this part of prayer is like the wide-angle camera lens.
Confession: This removes the barriers of sin. Be specific about what went wrong. Name the places where you have been separated from God. Let each one go. Trust God.
Thanksgiving: Offer your thanks to God for your day, the people in your life, the joys and the pains.
Supplication: This is the asking part. This is where we usually begin. We sound like spoiled children, saying, "Gimme, gimme." Sometimes we ask on behalf of others, and sometimes we ask on behalf of ourselves. We should not begin our prayers by making requests. When we arrive at the supplication point in our prayers, we should simply ask with the *assurance* that our request(s) will be answered. What we are requesting might be small and believable or huge and miraculous.

The Lord's Prayer is a perfect example of praying ACTS. Let's try it together now. *Pray the Lord's Prayer in unison.* 🕐

It may be helpful for you to change your prayer pattern frequently by trying different times and methods of prayer. The important thing is to never refuse to pray. The times when you are tempted not to pray are the times when you need to pray even more often. If the thought to pray ever enters your mind, pray right then!

For most people, praying alone comes much more easily than praying with others. That involves risk and fear. Yet, when we work through those feelings, we are able to build great friendships and discover that all are blessed by group prayer. Listen as the author of this retreat shares a personal story about praying with others:

I remember one of the first times I was ever in a prayer group. I was a public school teacher in a very oppressed inner-city location. When Janice, Betty, and I discovered that we were all actively seeking to grow spiritually, we decided to meet early in the mornings before our official school time began. The three of us would meet in one of our rooms, close the door, and pray. We would choose a verse for the day. Sometimes we drew the verse from a little plastic loaf of bread that held pieces of paper with scripture verses written on them. Sometimes the verse came from our own devotional reading. Then we would share prayer concerns, hold hands, and pray. They were rich, comforting prayers. I couldn't wait for those early morning get-togethers.

When have you found it rewarding to pray with others? *Encourage participants to respond freely; then proceed with the closing.* 🕐

Close   (4 minutes)

Slowly read aloud Psalm 103 to the group. 🕐

LUNCH AND FREE TIME   (12:15–1:30)

SESSION 3   (1:30–3:00)

Open   (3 minutes)

Read aloud the lyrics of the song "Day by Day." 🕐

Journal   (15 minutes)

Remember the story about Jesus walking on the water and Peter stepping out to walk to him? Listen as I read the story aloud. *Read aloud Matthew 14:22-33.* 🕐

Doubt and fear are part of faith. We often feel inadequate. When are the times you feel as if you are wearing someone else's shoes and they are way too big? Do these occasions involve relationships, your job, spiritual growth, friendships? Journal about these times now, as well as about your prayer life during these times. We'll come back together in about fifteen minutes. 🕐

Talk (30 minutes)

Read this section several times until you can paraphrase and present it in your own speaking style.

Prayer helps us grow. We grow through prayer because God *allows* us to grow *each day*—during good times as well as difficult times when we are plagued by doubt and fear and other heavy burdens. How do we grow? By broadening our perspective; by coming to recognize the difference between wants and needs; by risking and trusting. Prayer is sometimes a battlefield as we struggle between right and wrong desires. Prayer is a dimension of our faith pilgrimage, which is always a matter of trusting in God's goodness and love. God speaks to us in many ways. Through our conscience, we know or can sense what is right and what is not right for us. God also speaks to us through other people in our lives—even through strangers. God speaks to us through nature. If we live a prayer-filled life, we can hear God's words in many ways.

There are times in all of our lives when our prayer life is not fulfilling—when our prayer life is dry and bland. At those times, more than any others, it is more important to "fight the good fight" and keep working on our prayer life. We must continue through the fruitless season until we experience more fulfilling prayer.

Intercessory prayer, or praying for others, plays an important part in our spiritual growth through prayer. During this part of our prayer, we place other people's cares and concerns above our own. (As we mentioned in Session 2, intercessory prayer is part of supplication when we follow the ACTS model of prayer.) When we pray for others, we need to be careful not to tell God what we think is best for them. Instead, we express our love and concern and ask God to envelope them in his love and his will. Our job after prayer is simply to wait.

Let's consider a few important ideas related to intercessory prayer. I will read three statements aloud, one at a time. As I read each statement, write it in your journal and reflect on it for a moment. Then we'll have a time of open sharing and discussion. *After reading each of the following statements, pause for a minute or two so that participants may reflect. Then encourage them to share their thoughts and experiences related to that idea.* 🕐

1. Your mind is a channel that touches another's mind.
2. You can show your love for another by praying for that person.
3. You can grow in your forgiveness of others by praying for them.

As we conclude our study of prayer today, it is appropriate for us to consider the words of Paul in 1 Thessalonians 5:16-18. *Have someone read aloud 1 Thessalonians 5:16-18.* 🕐

Paul says that we are to give thanks *in everything*. We are to pray *without ceasing*. How is this possible? Listen as the author of this retreat offers some suggestions:

Prayer doesn't require quiet, stillness, or time alone. Actually, we can pray anytime, anywhere—while driving, walking, taking a bath, getting a drink of water, eating meals, getting dressed, or any time during the day. Sometimes we will have a lot to say; other times our prayers may be as short as just a few words. Some people call these short prayers "flash prayers" or "arrow prayers."

I learned another helpful way to remember to pray without ceasing from my friend Jodi. She wears her watch upside down at times when she wants to remember to pray for something immediate or specific. Each time she looks at it, she is reminded to pray. In fact, she wore her watch upside down during the weeks that I was writing this book, continually reminding herself to whisper intercessory prayers for me!

Invite participants to share their own ideas with one another. 🕐

Scripture Surf   (30 minutes)

Write the following scripture references on newsprint, a chalkboard, or a dry erase board; or instruct participants to write them in their journals as you read the references aloud.

Divide into small groups of *(state a number appropriate for your group)*. Choose three to four of these scripture passages and "surf" together for insights on listening.

Philippians 4:6
James 5:15-16
Psalm 103, 145, 150
Matthew 21:18-22
Galatians 6:7-10
Hebrews 11:1-3
James 1:19-20

We'll come back together in about twenty-five minutes. 🕐

Close   (10–12 minutes)

Have someone read John 15 aloud. 🕐 *Now play a recording of meditative music (approximately five to seven minutes in duration) and read aloud the following instructions.*

As you listen to the music, close your eyes and imagine the Master Gardener clipping your vines and reshaping your greenery. Think about your prayer life. Journal if you feel motivated to do so. After approximately five to seven minutes, we will come back together for our closing worship. I will let you know when time is up. 🕐

CLOSING WORSHIP   (3:00–4:00)

Lighting of the Candle

Light a white pillar candle in silence. (You will want this service to be in a quiet space—either outside or inside.)

Worship Song

Sing together the hymn "Spirit of the Living God." ♪

Special Music

If possible, play the song "Just Ask, and You Will Receive," included on Colleen Haley's CD From the Heart, *or choose another appropriate song.* ♪

Prayers of the People of God

Invite participants to share prayer concerns and requests. After allowing several minutes for silent prayer, close by saying the Lord's Prayer in unison. 🕐

Meditation

In advance, read the following story several times until you can paraphrase and present it in your personal speaking style.

It is only when we are still that the heart takes time to see. There was a little girl who liked to talk. In fact, she talked all the time! One day, she was telling her daddy a wonderful story while he was trying to read the newspaper. She crawled into his lap, wrinkling the paper, and held his face with her tiny hands as she said, "Daddy, listen to me with your ears and your eyes."

That's what God calls us to do—to listen with our very being! How will you begin to do just that? What small steps can you take to increase your "sacred listening"?

A Time of Sharing

Invite participants to share their responses with the group as they are comfortable. Be sure to say that it is OK for anyone to pass. 🕐

Worship Song

Close with the hymn "Sweet Hour of Prayer." ♪

RETURN HOME   (4:00)

Thank each person for her participation and make any necessary closing remarks. 🕐 *Now it is time for the design team to clean, pack up, and evaluate the day.*

Weekend

Retreats

The Weekend Retreat Model

◆

This retreat model is intended to be used as a weekend or three-day retreat. Weekend retreats provide optimal opportunity for spiritual growth and fellowship. Something happens when a group spends a few days together!

Although the retreats are designed and written for *groups* of women, individuals also may use them as personal retreats, making adjustments in the schedule and instructions as appropriate. Whether alone or in a group, the participant will be challenged through journaling, keeping silence, and "sacred stretching"—a time when God calls her to grow in her faith journey. These retreats provide avenues for great spiritual growth and new models for spiritual disciplines that can be incorporated into daily life.

This part of the book is divided into two sections: *Retreats Based on Themes* and *Retreats Based on Books*. The themes include four categories: priorities, needs, prayer, and spirituality. The retreats based on books represent a slice of what is available in the field of personal spiritual growth. (Other suggested books are listed in the Additional Resources section of the Appendix.) All provide a wealth of material for the avid learner.

Preparation is vital to the success of your retreat. First, you will want to read "How to Use This Book: Planning and Preparing for Retreats" (pp. 11-15) thoroughly. Then, before the retreat, prepare nametags, journals, and song sheets; gather the necessary supplies and materials; and consider any special needs of participants. See that the retreat space is cozy, appropriately arranged, and ready for you to begin as soon as all the participants have arrived and settled in. One or two members of the design team may want to arrive the night before to have ample time for setting up. Here are some questions to ask yourself:

- Will you be sitting on the floor or on couches, or will you be using tables and chairs or back jacks?
- Where will your worship space be? Do you need to create an altar? Will you need candles, flowers, a Bible, a special cloth? (I sometimes have used an altar cloth that participants can write their names on with a permanent ink pen. This can become a permanent worship cloth for future retreats.)
- What will the participants see, hear, and experience the moment they arrive?

The following weekend retreat schedule will help you plan your retreat; feel free to make revisions and additions to the schedule to meet your needs. Remember that the time allotments are estimates and are offered as suggestions.

Day 1

3:00 P.M.–6:00 P.M.	Arrive leisurely and relax
6:00 P.M.–7:00 P.M.	Dinner together
7:00 P.M.–7:30 P.M.	Group announcements and get-to-know-you activities
7:30 P.M.–9:00 P.M.	Session 1
9:00 P.M.–9:45 P.M.	Evening Worship

Day 2

8:00 A.M.–9:00 A.M.	Breakfast together (have coffee ready for the early risers)
9:00 A.M.–9:45 A.M.	Morning Watch
9:45 A.M.–11:45 A.M.	Session 2
11:45 A.M.–12:00 P.M.	Break
12:00 P.M.–1:00 P.M.	Lunch
1:00 P.M.–5:00 P.M.	Free time (sleeping, reading, craft activity, table games, etc.)
5:00 P.M.–6:00 P.M.	Singing and sharing
6:00 P.M.–7:00 P.M.	Dinner together
7:00 P.M.–8:00 P.M.	Session 3

8:00 P.M.–9:00 P.M.	Free time (time to stretch, take restroom breaks, visit, and grab blankets if having worship outside, while leaders set up for worship)
9:00 P.M.–9:45 P.M.	Evening Worship

Day 3

8:00 A.M.–9:00 A.M.	Breakfast together
9:00 A.M.–9:45 A.M.	Morning Watch
9:45 A.M.–11:00 A.M.	Session 4
11:00 A.M.–12:00 P.M.	Closing Worship
12:00 P.M. until . . .	Leisurely pack and return home (the design team may evaluate the retreat now or at a later time)

Remember to keep the format relaxed—do not overprogram. Encourage the women to arrive as early as their schedules permit in order to relax. One must be relaxed before one can be fed. Have nametags available when the first participant arrives. Nametags connect each participant to another and provide an easy way for the women to get to know one another. Ask participants to leave their watches in their suitcases so that they may be "fully present" for each part of the retreat and not anticipate the next activity or the schedule.

More than enough material is provided for each retreat session; simply choose what is needed for your group. A unique component to these retreats is Morning Watch, which is a block of time set apart for individual quiet time. Reproducible handouts for participants to use during this time apart are provided in the Appendix. Encourage every participant to make Morning Watch a priority. Many will take this new habit home with them. Another addition to the weekend retreat is Evening Worship. This is a moving time of worship, praise, and contemplation that may take place outside or inside by candlelight. It is appropriate that the setting be worshipful and conducive to your purpose. Often women will remain after the worship service to linger in the atmosphere that you have created. Be patient; God is working.

Throughout the retreat, be flexible, *feel* the pulse of the group, and listen to the direction of the Spirit. God will guide you!

Getting First Things First— and Keeping Them There! (Priorities)

OVERVIEW

One of the hardest things about life today is the busy-ness in which we all are caught. This model helps women simplify their daily lives as they learn how to put what is truly important first in their lives. Participants will explore holy habits and healthy balance that will help them to keep God first in their lives.

PREPARING FOR THE RETREAT
- Review "How to Use This Book: Planning and Preparing for Retreats" (pp. 11-15).
- Assemble the design team.
- Read through the retreat; make revisions and additions as appropriate for your group or situation.
- Pray for the retreat.
- Advertise; invite and recruit participants.
- Send correspondence noting details of the retreat. (Be sure to let participants know what items they are to bring.)
- Gather the supplies.

SUPPLIES AND MATERIALS
To be brought by the leader
- nametags
- cassette/CD player
- cassettes/CDs, including meditative music
- hymnals or other songbooks (see suggested hymns and songs throughout the retreat)
- newsprint and marker, chalkboard and chalk, or dry erase board and marker
- white pillar candle and matches or lighter
- paper, pens, pencils
- a journal for each participant (Note: For large groups, ask participants to bring their own.)
- medium-size basket
- recording of the song "Peace Be Still" (optional, see Session 1)
- *Opening to God* by Carolyn Stahl (optional, see Session 1)
- recording or music video of "Prayer and Plainsong" by Cynthia Clawson (Calla Lilly Productions, 1995) (optional, see Session 3)
- stationery and envelopes (see Session 3)
- handout of cinquain diagram (optional, see Session 4)
- Morning Watch handouts for Days 2 and 3, one for each participant (see Appendix)
- two or more washrags soaked in warm water (see Closing Worship)

To be brought by each participant
- Bible
- quilt or blanket
- pen or pencil

The Retreat   Day 1

ARRIVAL   (3:00 P.M.–6:00 P.M.)

Have nametags ready for the participants as they arrive. Designate one or more greeters to personally escort each participant to her room and invite her to relax by resting, sleeping, reading, walking, hiking, talking with others, and so forth.

DINNER   (6:00 P.M.–7:00 P.M.)

This is the first group activity. If space allows, form a large circle and say or sing the blessing. As leader, wait to be served last so that you may walk around the room and welcome everyone. Encourage the participants to sit with others whom they do not already know. Look for those who seem lost or who are alone. Assign persons from the design team to keep an eye on these participants and see that connections with others begin to take place.

GROUP ANNOUNCEMENTS/GET-TO-KNOW-YOU ACTIVITIES   (7:00 P.M.–7:30 P.M.)

After dinner, formally welcome everyone and make any necessary group announcements—such as telling the location of bathrooms, telephones, and first-aid kits, and reviewing the retreat schedule. Then begin a get-acquainted game or activity.

SESSION 1   (7:30 P.M.–9:00 P.M.)

Open   (5 minutes)

Play the selection "Look Inside Your Heart," included on Colleen Haley's CD From the Heart *(see p. 15), and sing along together, or choose another appropriate song.*

Read the following aloud:

You Renew Me

You, Lord, have washed the earth with fresh rain.
You renew the grass, the trees, the flowers,
You renew me.

You, Lord, hold the sun and shape the clouds.
You scatter the stars and design the moon.
You renew me.

You, Lord, send your breezes against my skin,
You make the leaves dance,
And you, O Lord, bend the mighty Georgia pines.
You renew me.

Lord, you indeed put a new song in my heart.
You renew me.

Talk   (5 minutes)

Read this section several times until you can paraphrase and present it in your own speaking style, reading the following excerpt from My Utmost for His Hightest.
Listen to this paraphrase of Psalm 139:

Thou art the God of the early mornings, the God of the late at nights, the God of the mountain peaks, and the God of the sea; but, my God, my soul has further horizons than the early mornings, deeper darkness than the earth, higher peaks than any mountain peaks, greater depths than any sea in nature—Thou Who art the God of all these, be my God. I cannot reach to the heights or to the depths; there are motives I cannot trace, dreams I cannot get at—my God, search me out.[1]

While we are on retreat, we need to focus on faith and our need for God in our lives. When was the last time you spent an hour in silence? A half hour? Sit back, relax, take a few deep breaths, and listen. *Play a recording of "Peace Be Still" or have someone sing the song for the group; or choose another song of a similar theme.* ♪

Journal   (15 minutes)

Pause now to write in your journal about what you do on a typical day and why you do it. We'll come back together in ten minutes. 🕐 When you read what you have written, how do you feel about it? *Pause for several minutes and allow participants to respond.* 🕐

Talk   (5 minutes)

Read this section several times until you can paraphrase and present it in your own speaking style, reading the following quotation from Gift from the Sea.
Anne Morrow Lindbergh writes in *Gift from the Sea:*

The problem is more basically: how to remain whole in the midst of the distractions of life; how to remain balanced, no matter what centrifugal forces tend to pull one off center; how to remain strong, no matter what shocks come in at the periphery and tend to crack the hub of the wheel.[2]

Entire books are written on practicing the presence of God in our lives. How do we do that? How do we begin in the midst of our chores and responsibilities and dreams and goals? We may practice the presence of God by living simply, praying throughout the day, journaling, and meditating on and absorbing the Scriptures. Let me repeat that: **We may practice the presence of God by living simply, praying throughout the day, journaling, and meditating on and absorbing the Scriptures.** How can you do these things in the midst of your busy life? You *decide* to do them. If you don't decide how to spend your time, someone else will decide for you. Your time is a gift from God, and it belongs to you. How will you use it? Let's use a guided journaling experience to think more about these ideas.

Journal   (10 minutes)

List ten significant events of your life. Think about how God was present in these experiences—how you experienced God in each of these events. List both positive and negative experiences. Remember, increasing the positives doesn't balance out the negatives; negatives are also learning and growing times. We'll allow ten minutes for this. 🕐

Explore   (10 minutes)

Briefly discuss the following questions as a full group; or, if your group is larger than twenty, you may want to break into smaller groups.

What did you learn about yourself?
Where were the surprises?
Where do you feel God leading you?
🕐

Talk   (5 minutes)

Read this section several times until you can paraphrase and present it in your own speaking style—with the exception of the author's words, which are to be read aloud.

What are the barriers to simplifying your life? Does your list possibly include any of these barriers?

• other people's needs

- things you "ought" to do
- things you "should" do

Our purpose as women of faith is to obey our Creator's will. Yet in order to do this, we sometimes define ourselves by our relationship to someone or something else. Listen to this example from the author of this retreat.

> I am Ellen, a child of God, a wife, mother, daughter, sister, niece, aunt, cousin, neighbor, friend, minister, writer. I am someone who loves quiet, early morning walks, music, art, and collections of quilts, angels, and Santas. I live in an intergenerational family. Sometimes I find it easy to find time to be with God because of who I am and how I live and because of the other people in my life. But the opposite is also true: Sometimes I find it difficult to find time to be with God because of who I am and how I live and because of the other people in my life. I often work hard to find time alone with God. Get my drift? We are many things as we relate to others. However, God calls us to simple things: to be still (Psalm 46:10) and to walk humbly with God (Micah 6:8). When I take time to be alone with God, to walk with God each step of the way, I am well assured of the direction and priorities of my life.

Who are *you*? How do *you* simplify? Let's spend a few minutes writing about this in our journals.

Journal (10 minutes)

List words to describe how you define yourself. Think about these questions: Who are you? How would you describe yourself to someone you've never met—on the phone, in a letter, or in a chat room on the internet? How do you spend your time? Do you have a pattern for spending time with God? What is your devotional time like? We'll allow five minutes for this. 🕐 Now find a partner and share your insights with each other. We'll allow another five minutes for this. 🕐

Talk (5 minutes)

Read this section several times until you can paraphrase and present it in your own speaking style.
How do we live with other people and not wear out in the process? Pastor and author James W. Moore tells a story of a "salty old saint" who says that she would rather wear out than rust out! How do we find the very thin line between wearing out and rusting out? How did Mother Teresa find this thin line? How did Martin Luther King, Jr.? Amy Carmichael? Dorothy Day? How do the women you know find this thin line?

What causes stress in your life? Work, family, extended family, neighbors, craft projects, the holidays, traffic, money, failure, worries about the future, too many commitments, church activities . . . ? Take time this weekend or after you return home to make your own list. Then prioritize your list. What are the "musts" in your life? You can't do everything. You will have to make choices in order to be a healthy seeker of the walk of faith. We all have the same twenty-four hours each day. By choosing some things, you are saying no to other things. Perhaps that "no" is not for all time; it is only for *this* time.

In her book *Women Who Do Too Much*, Patricia Sprinkle suggests that you determine which stresses are situational and which are caused by people. If a stress is situational, she suggests you pray about it and then decide if you can do anything to improve the situation. Ask yourself if there is any behavior of your own that you can change. If the stress is caused by a person, she suggests you ask yourself these questions: Does this person make demands on you? Are you responsible for this person? Other questions to consider include these: Have you overcommitted yourself to this person? Is this person a child you are raising? What can you do to better manage the situation? What are your options? Parenting classes? Fewer after-school activities? Think *change*. What change can you make? Change takes time, and change is difficult; but remember that your life can be enhanced through change.

In the end (or should it be in the beginning?), hand over to God every situation that you can do nothing about. Can you say confidently, "God is in control of my life"? Claim the power of this statement. Say it aloud now: "God is in control of my life." Listen to these words from Matthew 22:36-39:

"Teacher, which is the greatest commandment in the Law?" Jesus replied: "'Love the Lord your God with all your heart and with all your soul and with all your mind.' This is the first and greatest commandment. And the second is like it: 'Love your neighbor as yourself.'"

Close   (20 minutes)

Close with the guided imagery meditation "Reflection" from Opening to God *by Carolyn Stahl (Nashville: Upper Room Books, 1977), pp. 82-84, or you may choose to write your own guided meditation. For our purposes, a guided meditation is simply an imaginary story that requires participants to picture themselves in a place where they may come into contact with God. Using a lot of descriptive words, describe a beach or mountain scene; then ask a "wondering" question, such as, "What/Where is God calling you to do? . . . to be? . . . to go? Afterward, instruct participants to write about the experience in their journals. Allow twenty minutes for the entire exercise.*

EVENING WORSHIP (9:00 P.M.–9:45 P.M.)

Open

As you light a white pillar candle, say the following aloud: We are all connected by the Holy One. We are all challenged to carry the light within us.

Worship Song

Sing together the hymn "Spirit of the Living God." ♪

Words for Reflection

Read the following aloud:

Have you ever wondered why fish do not drown; why birds do not fall; why glass must be melted before it is shaped; why you are so unique—your eyes, your laugh, your thoughts, your fingerprints? We are called to live in our uniqueness and oneness with the Holy One.

A Time of Sharing

Let us pause for a time of deep listening. Find a partner and tell how it is with your soul. I'll let you know when it is time to come back together. 🕐

Words for Reflection

Read the following aloud:

Happiness is a butterfly which, when pursued, is always beyond your grasp, but which if you sit quietly, may alight upon you. —Nathaniel Hawthorne

Benediction

Close with these words: Go forth in peace, in the love of God, and may your rest be just what your body and soul desire.

Day 2

BREAKFAST   (8:00 A.M.–9:00 A.M.)

Have coffee ready for the early risers. Remember that this meal is an act of the total community. Join together in a large circle to greet the morning and to give thanks to God for the night's rest and for the food that is to be received. Encourage the women to sit beside new faces during breakfast.

MORNING WATCH   (9:00 A.M.–9:45 A.M.)

Reproduce the material on pages 178-79 and distribute to all participants as they leave breakfast and find a place apart for their Morning Watch. Remind them that Session 2 will begin at 9:45.

SESSION 2   (9:45 A.M.–11:45 A.M.)

Open   (1 minute)

Read aloud the following quotations:

The days that make us happy, make us wise. —John Mansfield

If I could, I would always work in silence and obscurity and let my efforts be known by their results. —Emily Brontë

Talk   (4 minutes)

Read this section several times until you can paraphrase and present it in your own speaking style. In order to have time for God, each of us must reorder our priorities. Henri Nouwen suggests that to grow spiritually we should have a relationship with our self, with others, and with God. Busyness is a status symbol today. There are hundreds of ads in magazines, on television, and on billboards that encourage us to be busy—consistently. There are so many calendar systems and organizational books. What is the key to living a life of (good) priorities? Constancy is the key. As Christian women, we need to find ways to consistently have God's peace that controls our daily lives. It's what we do *regularly* that makes a difference.

Journal   (5 minutes)

What are some synonyms for spirituality? Think of as many as you can. Your list might include time alone, time with God, music, peace, journey, consistency, countryside, snow, lakes, and so forth. We'll allow two minutes for this. 🕐

Now find a partner and share how these words interact with your life. We'll come back together in three minutes. 🕐

Talk   (8–10 minutes)

Read this section several times until you can paraphrase and present it in your own speaking style. Have someone read Psalm 46:10 aloud. 🕐 *What does Psalm 46:10 tell us about being open to God? Pause for a moment and let participants respond freely; then continue.* 🕐

Listen to these thoughts from the author of this retreat:

> I have a painting in my office that a special friend created. It is an oil painting of the lake at the retreat center where I try to spend as much time as possible. The proportion of the painting is really interesting; the majority of the painting is the reflection of the pine trees and clouds in the water. In the far right corner, my friend painted these words: "Peace, be still." This painting always causes me to take a deep breath and remember the presence of God—and I need that often in my day! God's presence—in me, in the place where I am, at that special retreat, and where you are right now. God is there. God is here. So I offer to you God's peace.

You can escape the busyness. There are many ways:

- discipline
- simplify your life and your stuff
- set priorities
- say no
- evaluate all the perimeters a commitment affects
- set time aside to *be* with God

- allow yourself time to be still
- remember God's presence

In her book *Women Who Do Too Much*, Patricia Sprinkle suggests we learn the three D's:

- Drop it—will it really matter if I don't do this?
- Delay it—Does this really have to be done today? (Be careful; this is not procrastination!)
- Delegate it—who else can do this job as good as or better than I can?

Life is about finding balance so that you may do all the things you love to do, which are gifts God has given you.

Journal   (15 minutes)

Reflect on your experiences of God at work in your life. Then journal your reflections. As Christians on the walk of faith, we need to learn ways to be *present* in our lives—to be aware of God's presence and to be present in return; to live life as a whole and not in thousands of tiny pieces. Where are you? Do you have a plan? Do you prioritize? Do you have perfect peace? We'll allow five minutes for this time of journaling. 🕐

Now share with a partner what your life "looks like." Talk together about the changes you would like to make. We'll come back together in ten minutes. 🕐

Talk   (5 minutes)

Read this section several times until you can paraphrase and present it in your own speaking style. Listen to Philippians 3:12-14:

Not that I have already obtained all this, or have already been made perfect, but I press on to take hold of that for which Christ Jesus took hold of me. [Sisters], I do not consider myself yet to have taken hold of it. But one thing I do: Forgetting what is behind and straining toward what is ahead, I press on toward the goal to win the prize for which God has called me heavenward in Christ Jesus.

Pause after reading each of the following points, inviting participants to respond briefly if they wish. We must make God first in all things. We can do this by:

- Practicing the presence of God. (You might want to read the little book by the same name.) Remember Psalm 16:8: "I have set the LORD always before me. Because [the LORD] is at my right hand, I will not be shaken."
- Guarding our daily quiet time with God, the Scriptures, and nature.
- Being diligent about worship. Remember Luke 4:16*b*: "[Jesus] went into the synagogue, as was his custom."
- Seeking larger chunks of time to spend with God.
- Taking care of God's people.

Think about these questions silently: What have you learned about seeking the priority of peace? How will this make a difference in your life?

Close   (15–20 minutes)

Close with the following guided imagery exercise, adapted from Patricia Sprinkle's book Women Who Do Too Much *(Grand Rapids: Zondervan, 1992), p. 32. Quietly play some meditative music in the background. Good choices are the recordings of David Lanz's "Pianoscapes" and Michael Jones's "After the Rain."*

Lie down on the floor and relax. *Pause.* Take several deep cleansing breaths. *Pause.* Become aware of your breathing. *Pause.*

Someone once suggested to me that as I pray, I might imagine myself as a stone before the sculptor begins carving. I should present myself before God in this way, desiring God's perfect image to be carved in my soul—to be made entirely like him. Imagine yourself before the throne of God. *Pause.* You are the stone and God is the carver. *Pause.* Ask the Holy One to shape you and allow that to happen. *Pause.* Imagine being so in tune with the Spirit of God that life flows smoothly and life works out. *Pause.* Allow yourself to yearn for God's tranquility. *Pause.* Turn that yearning into a prayer. *Pause.*

When you are ready, open your eyes. *Pause; when all have opened their eyes, continue.* Now journal your experience. 🕐

BREAK (11:45 A.M.–12:00 P.M.)

LUNCH (12:00 P.M.–1:00 P.M.)

This is another time for building community. Gather again in a large circle, give thanks, and encourage the women to sit beside some new faces.

FREE TIME (1:00 P.M.–5:00 P.M.)

This time is provided for sleeping, walking, crafting, sharing, playing games, or simply relaxing. If everyone is not comfortable with this amount of free time, feel free to adjust the schedule accordingly. Make sure that each woman finds something she wants to do.

SINGING AND SHARING (5:00 P.M.–6:00 P.M.)

Singing unites our spirits! Perhaps one or more individuals in your group are singers who may take turns leading the group in singing—and may even sing a few solos themselves. You may want to prepare one or more song sheets, use hymnals, or sing "old favorites." (If you prepare song sheets and use copyrighted material, be sure to include your church license number on these sheets. Check with your choir director or organist for this information.) This also is a good time to check in with the group and see how the retreat is going. Are there any problems? Any discoveries?

DINNER (6:00 P.M.–7:00 P.M.)

Form a circle and say or sing the blessing. Then enjoy more community-building time as you share food and fellowship.

SESSION 3 (7:00 P.M.–8:00 P.M.)

Open (5 minutes)

If possible, listen to the song (or view the music video) "I Love You, Lord" from "Prayer and Plainsong" by Cynthia Clawson (Calla Lilly Productions, 1995).
Read the following aloud:

Look to the LORD and his strength;
seek his face always. (Psalm 105:4)

Teach us to number our days aright,
that we may gain a heart of wisdom. (Psalm 90:12)

Shout with joy to the Lord, all the earth,
Burst into songs and make music. (Psalm 98:4, NCV)

Journal (5 minutes)

Make a list of ten things that you are thankful for, and a list of ten things that you do well. Quickly write those things you think of first. We'll pause for about five minutes. 🕐

Now, as you read over your lists, listen to these words of wisdom. You might want to write them in your journal.

Never underestimate the power of pride in one task well done.
What I can do is what I can do, and what I can do is enough.

Talk   (5 minutes)

Read this section several times until you can paraphrase and present it in your own speaking style.
Time. We all have the same amount each day. Why is it, then, that some people seem to have more time than others? Could it be that some people use their time wisely? We all have similar experiences: too many telephone calls; unexpected visitors; too much to do with too little, or in too little time; lack of focus, discipline, planning, or objectives. Can you think of other time constraints that you struggle with personally? *Allow participants to respond freely; then continue.* 🕐

Journal   (10 minutes)

For the next five minutes, reflect on the following questions and record your responses in your journal. I'll let you know when time is up.

- Do I have a quiet place where I can listen to God?
- Do I want a quiet place? (It can simply be a corner in your bedroom, a bench in your yard or a nearby park, the living room that everyone avoids, and so forth.)
- Is quiet time a priority for me?
- These are the steps I will take to make a regular quiet time with God a priority in my life . . . 🕐

Now, for the next five minutes, respond briefly to the following in your journal:

- Name four people you can share deep pain with.
- How satisfied are you with the level of sharing in these close relationships?
- How could that level become even deeper?
- What things can you do to strengthen these relationships? 🕐

Explore   (5 minutes)

Find a partner and share together some of the reasons we hold back in relationships. Why is it that we are afraid to grow and share deeply with one another? Is it the fear of rejection, a lack of trust, intuition, vulnerability, poor communication, boundaries? We'll come back together in five minutes. 🕐

Journal   (5 minutes)

Read the following aloud:

You have to know how someone cares before you care how much they know.—Anonymous

To love a person means to see that person as God intended him [or her] to be.—Dostoyevsky

If you were to have a conversation with God, what would the Holy One say about the close relationships in your life and what you want from them? Write your answer in your journal. We'll allow five minutes for this. 🕐

Scripture Surf   (15 Minutes)

Write the following scripture references on newsprint, a chalkboard, or a dry erase board; or instruct participants to write them in their journals as you read the references aloud.
In silence, choose three to four of the following verses and "scripture surf":

Psalm 46:10
Zechariah 2:13
Psalm 23:2
Zephaniah 3:17
1 Peter 3:4, 11

Isaiah 30:15
Numbers 6:26
Proverbs 14:30
Isaiah 26:3
John 14:27
John 16:33
1 Corinthians 7:15
Philippians 4:7

Read each passage silently. Meditate on the words. Then journal as God's Great Spirit leads you. We'll allow fifteen minutes for this. 🕐

Close (10 minutes)

Have stationery, envelopes, and a basket ready for participants as you begin this exercise.

For the remaining time of this session, write a love letter from God to *you*. (*Announce how much time is remaining; try to allow ten minutes for this exercise, if possible.*) What things would God give words to? How are you doing on being the person God intends you to be? Include any scripture verses that are especially important. When you have finished, put the letter in an envelope and address it to yourself. Then place it in this basket so that it can be mailed to you at a later date. 🕐

FREE TIME (8:00 P.M.–9:00 P.M.)

During this time, participants may stretch, take restroom breaks, visit with one another, and prepare for Evening Worship (remind them to grab blankets if worship is to be held outside) while you and members of the design team set up for worship.

EVENING WORSHIP (9:00 P.M.–9:45 P.M.)

Lighting of the Candle

As you light a white pillar candle, say the following aloud: As we look upon this lighted candle, let us remember that we are connected and are called to carry the light within us.

Worship Song

Sing together the hymn "Lead Me, Lord." 𝄞

A Time of Reflection

Read the following aloud, pausing briefly after each question so that the participants may reflect silently.

Once, a child looking at a stained-glass window in church remarked: "Saints are people the light shines through." Does the light shine through you? *Pause.* How does it? *Pause.* Is it noticed by others? *Pause.* Whom do you know that is or was a saint?

A Time of Sharing

Find a partner and take turns finishing this sentence: If Jesus came today, I would . . . 🕐

A Time of Prayer

Jesus taught us how to pray. Let us pray together the Lord's Prayer. 🕐

Worship Song

Sing together the hymn "Precious Lord, Take My Hand." 𝄞

Benediction

Go now in the peace of God that passes all understanding.

Day 3

BREAKFAST (8:00 A.M.–9:00 A.M.)

By this time, you will note that the group has "jelled" and most are interacting as family. Enjoy this breakfast together after a group blessing.

MORNING WATCH (9:00 A.M.–9:45 A.M.)

Reproduce the material on pages 178-79 and distribute to all participants as they leave breakfast and find a place apart for their Morning Watch. Remind them that Session 4 will begin at 9:45.

SESSION 4 (9:45 A.M.–11:00 A.M.)

Open (5 minutes)

Sing the hymn "It Is Well with My Soul." You may want to have an individual sing the verses and the group sing only the refrain. ♪
Read the following quotation aloud:

Busyness is the enemy of spirituality.—Eugene Peterson

Journal (15 minutes)

What have you learned or experienced during this retreat that will make a difference in your life? Record your thoughts in your journal. We'll come back together in fifteen minutes. ⏰

Talk (15 minutes)

Read this section several times until you can paraphrase and present it in your own speaking style. Give yourself permission to:

- take time to be holy.
- rest when you are weary.
- exercise.
- accept your limitations.
- reward yourself.
- give thanks in all things.

What do you need to give yourself permission to do? Will you share it with the group now? *Allow participants to share freely; then continue.* ⏰

What about your goals? One goal worthy of thinking about is to leave a mark on others, through your life and your talents, that will point them toward God. How does your life point the way toward God? How does your speech point the way? Your actions? Why is it important to point the way toward God? *Again, allow participants to share freely.* ⏰

Journal (15–20 minutes)

Prepare in advance a handout providing the following cinquain diagram, and distribute copies to participants now; or write the diagram on newsprint, a chalkboard, or a dry erase board.
Reflect on all that you have heard and experienced during this retreat, and write a cinquain that expresses something about your relationship with the Holy One. We'll allow ten minutes for this; I'll let you know when time is up. ⏰

Cinquain Diagram
Line 1   title (one word)
Line 2   describes the Holy One (two words)
Line 3   action words or phrase about the title (three words)
Line 4   describes a feeling about the title (four words)
Line 5   synonym for the title (one word)

I invite you now to share your poem with the group, if you like. *Allow participants to share as they choose; then proceed with the closing.* 🕐

Talk   (5 minutes)

As I read an excerpt from Deena Metzger's book *Writing for Your Life,* listen for the seeds of truth. Ask yourself: Where does this take me in my journey of priorities?

Many years ago, Barbara Myerhoff was teaching a class at the University of Southern California in urban anthropology. As part of the course, the students were required to interview someone very different from themselves, someone with whom they would not normally converse. One young man in the class, who had lived an unusually protected and insulated middle-class life, was having such great difficulty in finding a subject that he considered dropping the course. However, on the day the paper was due, he arrived to the class ecstatic.

"I was at my wit's end," he said, "when it occurred to me to interview our Guatemalan housekeeper. Naturally, I was very nervous because I had never really spoken to her, and it was rather late at night. But as I had to do the paper, I went to her room and knocked at her door. When I entered, I explained my need, asking if it would be a terrible nuisance for her to tell me something about her life. She looked at me strangely and my heart sank. After what seemed a very, very long time, she said quietly, "Every night before I go to sleep, I rehearse the story of my life, just in case someone should ever ask me. Gracias a Dios."[3]

Close   (15 minutes)

As we close this session and prepare for our final worship experience together, journal your thoughts about the story you've just heard. Where did it connect with your life? Do you need to share your story? Do you need to hear other stories? We'll allow about fifteen minutes for this. 🕐

CLOSING WORSHIP   (11:00 A.M. –12:00 P.M.)

Open

Read the following aloud:

Do not go where the path leads. Rather, go where there is no path and leave a trail.
—Anonymous

Worship Song

Sing together the hymn "Open My Eyes, That I May See." 🎵

A Time for Giving Thanks

Create a litany together by completing this statement one by one: I am thankful for . . . 🕐

Homily and Hand Washing

In ancient times, when knights were baptized, they often would allow the baptism by immersion to take place while holding their bag of gold above the water. In some sense, the statement they were making was, "God, you have all of me except my money."
What have you held back from God? *Pause momentarily for silent reflection; then continue.*
We will spend a few moments silently washing one another's hands. While this takes place, think of surrendering the piece of yourself or your life that you have held back.
Note: You will need at least two or more washrags that have been soaked in warm water. Have the group sit in a circle. Model the ritual by taking the hands of the woman beside you and washing them with the soft, warm rag. If your group is small, continue in this manner around the circle, washing one another's hands one at a time. If your group is large, have the women break into pairs. When all have been renewed, place the cloths near your "altar." 🕐

A Time of Sharing

While we have been together at this retreat, we have become family. With your new family in Christ, share the peace of God with one another. *Allow participants to share warm embraces and words of blessing.* 🕐

Worship Song

Sing together the hymn "All Things Bright and Beautiful." 𝄞

Benediction

As God's women, let us continue to walk in the light of God.

RETURN HOME   (12:00 P.M. until . . .)

Thank each person for her participation in the retreat and make any necessary closing remarks. 🕐 *Now it is time for the design team to clean, pack up, and evaluate the retreat; or, if you prefer, the team may save the evaluation for a later time.*

Come to the Well (God Meets Our Needs)

--------------------------------◆--------------------------------

> **OVERVIEW**
>
> The story of the woman at the well, found in the fourth chapter of John, is the foundation of this study. We all come to God's well—whether it is to take something or to bring something. Whichever it is, God will and does provide.

PREPARING FOR THE RETREAT
- Review "How to Use This Book: Planning and Preparing for Retreats" (pp. 11-15).
- Assemble the design team.
- Read through the retreat; make revisions and additions as appropriate for your group or situation.
- Pray for the retreat.
- Advertise; invite and recruit participants.
- Send correspondence noting details of the retreat. (Be sure to let participants know what items they are to bring.)
- Gather the supplies.

SUPPLIES AND MATERIALS
To be brought by the leader
- nametags
- cassette/CD player
- cassettes/CDs, including meditative music
- hymnals or other songbooks (see suggested hymns and songs throughout the retreat)
- newsprint and marker, chalkboard and chalk, or dry erase board and marker
- white pillar candle and matches or lighter
- paper, pens, pencils
- a journal for each participant (Note: For large groups, ask participants to bring their own.)
- medium-size basket
- materials of your choice for making a "well" (see Session 1)
- pitcher of water (see Session 1)
- "My Frail Raft" by Robert Raines (see Evening Worship, Day 1)
- biblical woman's costume and dramatic reading volunteer (see Evening Worship, Day 2)
- handout of Psalm 18:19; Romans 15:13; and 1 Corinthians 15:10 (optional, see Evening Worship, Day 2)
- *Granddad's Prayers of the Earth* by Douglas Woods (optional, see Session 4)
- Morning Watch handouts for Days 2 and 3, one for each participant (see Appendix)
- chalice of juice and loaf of bread (see Closing Worship)

To be brought by each participant
- Bible
- quilt or blanket
- pen or pencil
- flashlight

The Retreat Day 1

ARRIVAL (3:00 P.M.–6:00 P.M.)

Have nametags ready for the participants as they arrive. Designate one or more greeters to personally escort each participant to her room and invite her to relax by resting, sleeping, reading, walking, hiking, talking with others, and so forth.

DINNER (6:00 P.M.–7:00 P.M.)

This is the first group activity. If space allows, form a large circle and say or sing the blessing. As leader, wait to be served last so that you may walk around the room and welcome everyone. Encourage the participants to sit with others whom they do not already know. Look for those who seem lost or who are alone. Assign persons from the design team to keep an eye on these participants and see that connections with others are made.

GROUP ANNOUNCEMENTS/GET-TO-KNOW-YOU ACTIVITIES (7:00 P.M.–7:30 P.M.)

After dinner, formally welcome everyone and make any necessary group announcements—such as telling the location of bathrooms, telephones, and first-aid kits, and reviewing the retreat schedule. Then begin a get-acquainted game or activity. ☾

SESSION 1 (7:30 P.M.–9:00 P.M.)

Open (5 minutes)

Play the selection "Come to The Well," included on Colleen Haley's CD From the Heart (see p. 15), or choose another appropriate song. Sing along if you like. ♪
Read the following aloud:

The value of a personal relationship is that it creates intimacy and intimacy creates understanding and understanding creates love.—Anaïs Nin

To grasp God in all things—this is the sign of your new birth.—Meister Eckhart

Talk (15–20 minutes)

Read this section several times until you can paraphrase and present it in your own speaking style. In advance: Create your own "well" as a focal point for the retreat. You might use a large bucket or tub, a commercially made pump-driven waterfall, or a large cardboard box with a bucket placed inside. (You may paint the box or cover it with butcher's paper that you have decorated to look like a stone well.)

During the retreat: After you have poured water from a pitcher into the "well," say the following aloud: Think about the emptiness of this pitcher and the way we tend to live our lives. Our lives are far too full; our children's lives are too full—full of stuff and activities and busyness. But we can empty those things from our lives; we can fill ourselves with God. It is only when we are empty that we come to the Well to be restored. Remember that a well must be used in order to work. It must continually be emptied so that it will continually be filled. If it is not used at all, the well eventually will run dry. Recognize the One who brought you here. The Scripture for this retreat is John 4:1-30. Let's read the passage aloud together in its entirety. *Prepare a handout in advance and distribute it now so that all are reading the same translation.* ☾

What strikes you as fresh and new as you read this encounter between the woman at the well and Jesus? What "aha" moments did you experience? At a retreat led by the author of this retreat, one woman had a wonderful "aha." She said, "We've simply traded our water jars for briefcases!" *Encourage participants to share their "ahas" with one another; then continue.* ☾

Journal   (20 minutes)

In your journal, write an overview of the story of the woman at the well. Begin by listing the characters from the story. We'll allow five minutes for this. 🕐

Did your list of characters include Jesus, the disciples, the woman at the well, the woman *leaving* the well (who was very different from the woman who came to the well), the people in the town, the man she was living with? *Pause so that participants may share any responses; then continue.*

Now take ten minutes to respond to the following questions in your journal: Where are you in this story? Why have you come on this retreat? Where are you (in your life) as opposed to where you want to be? 🕐

Each of us needs to recognize the "Well" (with a capital W!) in our daily lives—to recognize the Holy Presence and surrender to the Source of all life.

Close   (20–25 minutes)

Lead the group in the following guided imagery experience, pausing as indicated and appropriate.

Get in a comfortable position. Lie down on your back, if possible. *Pause.* Close your eyes. *Pause.* Take several deep breaths, blowing them slowly out. *Pause.* Quiet your soul. *Pause.* Imagine that you are dressed in biblical clothing. *Pause.* It is noon, and the heat of the sun beats down on the ground, on your shoulders, and on your head. *Pause.* It is dusty. *Pause.* You are walking toward the well to retrieve water for cooking. You hope against hope that you see no one. They always seem to talk about you just when you are out of earshot. But you know what they are saying. It always makes you feel sick, and you look to the ground as you think about it. *Pause.* When you arrive at the well, you see a man. *Pause.* He is no one you recognize, but he looks at you—almost *through* you. *Pause.* Then you realize his look is tender, full of compassion, patient; and he's waiting—waiting for you to speak. What will you tell him? *Pause.* When you are ready, become aware of your breathing. *Pause.* When you are ready, journal about what you have experienced. We'll come back together in fifteen minutes. 🕐

EVENING WORSHIP   (9:00 P.M.–9:45 P.M.)

Call to Worship

Leader: Come, come to the well!
People: We come, Lord, to your well!

Worship Songs

Sing together the following:
"Kum ba Yah"
"Jesus Let Us Come to Know You," by Michael Card
"Spirit of the Living God"
🎼

Prayers of the People of God

Invite the women to share their prayers aloud at this time. Open and close the prayer time. 🕐

Homily

Share the following trilogy of stories, read aloud by the leader or by three participants. 🕐

Story #1

Once, while walking along one of North Carolina's beautiful lakes, three friends came upon a family of ducks. The ducks were beautiful, but they seemed to be caught in a strong current that was moving in an opposite direction as a result of one of the lake's inlets. The ducks fought and fought to rid themselves of the current and be free from being caught by the water. What the ducks didn't seem to know was that had they quit fighting and let the water guide them in the water's direction, they soon would have been freed of the current and found joy on the smooth water of the lake. Do you see yourself in this story? Are you fighting the pull? Or are you allowing God to lead you where God needs you to go? Stop furiously fighting the current; relax into the flow.

Story #2

Shortly after Travis had fallen asleep in his "big boy bed," he fell out of the bed with a loud crash. When his mother went to check on him, he said something that she never forgot: "Mommy, I guess I was just too close to where I got in." Is that where you are on your walk with Christ? Are you too close to where you got in?

Story #3

While a director of Christian education was attending a youth camp with the youth from her church, they had an opportunity to watch a professional glass blower make beautiful glassware. The glassblower was constantly shaping the glass by placing it into an extemely hot fire. He would then use very precise tools to shape the delicate object he was making. The fire continued to shape the glass. You see, the heat allowed the glass to be soft enough to be formed with the tools of the glassblower. It was melted and reshaped, melted and reshaped, until cool. Is that what God is doing in your life? Are you being thrown into the fire so that you can be reshaped? Are you one of God's delicate objects?

Reflective Reading

In advance, write the following poem by Robert Raines on a chalkboard or dry erase board. Read the poem aloud together.

My Frail Raft

I love walking at the river alone
it is quiet there
the river is flowing on
ever on
like my life

You are with me
beside still waters
near swift waters
in the rapids
in the quiet

Grant me in my frail raft
not to struggle
against the current of your leading
but to yield
to the flow of your pressure

You are with me
beside still waters
near swift waters
in the rapids
in the quiet

Let pressure from within
yield clarity
let pressure from without
distill patience
let me sense in every pressure
your presence

You are with me
beside still waters
near swift waters
in the rapids
in the quiet[1]

Special Music/Worship Song

Have an individual or the full group sing "Amazing Grace." 𝄞

Benediction

Living God, surround us with your grace, instill within us your love, that we may be your women. Amen.

Day 2

BREAKFAST   (8:00 A.M.–9:00 A.M.)

Have coffee ready for the early risers. Remember that this meal is an act of the total community. Join together in a large circle to greet the morning and to give thanks to God for the night's rest and for the food that is to be received. Encourage the women to sit beside new faces during breakfast.

MORNING WATCH   (9:00 A.M.–9:45 A.M.)

Reproduce the material on pages 180-81 and distribute to all participants as they leave breakfast and find a place apart for their Morning Watch. Remind them that Session 2 will begin at 9:45.

SESSION 2   (9:45 A.M.–11:45 A.M.)

Open   (5 minutes)

Sing together the song "Morning Has Broken." 𝄞
Read the following aloud:

All you need is deep within you waiting to unfold and reveal itself. All you have to do is be still and take time to seek for what is within, and you will surely find it.—Eileen Caddy

There are voices which we hear in solitude, but they grow faint and inaudible as we enter the world.—Ralph Waldo Emerson

The soul can split the sky in two, and let the face of God shine through.—Edna St. Vincent Millay

Talk   (15 minutes)

Read this section several times until you can paraphrase and present it in your own speaking style—with the exception of the author's words, which are to be read aloud.

We often recognize others as children of God before we recognize ourselves as children of God. We, you and I, are children of God. Say this sentence after me, each time with a different emphasis: I am a child of God. *Pause.* I *am* a child of God. *Pause.* I am a child of God. *Pause.* We need to remember that God acknowledges our needs, our gifts, our wishes—all as part of the community of the Body of Christ. What is God asking, calling, nudging, whispering to you today? *Pause for a moment, allowing participants to reflect silently; then continue.*
Listen to these words from the author of this retreat:

I grew up in south Georgia. There I was known as Nick and Shirley's child, Dave and Rob's granddaughter, Amy's niece, Annie Laurie's granddaughter. These relationships defined who I was. Later I was known as an Aggie (one who went to Texas A & M University), a teacher, a church lady, a writer, a minister. Today I hope that I am known as God's child. We—you and I—are God's children, and this defines all we need to be and become.

The older I become, the more I learn that most of the pressures in this world are self-imposed. God asks us to do only a few things: to stand firm, and to be still and know that God is God. Yet, in this life, we live somewhere between fear and hope. Anxiety is what hovers between these two emotions. Did you know that each time the words *fear* and *anxious* are used in the Bible, they are preceded by something to the effect of "Don't be . . ."? Aha! Why is that lesson so difficult for us to learn? It must be because we think we are in charge—in charge of our lives, in charge of the lives of others, in charge of the things that can happen. Well, guess what? We aren't in charge. God is, thank heaven!

Soon after my father died, I attended a retreat with my church staff. The leader had a fistful of pretty ribbons tied in several big, clumpy knots. She tried to wave the bunch of ribbons but they just flopped back and forth. Then she untied the knots, and the ribbons flowed beautifully, gracefully, as if they were intended just for that purpose. Her analogy was beautifully simple: We can choose to live all knotted up or we can live flowing and free as God's children. I knew which one I wanted. The beauty of that simple illustration brought tears to my eyes. You see, I was a knotted ribbon. I was not the free-flowing graceful ribbon God intended me to be. I had been filled with fear, anxiety, and grief. How about you? Are you living all knotted up? Or are you a graceful child of God? Remember: *The cause of most anxiety is taking our focus off God.*

Turn to your neighbor and ask where she "lives"—all knotted up or free flowing. Let's take ten minutes to share with one another. 🕐

Scripture Surf   (35 minutes)

Write the following scripture references on a chalkboard or a dry erase board; or instruct participants to write them in their journals as you read the references aloud.

In small groups of three to five, "scripture surf" several of the following verses:

Genesis 21:17-20
Exodus 14:13-14
Deuteronomy 20:1-4
Jeremiah 42:11
Luke 1:30

Read each passage aloud—reading from several different translations, if possible. Share your insights with one another. When you have made your way through all of the scriptures, journal as God's Great Spirit leads you for the remainder of the time. We'll come back together in about thirty minutes. 🕐

Talk   (15 minutes)

Read this section several times until you can paraphrase and present it in your own speaking style—with the exception of the author's story, which is to be read aloud.

Have you ever tried defining faith and trust? Let's try it now as a group. First, what is trust, and what does it have to do with faith? *Pause momentarily for silent reflection; then continue.*

Webster's dictionary defines trust as "assured reliance; to hope confidently; one in which confidence is placed; to rely on truthfulness; to commit or place in one's keeping." And faith, Webster's explains, is "allegiance, fidelity to one's promises; firm belief in something for which there is no proof." So it seems to me that trust and faith *do* relate to each other; they are dependent on each other.

For the Christian, trust is simply assured reliance on God, and faith is our allegiance to God's promises. Have you ever had an experience that helped make these definitions concrete? *Pause momentarily for silent reflection; then continue.*

Listen to these words from the author of this retreat:

> Several years ago my husband, Kelly, and I took a trip to the Pacific Northwest. We experienced many things. One was a swinging bridge in Cappilano, just outside Vancouver, that spanned a gap a mile high and what seemed to be a mile wide. It took a lot of courage on my part to walk that bridge and not hold on to the sides. I knew that even if I held on, that would not help me if we encountered any dangers. That's how we need to live our life of faith. We don't need to hold on to the sides—we just need to hold on to our faith and *trust*.
>
> Do you remember what happened to Peter when he wanted to walk out on the water to meet Jesus? He did fine—until he took his eyes off Jesus and realized what he was doing.

Faith is keeping our eyes on Jesus. Faith and trust go hand in hand. It is walking out on a suspension bridge. It is walking toward Jesus. It is trusting God with our next step.

Scripture Surf   (35 minutes)

Write the following scripture references on a chalkboard or a dry erase board; or instruct participants to write them in their journals as you read the references aloud.

In small groups of three to five, "scripture surf" the following verses:

Luke 21:14-15
John 14:1
1 Peter 5:7
Hebrews 4:9
Matthew 6:25-34 (This is the ultimate advice!)

Read each passage aloud, reading from several different translations, if possible. Share your insights with one another. When you have made your way through all of the scriptures, journal as God's Great Spirit leads you for the remainder of the time. We'll come back together in about thirty minutes. 🕐

Talk   (5 minutes)

Read this section several times until you can paraphrase and present it in your own speaking style.
Replace your worry with rejoicing. How? Sounds simple, yet how do we begin? The first step is though prayer. Find a committed Christian, and you will find someone who has an active prayer life. Find a child who feels close to God, and she will tell you that she regularly talks to God. All who have walked with God view prayer as the main business of their lives. To pray is to change. To pray is to have transformed passions. Someone once said that listening is the first, second, and third requirement of prayer. To whom do you pray? Do you use public names for God, or do you use intimate, private names? One is not better than the other. God is beyond and beneath all of these. Prayer is communion with God; prayer is listening with God; prayer is conversation with God; prayer is sharing your heart with God. Prayer is all these things and many others.

Explore   (5–7 minutes)

Find a partner and discuss the answer to the following question: What are the blocks you experience to prayer?

We'll come back together in about five to seven minutes. 🕐

Close   (3 minutes)

Sing the hymn "Jesus, Remember Me" in rounds. 🎵

BREAK   (11:45 A.M.–12:00 P.M.)

LUNCH **(12:00 P.M.–1:00 P.M.)**

Gather in a large circle, give thanks, and encourage each participant to eat with at least one new friend.

FREE TIME **(1:00 P.M.–5:00 P.M.)**

This time is provided for sleeping, walking, crafting, sharing, playing games, or simply relaxing. If everyone is not comfortable with this amount of free time, feel free to adjust the schedule accordingly. Make sure that each woman finds something she wants to do.

SINGING AND SHARING (5:00 P.M.–6:00 P.M.)

Singing unites our spirits! Perhaps one or more individuals in your group are singers who may take turns leading the group in singing—and even sing a few solos themselves. You may want to prepare one or more song sheets, use hymnals, or sing "old favorites." (If you prepare song sheets and use copyrighted material, be sure to include your church license number on these sheets. Check with your choir director or organist for this information.) This also is a good time to check in with the group and see how the retreat is going. Are there any problems? Any discoveries?

DINNER **(6:00 P.M.–7:00 P.M.)**

Gather again as a total community for food and fellowship. Be sure to bless the meal together. This is a good time to make any announcements as well.

SESSION 3 (7:00 P.M.–8:00 P.M.)

Open (1 minute)

Read the following aloud:

The outward work will never be puny, if the inward work is great. —Meister Eckhart

How is it that an artist creates out of the materials of the moment, never again to be duplicated? This creation is true of painters, musicians, dancers, actors, teachers, ministers, ranchers, and of you and me. Each moment of our lives is a fresh canvas just waiting for divine inspiration.

Scripture Surf (25 minutes)

Write the following scripture references on a chalkboard or a dry erase board; or instruct participants to write them in their journals as you read the references aloud.

In small groups of three to five, choose three to four of the following verses and "scripture surf":

Matthew 6:22
Luke 11:1
Mark 5:21-43
Psalm 40:12
Psalm 31:9-10
Psalm 84
Psalm 91
Mark 9:14-29

Read each passage aloud, reading from several different translations, if possible. Share your insights with one another. When you have made your way through all of the scriptures, journal as God's Great Spirit leads you for the remainder of the time. We'll come back together in about twenty minutes. 🕐

Journal (5 minutes)

What difference have the scriptures we have read during this session made for you today? What change(s) will you put into practice? Record your thoughts in your journal. We'll come back together in five minutes. 🕐

Talk   (10 minutes)

Read this section several times until you can paraphrase and present it in your own speaking style.

One of the fastest growing elements in our economy is the recreation industry. These days people are wanting to spend more time enjoying their families and their favorite activities. In fact, people everywhere are so enamoured with recreation that many companies have gone to a four-day work week. What is recreation? Is it really re-creating—creating ourselves anew? How do we find *true* re-creation?

Elijah found he was re-created when he heard God's still, small voice. *Read 1 Kings 19:11-12 aloud, reading from the King James or New International versions of the Bible.* 🕐

In order to hear God's voice, we must spend time with God regularly. This is the most important step to finding true re-creation. Here are some additional steps that can be helpful:

Make peace with the past.
Share your journey with those around you.
Be honest about facing the "real you."
Be patient—all things come in God's time.
Dwell in scripture and prayer.
Be deliberate.
Gain your strength from within; be impervious to the "blowouts" of life.

Remember: It is the journey, not the destination, that is important; and God is the one who can accomplish the work begun in you. When you realize that life as you know it today may not last until tomorrow, you can begin to appreciate that each moment is a gift—a moment on your journey of faith.

Ask yourself this question: Am I a *driven woman* or a *called woman? Pause momentarily for participamts to reflect in silence; then continue.* A driven woman shows signs of stress, is compelled by time and circumstances, has limited people skills, and views her accomplishments as symbols of achievement. A called woman, on the other hand, is God generated. In other words, she walks out in faith with the Holy One toward the place where God is pointing. She allows God to generate her movement, her work, her life. Jesus did not choose driven people. He chose called people—simple men and women of faith.

To be "called women," we need to begin to think like stewards. A steward is someone who takes care of something until the owner returns. We are the stewards of ourselves—of our bodies, our minds, our spirits, our souls. God is the owner; our very lives are precious gifts he has entrusted to our care. Only when we are careful stewards of ourselves and our lives will we possess inner peace and joy.

Part of being a "called woman" is recognizing that being called is a two-sided coin. One side is the call—God's claim upon our lives. The other side is our response. What response will you make to God's call?

Have you ever had a desert experience—a time when you felt dry, barren, alone, or perhaps desperate? Though desert experiences are no fun, they can lead us to become totally dependent on God, which is the way we were meant to live every day of our lives. Many of us are living in the desert right now. Perhaps we are not experiencing any major trauma or crisis, but life just seems to be monotonous or overcrowded or unfulfilling or out of control. Life can become like an overflowing teacup; sometimes you simply have to take some stuff out of your life.

Think about it this way. You want a cup of hot chocolate, so you heat the water and pour it into your cup. Then, when you are ready to add the instant powder, there is no room for it! You haven't left room for what you really want. All you have is a cup of hot water. So you have to take out some of the water in order to make room for the chocolate. In the same way, our lives often are full of what we do not want or desire, which, ironically, can make us feel empty and barren.

Journal   (10 minutes)

What do you need to make room for in your life? What will you need to take out of your life? Record your thoughts in your journal. We'll come back together in ten minutes. 🕐

Talk   (4 minutes)

Read this section several times until you can paraphrase it in your own speaking style.

Listen to these words of wisdom: "Those who live in accordance with the Spirit have their minds set on what the Spirit desires" (Romans 8:5b).

We all need to remember the bumper sticker that says "What I am + God's help = enough." Delegate. Say no. Set your own limits. Give someone else an opportunity. Set your timetable. Pray about new opportunities and seek God's will. If possible, work with people you like, and you will find added energy. If you must work with difficult people, try to have the best attitude you can and pray for strength. Do whatever you must do in order to create "still waters" for yourself. Create peace in your life by breathing deeply, by imagining yourself in a wonderful place, and by stretching. Remember the most important thing: spend regular, intimate time alone with God.

Ephesians 2:10 says, "For we are God's workmanship, created in Christ Jesus." We are women of God, created to glorify God in all that we do!

Close   (5 minutes)

Play the selection "Jesus, Come into My Heart," included on Colleen Haley's CD From the Heart, *and sing along together; or choose another appropriate song.* 🎵

FREE TIME   (8:00 P.M.–9:00 P.M.)

During this time, participants may stretch, take restroom breaks, visit with one another, and prepare for Evening Worship (remind them to grab blankets if worship is to be held outside) while you and members of the design team set up for worship.

EVENING WORSHIP   (9:00 P.M.–9:45 P.M.)

Opening Ritual

Prior to the retreat, ask a participant to dress in biblical costume and play the role of the woman at the well. Provide a copy of the following script so that she may practice and memorize her lines. Just before beginning the worship service, have the participants gather outside the meeting room—the room in which the well you created for the retreat is located. Turn out the lights in the room and light a white pillar candle. Then, use the following words to invite the participants to enter the candlelit room.

As we enter into worship, let us hum together "Amazing Grace." Once inside, we will find a woman dressed in biblical costume, the woman at the well, who will tell us her story. *Lead the group into the room.* 🕐

Dramatic Presentation

Woman at the Well Soliloquy

You see, I wanted no trouble. That's why I came to the well in the middle of the day—after the others. I was tired—tired of the looks, the whispers, the discussions behind my back. That's why I came to the well in the heat of the day. And wouldn't you know it: When a woman wants a little privacy, there he was—just sitting there in the sun. I walked to the well anyway, and as I stooped to fill my water jug, he asked me—*me*—for a drink. Imagine the talk. This man, a Jew, was asking *me*, a Samaritan, for a drink of water.

I asked him, "Sir, how can you ask me for a drink?"

He said, "Woman, if you knew the gift of God and who it is that asks, you would ask him and he would give you living water."

This man, the Jew, was talking in code. Here he was, and he didn't even have a cup to draw the water with. And what was this talk about "living water"? So I asked him, "Sir, where can I get this living water so that I won't have to keep coming to this well?"

Then he began to tell me about myself! How could he know these things? He doesn't live around here; I had never seen him before. He told me things that no one else could have known. Then, he told me that a time is coming and now has come, when the true worshipers of God will worship God in spirit and truth—for they are the kind of worshipers God seeks. He said, "God is spirit, and his worshipers must worship in spirit and in truth."

I told this man that I know the Messiah, the Christ, is coming. When he comes, he will explain everything to me—to all of us. Then this man, the one without the cup for water, said, "I who speak to you am he." I tell you now, in this place, I know it was so. I knew it then. I know it now. I was so excited to tell everyone what I had seen and heard that I ran to the town, forgetting my water jug. Can you believe that? I forgot my water jug! But I have met the Christ! He is here!

Special Music

If possible, play the selection "The Woman at the Well," included on Colleen Haley's CD From the Heart. ♪

Scripture Reading

Have someone read aloud the following scriptures, or prepare in advance a handout of the scriptures and distribute copies now so that all may read aloud togther from the same translation. (Note: Participants will need flashlights.) 🕐

Psalm 18:19
Romans 15:13
1 Corinthians 15:10

Ritual of Healing

Invite each woman to come forward to the well one at a time; to feel the cleansing power of the water with her hands; and then, symbolically and silently, to leave something behind—or perhaps bring something to add to the well for others. As each woman comes to the well, have the group softly sing worship songs together. You may want to appoint a song leader or provide song sheets. ♪

Closing Reading

Have someone read aloud the following:

My daughters, do not forget what you have learned,
but keep my word so that your life will prosper.
Love and faithfulness will not leave you;
bind them to your heart,
write them on your heart.
Trust me with all your heart and acknowledge me in every course you take.
And I, the Lord your God, will see that your paths are smooth. (Proverbs 3:1-6, paraphrase)

Blessed is the woman who delights in the Word of the Lord,
She meditates on God's Word day and night.
She is like a tree planted by a stream of water.
Whatever she does, she prospers. (Psalm 1:1-3, paraphrase)

Day 3

BREAKFAST   **(8:00 A.M.–9:00 A.M.)**
By this time, the group has become family. Pray together and enjoy this final meal together.

MORNING WATCH (9:00 A.M.–9:45 A.M.)

Reproduce the material on pages 180-81 and distribute to all participants as they leave breakfast and find a place apart for their Morning Watch. Remind them that Session 4 will begin at 9:45.

SESSION 4 (9:45 A.M.–11:00 A.M.)

Open (15 minutes)

If possible, read aloud the children's book Granddad's Prayers of the Earth *by Douglas Woods (Cambridge, Mass.: Candlewick Press, 1999); or choose another appropriate book or poem to share.* 🕐

Explore (15 minutes)

Find a partner and share what happened during your Morning Watch experience. We'll come back together in about ten minutes. 🕐

After the group has come back together, ask if anyone would like to briefly share with the full group. Allow about five minutes for sharing; then continue. 🕐

Talk (15 minutes)

Read this section several times until you can paraphrase and present it in your own speaking style.

Rejoice: What does that word mean to you? To the others in your life? *Pause momentarily so that participants may reflect; then continue.*

Joy—children know how to live it, claim it, know it. One Christmas Eve a church presented a live nativity enacted by young children. The Christmas angel, whose name was Maddy, was the youngest of all the actors and actresses. When it came time for the Christ child to be born—to be lifted and held from the manger by Maddy's sister, Amanda, who portrayed Mary—the Christmas angel, Maddy, *knelt!* She knelt before the baby Jesus. She was in awe. She knew this was a holy moment!

In her book *The Song of the Seed*, Macrina Wiederkehr writes:

When I was a child there were many things that didn't faze me, things that bother me dreadfully now as an adult. Some of these things were hot weather, cold weather, getting caught in the rain, getting places on time, getting all my chores done. I seldom worried about catching a cold or getting dirty. I didn't worry about saying something that would sound silly—or crying if I was hurt. I always gave myself permission to daydream, to do useless things and to talk to things that wouldn't talk back. I always had time to play, and I never got bored.

I was more spontaneous—less inhibited—than I am now. I was so delightfully involved in life that I didn't notice many of the inconveniences that trouble me today. One last and very important memory is that I spent a lot of time with creation. I was aware of beauty without analyzing it. Although many of these gifts are still alive in me today, the radiance that once was mine has dimmed. I must make plans to allow the child to animate me again.[2]

As you were listening, when did you find yourself smiling? Do you remember your childhood days? For most of us, they were times of joy. Joy is finding the holy in the ordinary. It is realizing the sacredness of ordinary things. It is suspending chronos time, or clock time, so that the gift of the present moment is recognized. It is recognizing that each moment is a holy moment. Unfortunately, for most of us, our moments of joy seem to decrease as we age. So how can we recapture joy in our lives? Listen to what the Bible tells us about finding true, lasting joy:

- "I [Jesus Christ] am coming to you now, but I say these things while I am still in the world, so that they may have the full measure of my joy within them" (John 17:13).
- "Rejoice in the Lord always. I will say it again: Rejoice!" (Philippians 4:4).
- "I have told you this so that my joy may be in you and that your joy may be complete" (John 15:11).
- "Therefore my heart is glad and my tongue rejoices; my body also will rest secure" (Psalm 16:9).

Scripture Surf (20 minutes)

Choose three of the following passages and "scripture surf" in silence.

Matthew 4:18-20
Deuteronomy 5:1
1 Kings 19:11-13
Proverbs 1:23-28
Mark 4:9
Philippians 4:4-5
Romans 4:6-8
Matthew 5:3-12
John 15:11

Read each passage silently. Meditate on the words. Ask yourself: What truths speak to me? Then journal as God's Great Spirit leads you. We'll come back together in about twenty minutes. 🕐

Talk   (5 minutes)

Jesus Christ is the key to real joy. Our joy knows no time; it knows no place. Our joy is complete in Jesus. True joy does not depend on circumstances but comes from a consistent relationship with Christ. We can cultivate joy in many ways:

- Cultivate the mood to linger. God just may whisper to you what the Holy One has been trying to say for so long.
- Read aloud this passage from the book of joy: Philippians 2:1-18. After each verse, ask yourself if these characteristics are true for you.
- Be authentic to yourself and to Christ Jesus, who is in you. Do not let the pressures of the world rob you of your joy.

A word of caution: Burnout saps joy and comes from wearing too many hats. Burnout comes not from doing too much, but from doing that which doesn't have any real meaning. If what you do brings you joy, you will not burn out. (You may get weary at times, but that is different from burnout.) Seek to do the things that bring you joy.

Reread John 4:7-30 aloud now. 🕐

Why did the woman leave her water jar at the well? After all, its emptiness was the reason she had come to the well in the first place. The reason was that she had found *living water.* Have you?

Close   (5 minutes)

Sing together the selection "Look Inside Your Heart," included on Colleen Haley's CD From the Heart, *or choose another appropriate song.* 🎵

CLOSING WORSHIP   (11:00 A.M.–12:00 P.M)

A Time of Sharing

Say aloud, "What difference has this retreat made in your spiritual life?" Invite participants to respond freely; then continue. 🕐

Love Feast of Communion

Read aloud Mark 14:12-16. 🕐

Note: This service calls for a chalice of juice and one loaf of bread, symbolizing that we, though many, are one in Christ. Serve one another communion, speaking the name of the person you are serving as you share the bread and juice. As leader, model how this is to be done by taking a piece from the loaf, dipping it in the cup, and saying, "As we share the bread and the wine, we remember God's great love for us." After eating the piece of bread, hold the cup for the person to your right, and instruct her to take a piece of bread, dip it, and say, "[Name], as we share the bread and the wine, we remember God's great love for us." This process continues until all have been served. 🕐

A Time of Prayer

Open a time of prayer with your own words. 🕐 *Now allow participants to fill the silence by praying aloud as they feel led to do so.* 🕐 *Conclude by saying the Lord's Prayer in unison.* 🕐

Closing Worship Song

Stand in a circle and sing together the hymn "Shalom to You." 🎵

RETURN HOME   (12:00 P.M. until . . .)

Thank each person for her participation in the retreat and make any necessary closing remarks. 🕐 *Now it is time for the design team to clean, pack up, and evaluate the retreat; or, if you prefer, the team may save the evaluation for a later time.*

Windows of Prayer (Prayer)

◆

OVERVIEW
After a historical presentation of the spiritual discipline of prayer, participants explore various personalities and prayer styles and their meaning for our lives. Prayer as process, method, and journey are considered, and the powerful benefits of personal transformation are brought into focus.

PREPARING FOR THE RETREAT
- Review "How to Use This Book: Planning and Preparing for Retreats" (pp. 11-15).
- Assemble the design team.
- Read through the retreat; make revisions and additions as appropriate for your group or situation.
- Pray for the retreat.
- Advertise; invite and recruit participants.
- Send correspondence noting details of the retreat. (Be sure to let participants know what items they are to bring.)
- Gather the supplies.

SUPPLIES AND MATERIALS
To be brought by the leader
- nametags
- cassette/CD player
- cassettes/CDs, including meditative music
- hymnals or other songbooks (see suggested hymns and songs throughout the retreat)
- newsprint and marker, chalkboard and chalk, or dry erase board and marker
- white pillar candle and matches or lighter
- paper, pens, pencils
- a journal for each participant (Note: For large groups, ask participants to bring their own.)
- medium-size basket
- *Prayer and Temperament* by Chester Michael and Marie Norrisey (see Session 2)
- *Please Understand Me* by David Keirsey and Marilyn Bates (see Session 2)
- Keirsey Temperament Sorter and answer sheet, one for each participant (Prometheus Nemesis Book Company, Box 2748, Del Mar, Calif. 92014; 714-540-5288; see Session 2)
- recording of a Native American prayer (you can locate one easily at a local music/audio store; see Session 2)
- handout of steps for using *lectio divina* (optional, see Session 2)
- handout presenting overviews of personality and prayer types (optional, see Session 2)
- handout of boldface prayer exercises and techniques (optional, see Session 3)
- "The Carpenter and the Unbuilder" by David M. Griebner in *The Weavings Reader* (Nashville, Upper Room Books, 1993) (see Evening Worship, Day 2)
- chalice of juice and loaf of bread (see Evening Worship, Day 2)
- handout of eight ways of praying (optional, see Session 4)
- Morning Watch handouts for Days 2 and 3, one for each participant (see Appendix)

To be brought by each participant
- Bible
- quilt or blanket
- pen or pencil
- flashlight

The Retreat Day 1

ARRIVAL (3:00 P.M.–6:00 P.M.)

Have nametags ready for the participants as they arrive. Designate one or more greeters to personally escort each participant to her room and invite her to relax by resting, sleeping, reading, walking, hiking, talking with others, and so forth.

DINNER (6:00 P.M. –7:00 P.M.)

This is the first group activity. If space allows, form a large circle and say or sing the blessing. As leader, wait to be served last so that you may walk around the room and welcome everyone. Encourage the participants to sit with others whom they do not already know. Look for those who seem lost or who are alone. Assign persons from the design team to keep an eye on these participants and see that connections with others begin to take place.

GROUP ANNOUNCEMENTS/GET-TO-KNOW-YOU ACTIVITIES (7:00 P.M.–7:30 P.M.)

After dinner, formally welcome everyone and make any necessary group announcements—such as telling the location of bathrooms, telephones, and first-aid kits, and reviewing the retreat schedule. Then begin a get-acquainted game or activity. 🕐

SESSION 1 (7:30 P.M.–9:00 P.M.)

Open (5 minutes)

As you light a white pillar candle, say aloud: We light this candle in recognition of God's presence with us. 🕐

Sing together the hymn "Lead Me, Lord." 🎵

Talk (5 minutes)

Read this section several times until you can paraphrase and present it in your own speaking style—with the exception of the author's words, which are to be read aloud.

Windows of prayer . . . Windows—you can look in them or out of them. Prayer windows, then, make sense. We receive prayers, and we say prayers. What is prayer? It is an attentive relationship to the living God. The heart of all prayer is attentiveness. Prayer is loving God with all our hearts. It is resting quietly in the peace of God. It is being aware of the presence of God. It is being engaged with God. Prayer is opening to God with our hearts, souls, and minds. Tilden Edwards has been quoted as saying that prayer is in being, not doing. In other words, prayer is conscious communion with the deity. Listen to that again: *Prayer is conscious communion with the deity.*

Prayer is a powerful tool that helps us name our fears and wounds. More than that, prayer leads to the *healing* of our woundedness. Prayer also enables us to stretch and be strengthened in the gifts we have been given. Listen to these words from the author of this retreat:

My friend Colleen is a wonderful musician. If you have ordered her CD *From the Heart*, which corresponds with these retreats, you already know that. Well, in the beginning, she was a bit uncomfortable performing her music. She couldn't figure out why anyone would want to hear it—much less hear her talk about it! She prayed about it for a long time, others prayed about it, and God gave her a lot of courage. God also has blessed her with many songs! I don't know how she remembers them all. Colleen's music praises God, brings others closer to the Holy One, and is a blessing to all. Colleen's gift of music grows through her prayers.

Will a lot of prayer make you a great musician like Colleen? Probably not, unless you also share that gift. But a lot of prayer will make you the best that *you* can be. And your life will be richer because of it.

Scripture Surf   (35 minutes)

Write the following scripture references on newsprint, a chalkboard, or a dry erase board; or instruct participants to write them in their journals as you read the references aloud.

In small groups of three to five, "scripture surf" the following verses:

Luke 11:1-4
Romans 8:26
Colossians 1:9
1 Thessalonians 5:17

Read each passage aloud—reading from several different translations, if possible. Share your insights with one another. When you have made your way through all of the scriptures, journal as God's Great Spirit leads you for the remainder of the time. We'll come back together in about thirty minutes. 🕐

Talk   (5 minutes)

Read this section several times until you can paraphrase and present it in your own speaking style—with the exception of the author's words, which are to be read aloud.

Because we are diverse in our gifts, ages, races, genders, and personalities, we are drawn together in the diversity of prayer. Listen to this memory shared by the author of this retreat:

I remember being in the chapel at Garrett Theological Seminary one summer day. It was time to say the Lord's Prayer. The worship leader gave permission for everyone to pray in his or her native language. It was the most beautiful moment: Chinese, African, Japanese, English, English with an Irish lilt—I just started to cry. I had never heard such beautiful "music," and we were all saying the same thing to the same God!

A friend wondered: "We are each unique and different, yet deep down are we alike?" If we look deep enough into another, who will you find? Perhaps you will find yourself! Perhaps you will find the essence of God. Though we may pray using different words or languages, we all have the same need for prayer.

Why *do* we pray? We pray to discover reasons for loving God. The essence or ultimate purpose of prayer is to know God, to enjoy God, and to glorify God—forever! We pray to be strong in God. We pray for nourishment of our soul. We pray to be peace filled.

Journal   (5 minutes)

Respond to these questions in your journal: How is your hunger for God expressed in your life? Have you tried substituting other things for communion with God? We'll come back together in about five minutes. 🕐

Talk   (5 minutes)

Read this section several times until you can paraphrase and present it in your own speaking style.

There are many different kinds of prayer. During this retreat, you will experience some prayer forms that may be new to you, some that may stretch you, and some that you may be uncomfortable with. Feel free to say "pass" to any prayer form that does not speak to you. Just as we have many different personalities, so also we have many different "prayer personalities." And that's OK! When we think of prayer, we generally think of verbal prayers—those that are spoken aloud or spoken silently to God. Yet there is another kind of prayer that is quite powerful: nonverbal prayer. We may not realize it, but we engage in nonverbal prayer every time we worship God—such as when we are:

• walking (into the sanctuary, toward the altar or communion table, out of worship)

- standing (which represents honor and awe and dignity and mission)
- kneeling (which represents surrender)
- touching another (which can represent healing, baptism, and the invoking of the Holy Spirit)
- making the sign of the cross (which is a remembrance of the Trinity—on the mind, lips, and heart—often made upon entering a sanctuary and/or before a Gospel is read)

These things help us become more concrete in our worship.

Silence is another powerful form of prayer. Prayers of silence are found within all of nature. We often are silent as we watch a flock of birds, a rushing waterfall, the beautiful fall trees, or a newborn baby. We are silent, but we are in prayer. These prayers happen as we respond to our Maker as living, breathing creatures. In silence we rest and wait and look for God. When we sit in silence, we should dismiss any thoughts that disturb our solitude as if they were a leaf floating down a river or puffs of smoke or clouds on a spring day.

Another form of prayer is breath prayer. Richard Foster calls it "unceasing prayer." Its purpose is to help us experience oneness with God. Breath prayer is good to use before bedtime, first thing in the morning, and as a quiet mini vacation during a stress-filled day.

To begin, take a deep, cleansing breath. Then, with every breath, simply repeat a simple prayer. You might begin with one of these well-known breath prayers:

Lord Jesus, have mercy on me, a sinner.
God, be merciful to me.
Thank you, Jesus, for this day.

Or you might want to make up your own breath prayer. The purpose is to pray it so much and so often that it is always in your subconscious. Pray that God will plant it deep into your spirit.

Journal   (25 minutes)

Take a couple of minutes now to write your own breath prayer. Remember, keep it short. Now get comfortable and close your eyes. *Pause.* Take several deep breaths. *Pause.* For the next ten minutes, I want you to think about your breath prayer and simply repeat it over and over in your mind until you hear my voice.

What happened during your breath prayer? Record your thoughts in your journal. We'll come back together again in ten minutes.

Close   (5 minutes)

Sing or listen to the selection "Listen to the Words of Jesus," included on Colleen Haley's CD From the Heart (see p. 15) or choose another appropriate song.

EVENING WORSHIP   (9:00 P.M.–9:45 P.M.)

Note: Plan to have this service outside, if possible. Rather than standing, it would be more comfortable for participants to sit on quilts or benches or chairs. Be sure to bring flashlights to illuminate your path to and from the worship space. You may want to light a large candle in the center of the worship space.

Worship Songs

Sing the following folk songs as your worship time begins: "Jesus, Remember Me" and "Peace Like a River."

Scripture Reading

Read Psalm 46:10 aloud: "Be still, and know that I am God."
Repeat Psalm 46:10 in a whisper, asking the participants to whisper it back to you.

A Time of Silence

Tell the women that you will spend the next three to five minutes being still and quiet together.

A Time of Sharing

Invite the women, one at a time, to complete these sentences:

God has been a strength to me when . . .
I will praise you, Lord, for . . .
🕐

Worship Song

Respond by singing together the first verse of "Amazing Grace." 𝄞

Benediction

Say aloud the following: "If we are patient, and if we are open, we will learn—and we will *feel* the presence of God."

Day 2

BREAKFAST   (8:00 A.M.–9:00 A.M.)

Have coffee ready for the early risers. Remember that this meal is an act of the total community. Join together in a large circle to greet the morning and to give thanks to God for the night's rest and for the food that is to be received. Encourage the women to sit beside new faces during breakfast.

MORNING WATCH   (9:00 A.M.–9:45 A.M.)

Reproduce the material on pages 182-83 and distribute to all participants as they leave breakfast and find a place apart for their Morning Watch. Remind them that Session 2 will begin at 9:45.

SESSION 2   (9:45 A.M.–11:45 A.M.)

Note: Prior to this session, you will want to familiarize yourself with the book Prayer and Temperament *by Chester Michael and Marie Morrisey (Charlottesville, Va.: The Open Door, Inc., 1991), and the book* Please Understand Me *by David Keirsey and Marilyn Bates (Del Mar, Calif.: Prometheus Nemesis Books, 1978). These books take the Myers-Briggs Personality Indicator and relate it to prayer types. You will also need copies of the Keirsey Temperament Sorter—one for each participant—so that each participant may take the assessment and find out her personality type. You may purchase the number of copies you need for twenty-five cents each from Prometheus Nemesis Book Company, Box 2748, Del Mar, Calif. 92014; 714-540-5288.*

Open   (5 minutes)

As you light a white pillar candle, say the following aloud: As we light this candle, we remember that God is with us. This session is a window into prayer.
Sing together the hymn "It's Me, It's Me, O Lord (Standing in the Need of Prayer)." 𝄞
If possible, play a recording of a Native American prayer. You can locate one easily at a local music/audio store. 🕐

Talk   (5 minutes)

Read this section several times until you can paraphrase and present it in your own speaking style.
During this session we will be introduced to *lectio divina* prayer, or "divine reading." This form of prayer is simply listening with the heart to the holiness that is within. It is a way of reading the Scripture and then praying with the heart. This classic form of prayer is universal and relates to almost every prayer type. *Lectio divina* initially will take you about thirty minutes. As you become more comfortable with the process, however, you may find that you spend a much longer time in prayer. In the days and weeks ahead, you will want to allow yourself plenty of time to develop this method in depth.
Write the following steps on newsprint, a chalkboard, or a dry erase board; instruct participants

to write them in their journals as you read the steps aloud; or prepare a handout in advance and distribute copies now.

In *The Song of the Seed,* Macrina Wiederkehr offers a wonderfully simple and practical method of learning and using *lectio divina* in our personal prayer life.[1] It might be paraphrased this way:

1. Quiet the soul. Keep silence for five minutes.

2. Reflective reading and deep listening. Choose and read aloud a scripture passage. Read slowly. Remember that haste is the enemy of reflection.

3. Contemplate the Word. Wait, abide, rest, sit, totally surrender to the Word. This will take about twenty minutes.

4. Prayer. The response to the Word of God.

5. Journaling. Writing your insights, prayers, concerns and experiences with the Scripture.

This form of prayer enriches many in prayer life. However, if it does not speak to your soul, choose from it what is helpful and simply discard the rest. Find the prayer form that is right for you!

Explore   (35 minutes)

This session is about prayer temperaments, which are intrinsically related to personality temperaments. Discovering your personal prayer temperament will lead you to say, "Aha! This is the way I need to pray!" It will introduce you to new prayer methods that will enrich not only your prayer life but also your personal life and relationships. For the remainder of this session, we will be taking an inventory and exploring our individual prayer/personality types. *Hand out copies of the Keirsey Temperament Sorter and answer sheet now.* 🕐

The Keirsey Temperament Sorter[2] has seventy questions with two possible answers each. You are to choose the answer that speaks to you first. Do not think too long about any question, and do not think about what you *should* say. Your first answer will be your best. Score the sorter according to the answer sheet.[3] When you have done this, you will have four pairs of numbers with four pairs of letters directly underneath them. The letter that corresponds with the highest number in each pair is part of your formula. Keep the letters in order; you will use them to identify your prayer/personality inclinations. 🕐

Let's begin. We'll come back together in about thirty minutes. 🕐

Talk   (35 minutes)

Read this section several times until you can paraphrase and present it in your own speaking style.

There are sixteen basic types of patterns, each made up of four preferences. Those preferences include extraversion (E), introversion (I), sensation (S), intuition (N), thinking (T), feeling (F), perceiving (P) and judging (J). The letters that identify your type are simply indicators of your preferences. In other words, they are clues about how you like to learn, play, recreate, and enjoy relationship.

In *Prayer and Temperament* by Chester Michael and Marie Norrisey, we see that there are nine basic prayer temperments or preferences. Each is closely linked to the personality type. They include: Trinitarian Spirituality, Marian Devotion, Spirituality of the Desert Fathers and Mothers, Benedictine Spirituality, Augustinian Spirituality, Franciscan Spirituality, Devotio Moderno, Ignatian Spirituality, and Teresian Spirituality. *At this time, have several members of the design team briefly present descriptions of the personality types found in the Keirsey/Bates book, followed by descriptions of the prayer types found in the Michael/Norrisey book. (Be sure to ask the design team members well in advance so that they may be prepared.) You might find it helpful to prepare in advance a handout presenting overviews of the personality and prayer types and distribute* copies now. If time permits, it might be interesting to create a chart of the personality and prayer types and tally the types of participants. Be cautious, however, of labeling the participants. Remember that these are simply personality tendencies and prayer preferences. 🕐

Explore   (35 minutes)

Now we're going to divide into small groups according to our prayer types. Once we're in our small group, we'll share and discuss our responses to the following questions: What have you learned about yourself and your prayer preferences? What sounded right? What did not seem like a good fit? We'll come back together in about thirty minutes. 🕐

Close   (5 minutes)

As we close this session, take a few minutes to record the highlights of what you have learned about yourself. We'll allow about five minutes for this. I'll let you know when time is up, and we will take a short break before lunch. 🕐

BREAK   (11:45 A.M.–12:00 P.M.)

LUNCH   (12:00 P.M.–1:00 P.M.)

This is another time for building community. Gather again in a large circle, give thanks, and encourage the women to sit beside some new faces.

FREE TIME   (1:00 P.M.–5:00 P.M.)

This time is provided for sleeping, walking, crafting, sharing, playing games, or simply relaxing. If everyone is not comfortable with this amount of free time, feel free to adjust the schedule accordingly. Make sure that each woman finds something she wants to do.

SINGING AND SHARING   (5:00 P.M.–6:00 P.M.)

Singing unites our spirits! Perhaps one or more individuals in your group are singers who may take turns leading the group in singing—and may even sing a few solos themselves. You may want to prepare one or more song sheets, use hymnals, or sing "old favorites." (If you prepare song sheets and use copyrighted material, be sure to include your church license number on these sheets. Check with your choir director or organist for this information.) This is also a good time to check in with the group and see how the retreat is going. Are there any problems? Any discoveries?

DINNER   (6:00 P.M.–7:00 P.M.)

Form a circle and say or sing the blessing. Then enjoy more community-building time as you share food and fellowship.

SESSION 3   (7:00 P.M.–8:00 P.M.)

Open   (5 minutes)

Sing together one or more verses of the hymn "Take My Life, and Let It Be." 🎵
Write the following prayer on newsprint, a chalkboard, or a dry erase board; pray the prayer aloud together.

Give us
A pure heart
That we may see Thee,
A humble heart
That we may hear Thee,
A heart of love
That we may serve Thee,
A heart of faith
That we may live Thee.[4]

Explore   (10 minutes)

Find a partner and share your thoughts about today's Morning Watch experience. We'll come back together in about ten minutes. 🕐

Talk   (5–10 minutes)

Read this section several times until you can paraphrase and present it in your own speaking style. Write the following material appearing in bold print on newsprint, a chalkboard, or a dry erase board; instruct the participants to take notes as you read the material aloud. Or, if you prefer, prepare a handout in advance and distribute copies now.

Let's consider some prayer exercises and techniques that may enhance your prayer life—or that of someone you know. You may be familiar with some of these; others may be new to you. Keep an open mind and be willing to try something different; you may be surprised at the results! *Review the boldface material with the group, taking note of the leader instructions appearing in italics.*

Guided Imagery—an imaginary "tour" that makes us open to hearing God in different ways. This prayer method is extremely helpful for many people. Others are fearful of the experience. It is helpful if you can stretch out on the floor. Take several deep, cleansing breaths before beginning. Journaling is a must following the guided imagery exercise.
Note: This form of prayer is often very emotional for some participants. Whenever using guided imagery in a group setting, be sure that someone is available to listen to participants after the experience. A good resource is Opening to God *by Carolyn Stahl.* 🕐

Prayer Positions—varieties of body position that help to generate energy and concentration (e.g., kneeling; lying prostrate on the floor; standing or sitting in a chair with hands together, hands open toward the sky, and so forth).
Spend several minutes discussing and/or demonstrating helpful prayer positions: kneeling; lying prostrate on the floor; standing or sitting in a chair with eyes closed, eyes open, hands together, hands open toward the sky, and so forth. Ask participants to offer other suggestions. 🕐

Music—a great window into prayer, whether the genre be classical, contemporary Christian, instrumental, or something else.
Ask the participants to tell what kinds of music are helpful in their own personal prayer lives. 🎵

Art—another great window into prayer.
Share some collected pieces of art, including things such as icons, photographs or prints of famous masters, stained-glass pieces, and so forth. Ask: How can pieces of art such as this lead you into a spirit of prayer? What other forms of art can lead you into prayer? What about poems, novels, plays, movies? Allow participants to respond freely. 🕐

Tongsung Kido—*a Korean form of prayer in which everyone present prays aloud at the same time.*
Explain to the group that when using Tongsung Kido, the congregation is given a specific period of time and a common theme or prayer request. All who are present pray aloud at the same time. The voices of others are not distracting if one is concentrating on one's own prayer.

Explore   (5 minutes)

Let's try *Tongsung Kido* together now. For the next five minutes, pray aloud for those who have not heard the gospel message. *Note: Be sure to give participants permission to be in silent prayer if they find this exercise uncomfortable. Tell them that you will indicate when time is up.* 🕐

Journal   (10 minutes)

Note: Have some soothing music playing in the background while participants journal.
Reflect now on the experience we've just had. Record your thoughts in your journal. We'll allow ten minutes for this. 🕐

Close   (10 minutes)

Listen to these words from the author of this retreat:

> When I was a child, my parents were wonderful to tell me often that I could be anything I wanted to be. The possibilities had no bounds. I remember a host of dreams and desires: to be a nurse, a social worker, a mom, a teacher, an astronaut, an interpreter . . . The list goes on and on. What were your childhood dreams?

Find a partner and share what you are really good at doing and any new insights that you have learned about yourself. Your partner must listen only. Then your partner will tell you what she has heard. You are then to trade roles. Each person needs equal time. You will have eight minutes total, or four minutes each. 🕐

FREE TIME   (8:00 P.M.–9:00 P.M.)

During this time, participants may stretch, take restroom breaks, visit with one another, and prepare for Evening Worship (remind them to grab blankets if worship is to be held outside) while you and members of the design team set up for worship.

EVENING WORSHIP   (9:00 P.M.–9:45 P.M.)

Note: Have this worship experience outside, if possible. Remember to help make everyone comfortable by providing chairs, quilts, or blankets. Participants will need flashlights to illuminate the path to the worship area.

Greeting

Say aloud the following: This is the night that the Lord has made! Let us rejoice and be glad in it!

Worship Songs

Sing favorite "camp" hymns together, such as "Kum Ba Yah," "Precious Savior," and others. 🎼

The Message in Story

Share the story "The Carpenter and the Unbuilder," from The Weavings Reader *(Nashville: Upper Room, 1993), p. 249. Rather than reading the story aloud, try telling the story from memory.* 🕐

Prayers of the People of God

Open a time of prayer with your own words; then say aloud:
Remembering the Cloud of Witnesses, let us call aloud the names of those who have shaped our faith and have gone home to live with God. I'll begin by naming . . .

After everyone who wants to share has spoken, close the prayer time. 🕐

Scripture Reading

Have someone read aloud Mark 14:17-26. 🕐

Holy Communion

Prior to the retreat, ask someone to play the guitar, flute, or "jam box" at this time so that there is music and/or singing during Holy Communion. You also might want to play the selection "Come Remember" from Colleen Haley's CD From the Heart.

Let us now share in the bread and the wine of remembrance of the ultimate gift of Jesus Christ.

Note: This service calls for a chalice of juice and one loaf of bread, symbolizing that we, though many, are one in Christ. After breaking the bread, have the participants file by one at a time, taking the bread and dipping it into the chalice of juice. 🕐

Worship Song

Sing together "You Are Beloved," included on Colleen Haley's CD From the Heart, *or choose another appropriate song.* ♪

Blessing

Go forth, remembering that you are the beloved of God!

Day 3

BREAKFAST   (8:00 A.M.–9:00 A.M.)

By this time, you will note that the group has "jelled" and most are interacting as family. Enjoy this breakfast together after a group blessing.

MORNING WATCH   (9:00 A.M. –9:45 A.M.)

Reproduce the material on pages 182-83 and distribute to all participants as they leave breakfast and find a place apart for their Morning Watch. Remind them that Session 4 will begin at 9:45.

SESSION 4 (9:45 A.M.–11:00 A.M.)

Open   (15 minutes)

Find a partner and share your thoughts about today's Morning Watch experience. We'll come back together in about ten minutes. 🕐

As the larger group comes back together, ask if anyone would like to comment on their Morning Watch experience. Allow participants to respond briefly; then continue. 🕐

Talk   (10 minutes)

Read this section several times until you can paraphrase and present it in your own speaking style.

As God's people, we pray for many reasons. The primary reason is that there is a hole in our hearts that is hungry for God. When we pray, we maintain

- our relationship with God;
- our relationship with the earth;
- our relationship with our deepest self;
- and our relationships with others.

Despite our hunger for God, we can easily fall into narcissistic prayer, which is praying just for ourselves and our needs, desires, and wants. We need to be intentional about praying holistic prayers, which put God, rather than ourselves, at the center.

When we sit with God in silence, we are able to listen to what God has to say to us. In turn, the ability to sit in silence with God emerges from listening. When have you listened to God lately—really listened? *Pause momentarily to allow participants to reflect; then continue.*

There are many kinds of prayer or ways of praying. Let's take a look at some of these now. *Write the following list on newsprint, a chalkboard, or a dry erase board; instruct participants to take notes as you read the list aloud; or prepare a handout in advance and distribute copies now.*

1. Praise—praying with wonder and gratitude. Using all the senses in nature often leads to spontaneous prayers of praise.
2. Repetitious prayer—repeating the prayers of others. Young children often learn to pray this way: "Now I lay me down to sleep"; "Our Father, who art in heaven"; "God is great."
3. Creedal or traditional prayer—praying the prayers of our faiths and denominations.
4. Experimental prayer—praying in a way that is conducive to personal expression. Our journals fit in here.
5. Corporate prayer—praying with others in small or large groups.

6. Continual prayer—praying without ceasing. Brother Lawrence, the Trappist Monk, prayed without ceasing, even while working long days and nights in the monastery kitchen.

7. The life of prayer—living prayer in each moment, each conversation, each relationship. Mother Teresa certainly lived this sort of prayer life. Do you personally know anyone who lives this kind of life?

8. Intercessory prayer—praying for others with a sense of interceding on their behalf. This is a spiritual gift of many individuals.

Where do you feel the nudge to try something new? Remember that prayer is something each of us can add to our life at any moment. Prayer changes us. We can be part of a miracle through prayer.

Journal   (5 minutes)

Respond to the following statement in your journal: Confession in prayer is something each of us can add to our life at any moment. Prayer changes us. We can be part of a miracle through prayer. 🕐

Scripture Surf   (35 minutes)

Write the following scripture references on newsprint, a chalkboard, or a dry erase board; or instruct participants to write them in their journals as you read the references aloud.

Scripture is a window of prayer: It gives us words and ways to pray. In small groups of three to five, "scripture surf" the following verses:

Psalm 23
Jeremiah 1:4-10
Psalm 32:6-7
Psalm 29
Psalm 100
Acts 16:25
Matthew 5:44

Read each passage aloud—reading from several different translations, if possible. Share your insights with one another. When you have made your way through all the scriptures, journal as God's Great Spirit leads you for the remainder of the time. We'll come back together in about thirty minutes. 🕐

Close   (10 minutes)

Teach the group the following prayer. You might want to write the prayer on newsprint, a chalkboard, or a dry erase board.

O God, fill our minds with your knowledge.
Fill our hearts with your peace
Fill our body with your joy.

Work together to make up hand and arm motions for this prayer; then pray it together. 🕐

CLOSING WORSHIP   (11:00 A.M.–12:00 P.M.)

Prayer of Illumination

Read aloud the following prayer:

Open wide the window of our spirits, O Lord, and fill us full of light; open wide the door of our hearts, that we may receive and entertain thee with all our powers of adoration and love. *Amen.*[5]

Worship Songs

Sing together some of the group's favorite "camp" spirituals or hymns. 🎵

Special Music

Play the selection "Look Inside Your Heart," included on Colleen Haley's CD From the Heart, *or choose another appropriate song.* ♪

Scripture Reading

Prior to the retreat, ask a participant to write a paraphrase of Psalm 46 and share it with the group at this time. 🕐

A Time of Sharing

Invite the participants to join in a time of remembering what has happened during the course of this retreat. Allow the women to take turns completing this sentence.

I remember when . . . 🕐

When all have had a turn, invite the women to respond to this question:

Is there anything we have left unsaid?

Allow the participants to reflect and respond freely. Remember that all answers are authentic feelings. 🕐

Special Music

Prior to the retreat, invite someone in the group to provide special music at this time. If this is not a possibility, play a favorite contemporary Christian song. Perhaps a participant might be able to prepare and present interpretive movement to the song.

Closing Prayer

Invite the women to echo each line of this closing prayer:

Into Thy hands, we commend our spirits, O Lord.
Into Thy hands, we commend our prayers, O Lord.
Into Thy hands, we commend our uniqueness, O Lord.
We give thanks to You, O Lord.
Amen.

RETURN HOME   (12:00 P.M. until . . .)

Thank each person for her participation in the retreat and make any necessary closing remarks. 🕐 *Now it is time for the design team to clean, pack up, and evaluate the retreat; or, if you prefer, the team may save the evaluation for a later time.*

Becoming: A Journey of Spirituality for Women (Spirituality)

◆

OVERVIEW

"I'm not finished yet!" we often explain. We all know that we are never quite finished. The women who journey through this retreat will outline their past and current spirituality to identify trends and styles that can enhance and develop their future spiritual growth.

PREPARING FOR THE RETREAT
- Review "How to Use This Book: Planning and Preparing for Retreats" (pp. 11-15).
- Assemble the design team.
- Read through the retreat; make revisions and additions as appropriate for your group or situation.
- Pray for the retreat.
- Advertise; invite and recruit participants.
- Send correspondence noting details of the retreat. (Be sure to let participants know what items they are to bring.)
- Gather the supplies.

SUPPLIES AND MATERIALS
To be brought by the leader
- nametags
- cassette/CD player
- cassettes/CDs, including meditative music
- hymnals or other songbooks (see suggested hymns and songs throughout the retreat)
- newsprint and marker, chalkboard and chalk, or dry erase board and marker
- white pillar candle and matches or lighter
- paper, pens, pencils
- a journal for each participant (Note: For large groups, ask participants to bring their own.)
- medium-size basket
- *Dawn*, by Uri Shulevitz (optional, see Session 2)
- handout of selected Bible verses and various quotations (optional, see Session 2)
- Morning Watch handouts for Days 2 and 3, one for each participant (see Appendix)

To be brought by each participant
- Bible
- quilt or blanket
- pen or pencil

The Retreat Day 1

ARRIVAL   (3:00 P.M.–6:00 P.M.)

> *Have nametags ready for the participants as they arrive. Designate one or more greeters to personally escort each participant to her room and invite her to relax by resting, sleeping, reading, walking, hiking, talking with others, and so forth.*

DINNER   (6:00 P.M.–7:00 P.M.)

> *This is the first group activity. If space allows, form a large circle and say or sing the blessing. As leader, wait to be served last so that you may walk around the room and welcome everyone. Encourage the participants to sit with others whom they do not already know. Look for those who seem lost or who are alone. Assign persons from the design team to keep an eye on these participants and see that connections with others begin to take place.*

GROUP ANNOUNCEMENTS/GET-TO-KNOW-YOU ACTIVITIES   (7:00 P.M.–7:30 P.M.)

> *After dinner, formally welcome everyone and make any necessary group announcements—such as telling the location of bathrooms, telephones, and first-aid kits, and reviewing the retreat schedule. Then begin a get-acquainted game or activity.* 🕓

SESSION 1   (7:30 P.M.–9:00 P.M.)

Open   (5 minutes)

> *Sing "Listen to the Words of Jesus," included on Colleen Haley's CD* From the Heart *(see p. 15), or choose another appropriate song.* 𝄞 *Then read the following poem:*

There is a time for everything,
and a season for every activity under heaven:
a time to be born and a time to die,
a time to plant and a time to uproot,
a time to weep and a time to laugh,
a time to mourn and a time to dance. (Ecclesiastes 3:1-2, 4)

Talk   (3–5 minutes)

> *Read this section several times until you can paraphrase and present it in your own speaking style.*
> Some buzzwords of our time are *soul care* and *spirituality*. It has been said that the search for spirituality is one of the deepest issues in our present-day culture. Many people are simply empty—empty at the core—and they don't know why. Soul care means paying attention to what is happening in the deepest places of your soul. It's been said there is a hole in our hearts that is homesick for heaven. Isn't that beautiful? And yet, instead of filling the hole with God, who is all we need, we try to fill the hole with clothes, food, drink, activities, friends, and countless other things.
> We are here today on a journey of spirituality. As women, we are:

- spiritual beings with spiritual experiences
- nurturers, caring for one another
- in need of spiritual mothers
- often guilty of "water-skiing" over the important issues of life, causing us to wear masks
- devoted to our spirituality

> What is spirituality? It is attentively relating to God, finding God in the sacredness of the present moment. Did you hear that? The *present* moment. To know God, we must be intentional about relating to God in every moment; we must be attuned to God's presence with us at all

times and in all places. Unfortunately, our daily frenzy causes us to lose touch with God, and consequently, lose our capacity to be filled with God's peace. You see, we are already too "full."

Journal (30 minutes)

Write the following questions on newsprint, a chalkboard, or a dry erase board; or instruct participants to write them in their journals as you read the questions aloud.

What are you too "full" of? Think about this for a moment. *Pause for about thirty seconds.* Now take fifteen minutes and journal in response to the following questions.

- What is your understanding of spirituality?
- Who is God in your life? Can you identify and express your image of God?
- Is anything going on between you and God right now?
- Are there particular people or experiences that connect you with God or the meaning of hope for your life? 🕐

Time is up. Now I invite you to find a partner and discuss what you have written. If you are uncomfortable sharing with another, continue to wrestle with the questions privately. We'll allow another fifteen minutes for sharing or continued contemplation. 🕐

Talk   (3–5 minutes)

Read this section several times until you can paraphrase and present it in your own speaking style.

As women, we choose to be grasped by God, embraced by God, held in God's own hand. However, we often miss these opportunities by staying too busy, having no stillness or quiet, constantly intellectualizing, refusing to listen, or being unaware of the beauty of creation. Our need is deep; it is the Holy Presence we long for, and the peace of God can fill our longing.

Deep rivers move silently; shallow streams are noisy. What does this say to you about spirituality? *Invite participants to share their thoughts; then continue.* 🕐

In his book *Life Together,* Dietrich Bonhoffer reminds us: "One who wants fellowship without solitude plunges into the void of words and feelings, and one who seeks solitude without fellowship perishes in the abyss of vanity, self-infatuation, and despair."[1] Solitude and fellowship: both are essential. As we begin our journey today, let us consider first solitude.

Have someone read aloud Isaiah 50:4-5. 🕐

Journal/Close   (45 minutes)

If the weather is bad or it is too cold to go outside, invite the women to find a place of solitude wherever you are meeting.

To close this session, I invite each of you to go outside, find a quiet spot, and *listen.* Listen to God with your heart. Listen to God all around you. Listen—it is sometimes easier with your eyes closed. Listen—for thirty minutes, just listen. I'll announce when time is up. Then, after having listened, journal as the Spirit leads you. After ten minutes of journaling, we'll take a short break before moving on to our evening worship service. I will announce when it is time to stop journaling. 🕐

BREAK   (9:00 P.M.–9:05 P.M.)

EVENING WORSHIP   (9:05 P.M.–9:45 P.M.)

Note: You may choose to have this worship experience outside or in a quiet room. It is important that your worship space be relatively free of distractions and that every effort be made for the participants to be comfortable. You may choose for the women to sit on quilts, blankets, benches, or chairs. Have some quiet music playing as you gather for this time together.

Worship Songs

Sing some familiar "camp" songs such as "Seek Ye First" and "Kum Ba Yah." 🎵

Play the selection "Put Your Life in His Hands," included on Colleen Haley's CD From the Heart, or choose another appropriate song, and sing along together. ♪

Scripture Reading

Have someone read aloud Genesis 1:26-28 and Isaiah 64:8. 🕐

Meditation

> When my children were young we had a small desk and chairs in the kitchen for occupying their busy hands and minds while I prepared family meals. Horizontally, over the desk, I hung an inexpensive wardrobe mirror. The children were fascinated with watching themselves as they painted, created, or wrestled with homemade play-dough. Intensely, they studied their faces, often lost in the time. Their imaginations must have revealed the wonder of *who* and *why* they are—each a unique, wonderful creation by the Designer of the universe.

Why is it that we, the humans, the crowning glory of God's creation, so often pretend to be something or someone we are not? A tulip wants only to be a tulip. A dog wants only to be a dog. A pine tree does not try to be a weeping willow. A goldfish does not try to become a dolphin. Who is it that we are intended to be? How can we plan in intentional ways to live in oneness with God?

We begin the journey by *listening*. Listening to the presence of God. Listening to the created world around us. Listening to those God has placed in and around our lives. Listening to the movement of the Spirit within our hearts. We are created by God. We are molded by God. We belong to God. We intend to live in oneness with God. My prayer for each of you during the time we spend together is that you may hear the voice of God speaking to you and to your journey of becoming the one you are intended to become.

Prayer

Gracious God, lead us to the place where we may feel the movement of you within our hearts. Lead us to the place where we can listen to your will, your yearning for our lives. Slow us down to a way of being and knowing that praises you. Amen.

Worship Song

Sing the hymn "Go Now in Peace" in rounds, if possible, and return to your sleeping quarters quietly. ♪

Day 2

BREAKFAST   (8:00 A.M.–9:00 A.M.)

Have coffee ready for the early risers. Remember that this meal is an act of the total community. Join together in a large circle to greet the morning and to give thanks to God for the night's rest and for the food that is to be received. Encourage the women to sit beside new faces during breakfast.

MORNING WATCH   (9:00 A.M.–9:45 A.M.)

Reproduce the material on pages 184-85 and distribute to all participants as they leave breakfast and find a place apart for their Morning Watch. Remind them that Session 2 will begin at 9:45.

SESSION 2 (9:45 A.M.–11:45 A.M.)

Open   (20 minutes)

Choose a partner and discuss what happened during your Morning Watch. Each of you should talk about five minutes. After ten minutes have passed, I'll call the group back together. 🕐

When all have come back together, ask if anyone would like to share anything with the larger group. Allow about ten minutes for sharing; then continue. ⏱

Talk   (5 minutes)

If possible, read aloud the book *Dawn*, by Uri Shulevitz (New York: Farrar, Straus & Giroux, 1974), or choose another appropriate reading. ⏱

Explore   (20 minutes)

Read the following excerpt from the poem "The Wellsprings" aloud. Instruct participants to think about moments in their own lives as they listen.

I seek the sources of refreshment,
sustenance, and healing
that my spirit, like my body,
is constantly in need of.

I am made whole again
—my self is given back to me—
in solitude and silence.

So now I seek to silence word and thought
by being conscious of the sounds around me,
or the sensations of my body,
or my breathing.

I am energized by love.

So I recapture
and relive the times when I felt loved,
cared for, and treasured.

And I see myself going out in love
to friends,
to those who are in need,
and to every living creature.[2]

Take a few minutes now to relive silently the moments of your life that flashed into your mind's eye while listening to the poem. *Pause for two to three minutes; then continue.* ⏱

Now turn to your neighbor and share any "aha" moments that may have come to you. Discuss how we can "go out in love" to every living creature. We'll come back together in about ten to fifteen minutes. ⏱

Talk   (3–5 minutes)

Read this section several times until you can paraphrase and present it in your own speaking style.
Jeremiah 29:13 tells us, "You will seek me and find me when you seek me with all your heart." When we listen with the heart, we find communion with God; we find spiritual growth. As God's people, we are to have hope—the hope that we will have a future—for we find God when we seek God with our whole heart. We find ourselves "at home" with God. Listening with the heart is a gift from God. It is grace. It is like love that is sleeping in our hearts. Thomas Moore said that we cultivate silence, and thereby listening, not by forcing our ears to hear, but "by turning up the volume of the music of the world and the soul." The heart, then, is the place where we find God. I wonder if that is why we say someone "has a good heart." In Proverbs 4:23 we read, "Above all else, guard your heart, for it is the wellspring of life." Our heart seems to dictate how we live our lives because we always find time to do that which brings us joy and makes us happy. When we are restless, we fail to listen with our hearts and commune with God;

as a result, our hearts are not fed and our wellspring of life dries up. **Our deepest need is the movement of our hearts toward spiritual growth.**

Explore   (60 minutes)

In advance, prepare a handout of the following Bible verses and quotations. Divide the participants into small groups of three to five and distribute copies of the handout to each group. Instruct the groups to read and discuss the verses/quotations. Allow approximately thirty minutes for this exercise; then come back together as a full group and share any insights in the time remaining.

- Deuteronomy 6:4-6 (This is the basis of all of life.)
- Matthew 6:19-21 (Be careful what is important to you; it will be in your heart!)
- "The best and most beautiful things cannot be seen or touched; they must be felt with the heart." (Helen Keller)
- Matthew 5:8
- Psalm 51:10
- Psalm 19:14
- Above all else, guard your heart!

Talk   (10–15 minutes)

Read this section several times until you can paraphrase and present it in your own speaking style.
We need to clear the clutter out of our hearts through prayer. We know how quickly the clutter can pile up in our homes, creating a mess that requires many hours of time and energy to straighten. The same thing can happen in our hearts if we are not careful to clean them daily through prayer. Listen to the author of this retreat share a story from her own experience:

> I remember an occasion when someone was very unkind to my children. In fact, this someone was quite mean-spirited. Now, my children aren't angels, but I would put them up against any other children in the universe for having good, kind, loving hearts. It took me a long time and a lot—I mean *a lot*—of prayer to clean out my heart; to let go of angry, hurt feelings; to allow God to fully reign in my heart. It is interesting to note that it took my children nearly no time at all. What does that tell us about "becoming like a child" (Matthew 18:2-4)?

How would you respond to the author's question? How does "becoming like a child" help us clean the clutter out of our hearts? *Encourage participants to share their thoughts; then continue.*
Childlike humility helps us guard our hearts. And that requires prayer—regular prayer!
Have someone read aloud Philippians 4:4-7.
Rejoice in the Lord—not sometimes, but *always!* Can you say that you do that? Do you even try to do that? Paul tells us that if we will rejoice in the Lord and pray with thanksgiving, we will receive the peace of God, which "will guard [our] hearts and [our] minds in Christ Jesus" (Philippians 4:7*b*).
We are learning how important it is to listen for the divine whisper amid the human clutter. Rest in this thought: Glory to you who creates us, redeems us, and lives in our hearts now and forever.

Close   (15 minutes)

Sing the Gloria Patri, or another appropriate hymn of praise. Make up hand motions to accompany the words. Sing the song through once with words and hand motions; then "sing" it again with hand motions only! Conclude the session with these parting thoughts:

The deepest sound and silence of God take us into our spiritual hearts.—Ellen Shepard

Earth's crammed with heaven,
And every common bush afire with God. —Aurora Leigh

BREAK   (11:45 A.M.–12:00 P.M.)

LUNCH   (12:00 P.M.–1:00 P.M.)

This is another time for building community. Gather again in a large circle, give thanks, and encourage the women to sit beside some new faces.

FREE TIME   (1:00 P.M.–5:00 P.M.)

This time is provided for sleeping, walking, crafting, sharing, playing games, or simply relaxing. If everyone is not comfortable with this amount of free time, feel free to adjust the schedule accordingly. Make sure that each woman finds something she wants to do.

SINGING AND SHARING   (5:00 P.M.–6:00 P.M.)

Singing unites our spirits! Perhaps one or more individuals in your group are singers who may take turns leading the group in singing—and may even sing a few solos themselves. You may want to prepare one or more song sheets, use hymnals, or sing "old favorites." (If you prepare song sheets and use copyrighted material, be sure to include you church license number on these sheets. Check with your choir director or organist for this information.) This also is a good time to check in with the group and see how the retreat is going. Are there any problems? Any discoveries?

DINNER   (6:00 P.M.–7:00 P.M.)

Form a circle and say or sing the blessing. Then enjoy more community-building time as you share food and fellowship.

SESSION 3 (7:00 P.M.–8:00 P.M.)

Open   (1 minute)

Read aloud the following quotations:

Take joy in the sacrament of the present moment, for that is where we find God. —Casad

It is necessary that we find God, who cannot be found in noise. God is the friend of silence. See how nature—trees, flowers, and grass—grow in stillness; how stars, moon and sun run their course in silence. The more we receive through silence, the more we can give in the activity of our daily lives. In essence, it is not what *we* say, but what *God* says to us and through us. All our words are useless if they do not come from within. "As God speaks only in silence, this is a big problem for those searching for God."[3]

Explore   (5 minutes)

After reading aloud each of the following Bible verses, read the question that follows it and pause for thirty to sixty seconds, allowing participants a moment of silent reflection. Continue in this manner until you have completed all the verses.

I invite you to silently read four sayings of Jesus in your Bible as I read each of them aloud. I will give you time to locate each verse before I read it; then, after reading each verse, I will read a question and give you a moment to reflect silently. 🕐

John 8:12	"I am the light of the world." (We are called to be the light; are you light?)
John 6:35	"I am the bread of life." (God has all that you need; what do you need right now?)
John 10:4	"His sheep follow him because they know his voice." (Do you know God's voice?)
John 15:1	"I am the true vine." (Do you abide in love?)

Talk   (50 minutes)

Read this section several times until you can paraphrase and present it in your own speaking style—with the exception of the author's words, which are to be read aloud.

As any woman making a journey, we need to take a few things with us. Some of the tools that will help us on our spiritual journey are (1) journaling, (2) Sabbath, (3) spiritual friends, and (4) a day of prayer. Let's consider each one. *Note: You will want to limit your time to roughly ten minutes on each of the four spiritual tools.*

1. Journaling. It has been said that journaling allows us to live a chronicled life. Writing helps us know ourselves. Writing assists us in deepening our relationship with God by giving life to our words. Listen as the author of this retreat talks about her own experiences with journaling.

For many years, no one knew I kept a journal. Now, practically everyone I know knows about it, because I leave it everywhere! I use all kinds of spiral-bound books. I have found that journaling helps me remember some of the tough lessons that I have learned during my life. I don't journal every day, but most days I do. I keep all my journals; maybe one of my grandchildren will someday read them and learn some of life's lessons. My journal is also where I write my prayers. It gives me a record of my prayers; and often when I return to my journal, I find those prayers have been answered so beautifully. I urge you to keep a journal for three weeks. Why three? It is the holy number! Besides, after twenty-one days of doing a new routine, it becomes habit!

There are no "rules" for journaling. Be creative, be yourself, be truthful, and experiment. What will you journal about? Try journaling in response to one of the following:

- a Bible verse
- a poem
- a picture or photograph
- a memory
- your dreams
- your feelings
- the people and places in your life
- your prayers

Invite participants to talk about their own experiences or thoughts related to journaling. Encourage them to accept the challenge to keep a journal for three weeks; then continue. 🕐

2. Sabbath. The Sabbath, a day of rest, is biblical. In Genesis 2:2 we read, "By the seventh day God had finished the work he had been doing; so on the seventh day he rested from all his work. And God blessed the seventh day and made it holy, because on it he rested from all the work of creating that he had done." Check this out: God rested from *all* his work—and God had made the world during his "week at the office"! How about you? Can't you give it up and rest for just one day? Give it *all* up!

Now, your Sabbath doesn't have to be Sunday. Your Sabbath may come on a Monday or a Friday if that is your day off. On whatever day of the week your Sabbath falls, renew your soul—let your soul catch up with your body. How about it? Will you set aside one day a week to renew your soul? What will you do to renew your soul? Where will you find Christian renewal? Where are the places of Christian fellowship in your Sabbath?

Encourage participants to share, being careful to watch the time; then continue. 🕐

3. Spiritual friends. A spiritual friend is a significant person in your life who walks a life of faith; who is committed to the Living Christ; who listens without offering judgment; who loves unconditionally; who cries with you, plays with you, and prays with you. This person encourages you and helps you be better than you already are. Take a couple of minutes to develop a list of characteristics you would look for in a spiritual friend. I'll let you know when time is up. 🕐

Let's share our lists now. Did your list include any of these characteristics: trustworthy, able to keep confidences, mature, loving, patient, has a good sense of humor, faithful, is a lifelong learner, is a good listener? What else did you include? *Pause and allow participants to share; then continue.* 🕐

Star the three words on your list that are most important to you. *Pause for thirty to sixty seconds.* Now, do you know someone who fits that description? *Pause momentarily so that participants may reflect silently; then continue.*

Relationships with spiritual friends can happen spontaneously or by invitation. Spiritual friendships can be organized (meeting once or twice a month) or can grow out of existing relationships. Having one or more spiritual friends to share our faith journey with helps us *continue to grow.* She models for us. He guides us and listens to us. Sometimes we outgrow a spiritual friend and begin seeking a new relationship. There is a school of thought that suggests that spiritual friends, other than one's spouse, should be limited to one's own gender. There are merits both for and against this thought. If the spiritual friendship is sought through prayer, however, there can be great gifts to be gained from being open to any individual. Ask that the Holy Spirit guide you in discerning your spiritual friends.

What do spiritual friends do? They ask: How is it with your soul? Where are you growing in your prayer life? What is new in your life of faith? Where does your life need "weeding"? How can I help you? What should we pray about? Spiritual friends are a treasure: Guard them with your life! Does anyone have a special spiritual friend she would like to tell us about? *Encourage participants to share, being careful to watch the time; then continue.* 🕐

4. A regular time of prayer. Give yourself a priceless gift: a regular time of prayer. On one of your Sabbath days, unplug the phone, lock away the laundry, and spend the day in prayer. You don't have to stay at home. Go to a park, to your backyard, to a neighbor's empty house, to the country, or to a local retreat center. Retreat centers often have day rates that include a private room. Wherever you go, grab some sweet sleep or rest and holy prayer. This regular day of prayer will renew your spirit in ways you never thought possible. Perhaps a day of prayer is an impossibility for you at this stage in your life. What is the largest amount of time you can carve out of your month? Even if you begin with only an hour or two, you will be blessed in many ways. Listen to these words from the author of this retreat:

> I have always been a full-time wife, mom, and minister. I often need Sabbath spaces in my life. When our children were small, I would often "trade" time with a girlfriend. We would watch each other's children so that we could gain balance, peace, and love! I remember one time, after returning home from five hours at a nearby convent, my youngest son, Martin, said, "Mom, I like it when you go away to pray. You come home so much fun!" Ouch! Out of the mouths of babes!

Have any of you ever had that kind of experience? If so, tell us about it. If not, what would it take for you to set aside your own personal day of prayer? *Encourage participants to share, being careful to watch the time; then continue.* 🕐

Although these four tools—journaling, Sabbath, spiritual friends, and a regular time of prayer—can be extremely useful to us on our spiritual journeys, we must be careful not to structure our spiritual journeys too much, to make a box for them or to label them. We simply must remain open to God and God's direction for our lives. Sometimes we can come to God and our time is not as fulfilling as we had hoped. Our job is to keep coming to God—to stay as close to God as possible during these "dry" times. There is an old story that goes something like this: If a quarterback isn't throwing well, the coach doesn't take him out of practice. The coach makes him practice more! That's how it is with our spiritual lives. We need more practice when we are dry and unfulfilled.

Take a moment now to make a commitment to yourself and to God regarding the facet of your spiritual life that you want to work on: journaling, Sabbath, spiritual friendships, or a regular time of prayer. Write your commitment in your journal. *Pause for one to two minutes; then proceed with the closing.* 🕐

Close   (4 minutes)

Read aloud the following:

. . .He leads me beside *quiet* waters. (Psalm 23:2)

. . .He will *quiet* you with his love. (Zephaniah 3:17b)

[Your beauty] should be that of your inner self, the unfading beauty of a gentle and *quiet* spirit, which is of great worth in God's sight. (1 Peter 3:4)

Sing together one or more verses of the hymn "Lead Me, Lord." ♪

FREE TIME   (8:00 P.M.–9:00 P.M.)

During this time, participants may stretch, take restroom breaks, visit with one another, and prepare for Evening Worship (remind them to grab blankets if worship is to be held outside) while you and members of the design team set up for worship.

EVENING WORSHIP   (9:00 P.M.–9:45 P.M.)

Lighting of the Candle

Light a white pillar candle as you say the following: We light this candle remembering that you, O God, created and are creating.

Special Music

Play the selection "Put Your Life in His Hands," included on Colleen Haley's CD From the Heart, *or choose another appropriate song.* ♪

Hymn

Sing together the hymn "When Morning Guilds the Skies." ♪

Scripture Reading

Have someone read aloud Jeremiah 29:11-13. 🕐

Meditation

Listen to this story told by the author of this retreat:

> When my husband and I celebrated our twentieth wedding anniversary, we went to the Pacific Northwest. There I met a Native American—a carver who is a member of the Wolf Clan—a man of the Creator. His "job" (my word, not his) is to carve totem poles—poles taller than thirty feet. In his words, his activity—his job—is releasing the beauty that is already within the wood. He told me that he is partners with the Creator, finishing the work that was begun by his people through the symbols in his carving. He said, "The story never changes; we are changed by hearing the story in some new way."

Isn't that the way it is for us? The story never changes; we are simply and wonderfully changed through hearing it.

Consider yourself a story pole, waiting to release a story. What parts need to be carved away? Where is the beauty within? Spend a few moments naming the beauty within you, placed there by the Creator. Ask yourself, "What does this have to do with my perception of being called a woman of God?" *Allow one to two minutes of silence; then encourage participants to share their thoughts with the group.* 🕐

Prayer

Spirit of God, Weaver of Stories, Creator of Stories, make us new this day so that we may be the women you intend us to become. Stop our daily frenzy and cause us to rest in you. We are too full, and there seems to be no space, no time, no words. Lord, we give it all to you so that our time is your time. Take care of our souls. We love you. Amen.

Closing Hymn

Sing together the hymn "Shalom to You." You may choose to sing it through several times. 𝄞

Day 3

BREAKFAST   (8:00 A.M.–9:00 A.M.)

Again, have the coffee ready for the early risers. By this time, you will note that the group has "jelled" and most are interacting as family. Enjoy this breakfast together after a group blessing.

MORNING WATCH   (9:00 A.M.–9:45 A.M.)

Reproduce the material on pages 184-85 and distribute to all participants as they leave breakfast and find a place apart for their Morning Watch. Remind them that Session 4 will begin at 9:45.

SESSION 4   (9:45 A.M.–10:45 A.M.)

Open   (5 minutes)

Read aloud the following quotes:

Why indeed must "God" be a noun? Why not a verb—the most active and dynamic of all? —Mary Daly

The blessings for which we hunger are not to be found in other places or people. . . . They are at home in the hearth of your soul. —John O'Donohue

Sing together the hymn "Lead Me, Lord." 𝄞

Journal   (40 minutes)

Make a list of several quotations of your choosing and ask the women to spend twenty minutes journaling in response to them. Tell them that you will ring a bell when time is up. 🕐
Now, take your Bible and journal with you to a quiet place and read the first chapter of the book of James. Then journal about it. We'll allow another twenty minutes for this. Please return and rejoin the larger group when you hear the ringing bell. 🕐

Explore   (20–25 minutes)

Find a partner and share what happened during your Morning Watch experience. We'll come back together in about twenty to twenty-five minutes. 🕐

Close   (5 minutes)

Close by singing together again the hymn "Lead Me, Lord." 𝄞

CLOSING WORSHIP   (11:00 A.M.–12:00 A.M.)

Lighting of the Candle

Light a white pillar candle as you say aloud the following: We light this candle remembering that you, O God, created and are creating.

Worship Song

Sing together the worship song "I Could Sing of Your Love Forever." 𝄞

Scripture Reading

Ask someone to read aloud James 1:17. 🕐

Meditation

Read aloud the following story told by the author of this retreat:

> One Lenten season, my husband and son made a processional cross for our church. They made it from our Christmas tree. I remember well how they spent time trimming and pruning away the branches. How I wished that I could trim away the dead parts of myself. I remember how they sawed the trunk, carefully choosing the place where they would cut. How I wished that I were more careful. I remember how they made the cross, tying the two pieces of wood together with a leather strap. How I wish I could begin again—being made new in Christ. Then they made a rectangular base for the cross and nailed the cross to it. The cross stood straight and tall. It was carried into worship each week by a child. How I wished I stood straight and tall for Christ. The cross is beautiful. It remains today in my friend Nancy's office. It has a soft purple cloth around the base. I wonder: Was that cross for our congregation only, or was it also my lesson to learn that spring?

A Time of Sharing

If you are so moved, share what is in your heart as a result of our time spent together on this retreat. Allow participants to share as they choose. 🕐

Closing Prayer

Great Spirit of God, we are trying to *become* your women. We ask you to be the carpenter of our souls. Chip away the outer pieces that need to be removed. Eliminate the inner parts that have nothing to do with you. Refine us into your image that we might be your representatives in the world. Stop our busyness that we might rest in you and *become* who you want us to be. You have our names written on your hand and in your heart. Help us know and remember that! We love you, Lord. Amen.

RETURN HOME (12:00 P.M. until . . .)

Thank each person for her participation in the retreat and make any necessary closing remarks. 🕐 *Now it is time for the design team to clean, pack up, and evaluate the retreat; or, if you prefer, the team may save the evaluation for a later time.*

God's Simple Path

◆

OVERVIEW

This retreat is based on Mother Teresa's book *A Simple Path,* and Macrina Wiederkehr's *Song of the Seed: A Monastic Way of Tending the Soul.* Participants work through the parable of the sower, found in Matthew 13, and search to find places of fertile soil in which to tend a deep yearning for God and nurture their own spirituality.

PREPARING FOR THE RETREAT
- Review "How to Use This Book: Planning and Preparing for Retreats" (pp. 11-15).
- Assemble the design team.
- Read through the retreat; make revisions and additions as appropriate for your group or situation.
- Pray for the retreat.
- Advertise; invite and recruit participants.
- Send correspondence noting details of the retreat. (Be sure to let participants know what items they are to bring.)
- Gather the supplies.

SUPPLIES AND MATERIALS
To be brought by the leader
- nametags
- cassette/CD player
- cassettes/CDs, including meditative music
- hymnals or other songbooks (see suggested hymns and songs throughout the retreat)
- newsprint and marker, chalkboard and chalk, or dry erase board and marker
- white pillar candle and matches or lighter
- paper, pens, pencils
- a journal for each participant (Note: For large groups, ask participants to bring their own.)
- medium-size basket
- *A Simple Path* by Mother Teresa
- *Song of the Seed: A Monastic Way of Tending the Soul* by Macrina Wiederkehr
- handout of steps for using *lectio divina* (optional, see Session 2)
- chalice of juice and loaf of bread (see Evening Worship, Day 2)
- *Old Turtle* by Douglas Wood (optional, see Session 6)
- Richard Foster's book *Celebration of Discipline* (optional, for leader's reference only; see Session 3)
- Morning Watch handouts for Days 2 and 3, one for each participant (see Appendix)

To be brought by each participant
- Bible
- quilt or blanket
- pen or pencil

The Retreat   Day 1

Note: The schedule for this retreat has been modified to allow for a total of six group sessions.

ARRIVAL   (3:00 P.M.–6:00 P.M.)

Have nametags ready for the participants as they arrive. Designate one or more greeters to personally escort each participant to her room and invite her to relax by resting, sleeping, reading, walking, hiking, talking with others, and so forth.

DINNER   (6:00 P.M.–7:00 P.M)

This is the first group activity. If space allows, form a large circle and say or sing the blessing. As leader, wait to be served last so that you may walk around the room and welcome everyone. Encourage the participants to sit with others whom they do not already know. Look for those who seem lost or who are alone. Assign persons from the design team to keep an eye on these participants and see that connections with others begin to take place.

GROUP ANNOUNCEMENTS/GET-TO-KNOW-YOU ACTIVITIES (7:00 P.M.–7:30 P.M.)

After dinner, formally welcome everyone and make any necessary group announcements—such as telling the location of bathrooms, telephones, and first-aid kits, and reviewing the retreat schedule. Then begin a get-acquainted game or activity. ⏱

SESSION 1: SILENCE   (7:30 P.M.–9:00 P.M.)

Open   (5 minutes)

Say the following aloud: This time is provided for you to step back and take a new look at your life—not so much to learn as to remember and to feel some of what you may have forgotten. A retreat is the time and space to remember the sacred truths that are buried within your soul. Quiet your soul so that God may teach you. There are many things we can learn only when we are quiet and silent before God.

Play the selection "Put Your Life in His Hands," included on Colleen Haley's CD From the Heart *(see p. 15), or choose another appropriate song.* 🎵

Journal   (15 minutes)

In your journal, draw a picture representing your unique spiritual path. Identify the significant events, people, and places that you have encountered along the way. You may not remember everything your drawing needs; feel free to come back and add to it over the weekend. We'll come back together in fifteen minutes. ⏱

Explore   (20 minutes)

Now divide into small groups of three to four and, one at a time, share one significant thing from your spiritual path. Without showing your picture, describe this one thing so that the others can picture it. We'll allow twenty minutes for this. ⏱

Talk (15 minutes)

Read this section several times until you can paraphrase and present it in your own speaking style.
This weekend we will travel a path—a simple path, a path of grace. As we travel the path, the blessing of God will come upon us, and from us, and mold us into the image of Jesus Christ. We must remember that the path does not produce the change; it simply puts us in the place where change can occur. The change is God's work, not ours.

Read aloud John 14:1-7.
Listen to these words from the author of this retreat.

Jesus is . . .
   a light Heart
   a warm Home
   the Way to live
   the Path to follow
   the Truth to be told
   the Life to be lived.

Jesus is . . .
   our Father
   our Mother
   our Healer
   our Creator
   our Savior
   our Master and Guide.

Jesus is my All in All.

Write the following steps on newsprint, a chalkboard, or a dry erase board and instruct participants to make notes as you review the material together.
As we learn about walking the simple path this weekend, we will look at the steps along the path that are ways to receiving God's grace. These steps are ways of "sowing the Spirit." We will experiment with ways to embed the Word into our minds, hearts, and souls. According to Mother Teresa, there are five steps, and each one leads naturally to the next. The steps are silence, prayer, faith, love, and service. God's simple path makes a circle as the words lead one to another. Can you picture it?

Silence leads to prayer
Prayer leads to faith
Faith leads to love
Love leads to service
Service leads to peace
Peace leads to prayer. . . .

The first step of the path is silence. Jesus showed us the way to silence in his own life: time alone for prayer. *In advance prepare a handout presenting the following statements and scripture references and distribute copies now; or write them on newsprint, a chalkboard, or a dry erase board and instruct participants to make notes as you review the material together. You may choose to read part or all of the scripture passages as time permits.*

• Jesus spent forty days in the wilderness to prepare for his ministry (Matthew 4:1-11).
• Jesus spent the night alone before he chose the twelve (Luke 6:12).
• Jesus sought the lonely mountain with three disciples for the transfiguration (Matthew 17:1-2).
• Jesus prepared for the crucifixion in prayer at Gethsemane (Matthew 26:36-44).
• Jesus connected other significant acts of ministry with solitude. After feeding the five thousand, he went alone to pray (Matthew 14:23).
• Jesus told the twelve to come away by themselves to pray (Mark 6:31).
• Jesus withdrew after healing the leper (Luke 5:12-16).

Solitude was a regular practice with Jesus. Today he calls *us* to silence and solitude because it is essential for prayer and for listening to God. It's been said that there are few persons who are still enough to hear God speak.

Journal   (1 minute)

What is silence? *Pause momentarily; then continue.* In your journal, write a word or phrase to complete this sentence: "Silence is . . . *Pause for one minute so that participants may write; then continue.* 🕐

Talk   (2 minutes)

Read this section several times until you can paraphrase and present it in your own speaking style.
Perhaps you wrote one of these words or phrases: surrender, something I long for, a paradox, not babble, free, cleansing, perspective, armor, essential, serendipity, serenity. Sister Wendy Beckett said this about silence: "The capacity for silence—a deep, creative awareness of one's inner truth—is what distinguishes us as human."[1] Mother Teresa wrote in *A Simple Path*: "It is in the silence of the heart that God speaks. God is the friend of silence—we need to listen to God because it's not what we say but what [God] says to us and through us that matters."[2]

Journal   (5 minutes)

For the next five minutes write about how God has used silence to speak to you. 🕐

Talk   (2 minutes)

Read this section several times until you can paraphrase and present it in your own speaking style—with the exception of the quotation by Macrina Wiederkehr, which you are to read aloud.
Silence is a way to receive. Most of our days are filled with relationships, demands, requests, reactions, noise, and so forth. There is little or no harmony at all to our days. In silence, we settle down and receive and are energized through the love of Christ. Silence creates space. In her book *Song of the Seed: A Monastic Way of Tending the Soul*, Macrina Wiederkehr says it like this:

Long ago when I was learning to type, I used to delight in typing letters to my friends without pressing the space bar. Now when you don't press the space bar, you've got a real mess, and there is much decoding to be done. It is the spaces in between that enable us to understand the message.

Life is very much the same. It is the spaces in between that help us understand life. But, you see, some of us keep forgetting to press the space bar.[3]

Lifewithoutspacemakesnosense.
Life without space makes no sense.

Journal   (5 minutes)

Where is there "space" in your life? Journal about this for five minutes. 🕐

Talk   (2 minutes)

Read this section several times until you can paraphrase and present it in your own speaking style.
Silence allows us to find our true selves; we find our true selves in the silence of our hearts. If we are not silent, we do not have time to ask ourselves the questions of our hearts or listen to God's answers. All we have is a chaotic jumble of feelings that we never sort out. When we experience a silence of the heart, it is as if we have received a gift from God. Silence brings us back to the One who formed us. In silence we can be ourselves—the persons God created us to be. All false pretenses fall away. In silence we find out who we really are.

Journal   (5 minutes)

What keeps you from silence? Write about this for the next five minutes. 🕐

Talk   (2 minutes)

Read this section several times until you can paraphrase and present it in your own speaking style—with the exception of the quotation by Henri Nouwen, which you are to read aloud.
There is a silent self in all of us, yearning to be nurtured. Yet this silent self constantly is being eroded away by pressures, work, and relationships. The emptiness we feel can be filled only by God. Catherine of Siena, a fourteenth century saint, encourages us to find a cell within our-

selves where we can go to pray and to be with God. Susanna Wesley, who was the mother of seventeen children, used to create a prayer closet by drawing her long shirts and petticoats over her head.

Sometimes we simply avoid silence.

In his book *With Open Hands*, Henri Nouwen writes:

There are two silences, one is frightening and the other is peaceful. For many, silence is threatening. They don't know what to do with it. . . . To be calm and quiet all by yourself is hardly the same as sleeping. In fact, it means being fully awake and following with close attention every move going on inside you.[4]

Journal   (10 minutes)

What causes you to avoid silence? Write about this for five minutes.

Take several deep breaths. *Pause.* Now listen to this song as you move into silence. After keeping silent for the duration of the song, take a few minutes to write about something you felt or experienced during the silence. I'll let you know when time is up. *Play the selection "Beloved" from Collen Haley's CD* From the Heart, *or choose another appropriate song.*

Close   (1 minute)

Read the following aloud: Sometimes God whispers so that we can get close to the Holy One.

EVENING WORSHIP (9:00 P.M.–9:45 P.M.)

Note: Try to have this worship experience outside or in a candlelit room. If outside, make sure that the participants will have chairs, benches, quilts, or blankets to sit on. You may want to prepare a special centerpiece for your worship table by filling a clear vase with layers of different kinds of seeds.

Gathering

As everyone gathers, play instrumental music in the background—either from a cassette or CD or from a musician in the group—or simply have everyone hum a familiar tune such as "Amazing Grace."

Call to Worship

We have come to this sacred space to worship together. Let us begin our worship with a song.

Special Music

Play the selection "The Seed Becomes a Prayer," included on Colleen Haley's CD From the Heart, *or choose another appropriate song.*

Scripture Reading

Have someone read aloud Matthew 13:1-9.

Invitation to Meditation and Prayer

There is a story told of one who asked a rabbi, "Why did God speak to Moses from the thorn bush? Why not in the loud thunder or from a mountain or from the rushing water?"

The rabbi answered: "To teach us that there is no place on earth where God's glory is not, not even in a thorn bush."

Where are the many places you have seen the "seeds" that God has planted in your life? Reflect on this in a moment of silent meditation and prayer. *Pause for approximately two minutes; then continue with the closing prayer.*

Closing Prayer

Gracious God, we ask you to gather all our "seeds" into your care and bless them. We pray especially for our families; for those who have planted seeds; for those who need seeds planted for them; for the seeds that we would plant in the future. These things we ask in your name. Amen.

Benediction

Sing "Go Now in Peace" or another musical benediction. (Note: This tune may be sung in rounds.)

Day 2

BREAKFAST   (8:00 A.M.–9:00 A.M.)

Have coffee ready for the early risers. Remember that this meal is an act of the total community. Join together in a large circle to greet the morning and to give thanks to God for the night's rest and for the food that is to be received. Encourage the women to sit beside new faces during breakfast.

MORNING WATCH   (9:00 A.M.–9:45 A.M.)

Reproduce the material on page 186 and distribute to all participants as they leave breakfast and find a place apart for their Morning Watch. Remind them that Session 2 will begin at 9:45.

SESSION 2: PRAYER   (9:45 A.M.–10:45 A.M.)

Open   (5 minutes)

Read the following Scripture verse aloud:

I will go before [you], and make the crooked places straight. (Isaiah 45:2 KJV)

Play the selection "The Seed Becomes a Prayer," included on Colleen Haley's CD From the Heart, *or choose another appropriate song. Sing along together, if you like.*

Talk   (3 minutes)

Read this section several times until you can paraphrase and present it in your own speaking style.
It is difficult to follow God's guidance when we are on rigid paths of our own. We should not follow where the path leads; rather, we should go where there is no path and leave a trail. One way that we can follow God's guidance is through prayer. The fruit of silence is *prayer*. By living in the silence, we come to prayer—being in communion with God, conversing with God, listening, waiting, sharing our innermost thoughts. It becomes a way of life.

Journal   (10 minutes)

How and when do you experience prayer in your life? How do others experience prayer? Journal in response to these questions for the next five minutes.
Now find a partner and share your answers together. We'll allow another five minutes for this.

Scripture Surf   (20–25 minutes)

Write the following scripture references and questions on newsprint, a chalkboard, or dry erase board; or instruct participants to take notes as you read the references and questions aloud.
In small groups of (*state a number appropriate for your group*), read the following scripture passages aloud:

James 5:7-8
Mark 4:1-9
Matthew 13:1-23

Spend the next fifteen minutes sharing your responses to the following questions as you are comfortable:

- What do these verses have to do with prayer?
- Where does the soil need the most work in your life?
- Where is there good soil in your life?
- What weeds need to be pulled from your life?
- Where are the obstacles to prayer in your life?
- Do you lack for depth in your prayers or prayer life?
- Do you have a prayer life?

I'll let you know when time is up. 🕐

Talk   (10–15 minutes)

Read this section several times until you can paraphrase and present it in your own speaking style—with the exception of the author's story, which is to be read aloud.
Listen to this story told by the author of this retreat:

> One young couple I know adopted a baby from Bulgaria. His name is Alec. Many friends and family in their church had anticipated, waited, and prayed for this child and his family. The day of his baptism arrived. Alec was about six months old, and he was aware of absolutely everything! As the family made their way to the altar, Alec—upon seeing the sanctuary and the chandeliers, smelling the flowers, hearing the organ play and the people sing, and looking at all the people—began to clap his hands with joy and look with wonder at everything he saw. He knew this was a holy moment. *That was prayer, communion with God.*

Hear that again: Prayer is communion with God. In prayer, it is the *heart* that prays. Our hearts can be moved to pray by many things, such as music, nature, scripture, and silence. Likewise, there are many methods or ways of praying.

One of the most effective ways to enrich your prayer life is through the ancient method of meditative prayer called *lectio divina* or "divine reading," which is a way of reading the Scripture and praying with the heart. Initially, *lectio divina* will take you about thirty minutes to complete. As you become more comfortable with the process, however, you may find that you spend a much longer time in prayer. You will want to allow yourself plenty of time to develop this prayer method in depth. It will allow the depth of the Word to soak into your soul. It will provide you with a sense of peace and a keener understanding of God's Word.

Write the following steps on newsprint, a chalkboard, or a dry erase board; instruct the participants to write them in their journals as you read them aloud; or prepare a handout in advance and distribute copies now.
Here is a wonderfully simple and practical method of learning and using *lectio divina* in our personal prayer life.

- Quiet the soul. Keep silence for five minutes.
- Reflective reading and deep listening. Choose and read aloud a scripture passage. Read slowly. Remember that haste is the enemy of reflection.
- Contemplate the Word. Wait, abide, rest, sit, totally surrender to the Word. This will take about twenty minutes.
- Prayer. The response to the Word of God.
- Journaling. Writing your insights, prayers, concerns, and experiences with the Scripture.

Lectio divina may not be your favorite method of prayer. However, it has survived the test of time through the centuries and is one method that deserves a place in your prayer repertoire. Another helpful form of prayer rooted in *lectio divina* is *centering prayer,* which is the contemplation of one word over and over whether aloud or silently. Centering prayer is being aware of God's presence through prayer; in other words, it is resting in God's presence. This practice can be especially effective in your personal prayer life. You can do it anywhere at any time—even during a brief break from your work or while sitting in a traffic jam. The word you choose to pray may come from a line of scripture, or it simply may be a word such as *Jesus, light, love,* or *listen*. Whatever word you choose, it will travel with you throughout the day.

Breath prayer is yet another effective method of prayer that has been part of the Christian tradition since the sixth century. Breath prayer has its roots in the Psalms, yet it is neither limited to the Psalms nor to scripture. A breath prayer is a short, simple prayer that can be spoken in one breath and repeated again and again. One of the more familiar breath prayers is "Lord Jesus, Son of God, have mercy on me, a sinner," or simply "Lord Jesus, have mercy on me." The phrases can be taken from scripture, or they can be simple sentence fragments of your own, such as "Lord Jesus, bless me with your love." The idea is to repeat the phrase over and over. At times you may want to use centering prayer in conjunction with breath prayer.

Allow God to help you shape your own personal breath prayer. You may find that the same breath prayer will be part of your prayer life for many months. Listen and wait with the experience to know what God is teaching you. In *Prayer: Finding the Heart's True Home*, Richard Foster writes, "Breath prayer is discovered more than created. We are asking God to show us his will, his way, his truth for our present need."[5]

Close   (2 minutes)

Reread Isaiah 45:2 aloud.

As we reflect on these words from Scripture, let us hear the words of Sue Monk Kidd:

Wherever we walk in life, whether through grief, uncertainty, worry or despair, there is One who not only travels with us in the present, but goes before us into the future, making the path straight. When the way grows crooked, watch with care. For that is when God appears like a mother's kiss or a spring of water breaking into a thirsty moment. We are never alone in our need.[6]

BREAK   (10:45 A.M.–11:00 A.M.)

SESSION 3:   FAITH (11:00 A.M.–12:00 P.M.)

Open   (5 minutes)

Play the selection "Jesus, Come into My Heart," included on Colleen Haley's CD From the Heart, *or choose another appropriate song. Sing along together, if you like.* ♪

Scripture Surf   (15 minutes)

Have a different person read each of the following scripture verses aloud for the full group. Instruct the participants to meditate on the words as they listen.

Romans 3:20-31
Ephesians 2:8-10
Lamentations 3:21-26
James 2:14-26
Matthew 17:18-21
Hebrews 11–12:1

Journal   (5 minutes)

We have discovered that the fruit of silence is prayer. Now let us consider the fruit of prayer: faith. Faith comes as a result of prayer. Faith is trusting. A person of faith, then, is one who trusts God. A person of faith tries to grow her or his faith and become more faithful. What persons do you know who are faithful—from history, from your family, from your present life? *Pause momentarily so that participants may reflect silently; then continue.*

Are *you* faithful? Journal your response now. We'll allow three to five minutes for this. 🕐

Talk   (3–5 minutes)

Read the following aloud:

Faith is to believe what we do not see, and the reward of this faith is to see what we believe.
—St. Augustine

Listen to three stories of faithful women told by the author of this retreat.

---

1. Faith Is "Stepping Out"

A friend of mine had an opportunity to take a new job in a new city. It meant having to leave her roots, her friends, and a job she loved. It meant moving her children—all teenagers. It meant that her husband would leave his job without the certainty of a new job. Yet she and her family felt compelled to go where God was calling her. She stepped out on faith. When have you stepped out on faith?

2. Faith Is Contagious

My daughter Meg went on a junior high mission trip to a small town in Mexico where they worked with the children in an orphanage. Her experience was tremendous. When she spoke of the children, she said, "You know, Mom, those children had nothing that we would consider important, yet they were so happy, so *pure.*" Meg was motivated to find that purity of faith in her own life.

3. Faith Is Not Waiting and Doing Nothing

An orphan girl in India was desperate to find a home. One day she approached a visiting missionary teacher from a nearby village and asked the woman for help. The teacher had no room in her home for the girl, and no money to make a place for her. "But I will pray and ask God for his help," she said, "and you do the same."

That evening, the teacher returned to her home and found a letter from a friend in the United States. It contained a small sum of money—enough to begin providing for the orphan girl. Taking this as a sign of encouragement from God, she summoned a messenger the following morning and asked him to go to the neighboring village—a day's walk from her home—and bring the girl back.

To the teacher's surprise, the messenger returned with the girl in half the expected time. "How did you travel so quickly?" the teacher asked the girl. The girl's answer demonstrated the strength of her faith. "We both prayed to God for help," she reminded the teacher. "I thought I might as well start walking." She had been halfway to the teacher's house when the messenger met her on the road. She had faith that God would meet her needs, and God did.

Journal   (10 minutes)

Which of these three stories speaks to your heart the most, and why? Write about this in your journal for the next ten minutes. 🕐

Explore   (10 minutes)

Now I invite you to share your thoughts with the group as you are comfortable. *Encourage participants to respond freely; then continue.* 🕐

Journal   (5 minutes)

Consider this question silently: On a scale of one to ten, with one being the lowest and ten being the highest, what is your current level of faith? Take a few minutes to record your thoughts in your journal. 🕐

Close   (5 minutes)

Play a three to five minute selection of meditative music—preferably an instrumental selection, so that there are no words to distract participants' thoughts.

Our faith is a gift from God that is meant to grow and mature through prayer. Without faith, we cannot believe in anything that is beyond our ability to comprehend—such as believing there is an ocean simply because we have seen a river; or believing in love even though we may not have felt it; or believing that every time we switch on the lights, they actually will come on; or believing that something as heavy as an airplane can actually fly.

What can you do to increase your faith? Seriously consider this question in silence for the duration of the music. When the music has ended, we will break for lunch. 𝄞

LUNCH (12:00 P.M.–1:00 P.M.)

This is another time for building community. Gather again in a large circle, give thanks, and encourage the women to sit beside some new faces.

SESSION 4: LOVE (1:00 P.M.–2:30 P.M.)

Open (3 minutes)

Sing together "Jesus Loves Me" and "Blest Be the Tie That Binds." 𝄞

Talk (5 minutes)

Read the following aloud.
Listen to these words from the author of this retreat:

Love—perhaps it is the most often used yet least understood word in our language. What is your picture or image of love? Several images come to my mind as I write this: The moment my husband and I met; the births of our three children; the period when we cared for my father-in-law as he was dying from cancer; a pink silk bag from my paternal grandmother that contained the cut-up pieces of love letters from her husband during World War I; a scrawled note from my preschool son to the Tooth Fairy about losing the ever-important tooth in a fight; a bookmark in my Bible made by my daughter in kindergarten, which said how much she loved having lunch with me on my day off. . . . The list goes on and on. What are your images of love?

Read aloud 1 John 4:18.
Jesus taught that perfect love, God's love, casts away fear. God's love gives us confidence against the fear of the world.

Mother Teresa said, "There are many in the world who are dying for a piece of bread but there are many more dying for a little love."[7] We have a natural hunger for love, just as we have a hunger for God. Yet we can't respond to the need for love without God's grace. It is only in being loved by God that we know how to love. Listen to this excerpt from *Chicken Soup for the Soul*:

In one seat a wispy old man sat holding a bunch of fresh flowers. Across the aisle was a young girl whose eyes came back again and again to the man's flowers. The time came for the old man to get off [the bus]. Impulsively he thrust the flowers into the girl's lap. "I can see you love the flowers," he explained, "and I think my wife would like for you to have them. I'll tell her I gave them to you." The girl accepted the flowers, then watched the old man get off the bus and walk through the gate of a small cemetery.[8]

Journal (10 minutes)

Write about a time when you experienced sudden love from a stranger. We'll come back together in five minutes. 🕐
After the journaling exercise, ask for one volunteer who is willing to share her experience with the group. Allow another five minutes for sharing. 🕐

Explore (25 minutes)

Love—is there any word that evokes more feeling in us? Is there any more desired trait? To many, love is the ultimate virtue. To others, it is the end of our journey of seeking. Let's dig a little deeper into the meaning of love with the help of God's Word.

Read aloud 1 Peter 4:8. 🕐

"Love covers a multitude of sins." What does that mean? How do you know it is true? *Encourage participants to respond briefly as they are comfortable, allowing approximately three to five minutes.* 🕐

Have someone read aloud 1 John 4:8.

God gives freely—with no motive other than to express God's nature. When have you been given God's love? When have you felt God's love? When have you taken notice of God's love? *Encourage participants to respond briefly as they are comfortable, allowing approximately three to five minutes.* 🕐

Have someone read aloud Galatians 5:22-25.

Love is listed as the first fruit of the spirit. How is love evident in your life? *Encourage participants to respond briefly as they are comfortable, allowing approximately three to five minutes.* 🕐

Have someone read aloud John 13:34-35.

Mother Teresa has said, "It is not how much you do but how much love you put into the doing and sharing with others that is important."[9] What are some of the limitations that prevent us from loving others as Christ commanded? *Encourage participants to respond briefly as they are comfortable, allowing approximately three to five minutes.* 🕐

Journal   (7 minutes)

How do we learn of love? Write your response in your journal. We'll come back together in three minutes. 🕐

After the journaling exercise, allow three minutes for participants to share a few brief thoughts. 🕐 *Conclude with these words:* We can learn of love only as we learn of God. Jesus said, " . . . learn from me" (Matthew 11:29). There is no other way to learn of love.

Scripture Surf   (15–20 minutes)

Write the following scripture references on newsprint, a chalkboard, or a dry erase board; or instruct participants to write them in their journals as you read them aloud.

In silence, "scripture surf" the following verses.

1 John 4:7-8
1 Corinthians 13
John 3:16
John 15:9-17

Read each passage silently. Meditate on the words. Then journal as God's Great Spirit leads you. You have fifteen to twenty minutes to do this. 🕐

Journal   (3 minutes)

Love is first being with someone and then reacting to his or her need. How have you experienced this to be true? Journal your response for the next three minutes. 🕐

Talk   (5–7 minutes)

Read this section several times until you can paraphrase and present it in your own speaking style—with the exception of the author's words and the excerpted material, which are to be read aloud.

Let's hear again Mother Teresa's words: "Every act of love is a prayer. . . . It is not how much you do but how much love you put into the doing and sharing with others that is important.[10] How much love do you put into doing and sharing? Do you give it freely? *Pause momentarily for silent reflection; then continue.*

There is an old story of a Hassidic rabbi who was confronted by one of his youthful disciples. In an eager emotional display of emotion, the young student said, "Master, I love you!" The teacher looked at his student and asked, "Do you know what hurts me?"

The young man, surprised and puzzled, said, "I'm confused; I said, 'I LOVE YOU!'"

The rabbi responded, "How can you love me if you do not know what hurts me?"

God asks us the same question. What is it we do that hurts God? *Pause momentarily so that participants may reflect silently; then continue.*

Hear these words from Isaiah 45:2: "I will go before [you], and make the crooked places straight" (KJV). Sue Monk Kidd wrote:

Wherever we walk in life, whether through grief, uncertainty, worry, or despair, there is One who not only travels with us in the present, but also before us into the future, making the path straight. When the way grows crooked, watch with care. For that is when God appears like a mother's kiss or a spring of water breaking into a thirsty moment. We are never alone in our need.[11]

Listen to these words from the author of this retreat:

> Love is like being with someone without a clock. I have a friend named Kent. He has neither a watch nor a concept of time. When Kent is with me, he is fully with me; he's not thinking of his "to do" list, where he needs to go next, the multitude of errands he must run; he simply is with me. Are you like this with anyone? Are you like this when you spend time with God? This is loving without anticipating the results.

Journal   (5 minutes)

Listen closely to this statement: Love makes one capable of doing ordinary things in extraordinary ways. Take a few minutes to list some of the ordinary things you do with love, such as packing your child's lunch or making the bed. Listen to these words from the author of this retreat:

> My husband, Kelly, leaves for work very early in the morning, and sometimes the children and I don't see him until evening. But he is wonderful at leaving a love note on the kitchen counter for us—individually or collectively. These notes are so important to us that often they will wind up on someone's bulletin board or in a notebook or wallet.

Make a brief list of ways you can be more loving. We'll come back together in about five minutes. 🕐

Close   (5 minutes)

Read the following aloud: God's love is reaching and longing and waiting.

Play again the selection "The Seed Becomes a Prayer," included on Colleen Haley's CD From the Heart, *or choose another appropriate song. Sing along together, if you like.* 𝄞

FREE TIME   (2:30 P.M.–5:00 P.M.)

This time is provided for sleeping, walking, crafting, sharing, playing games, or simply relaxing. If everyone is not comfortable with the amount of free time, feel free to adjust the schedule accordingly. Make sure that each woman finds something she wants to do.

SINGING AND SHARING   (5:00 P.M.–6:00 P.M.)

Singing unites our spirits! Perhaps one or more individuals in your group are singers who may take turns leading the group in singing—and may even sing a few solos themselves. You may want to prepare one or more song sheets, use hymnals, or sing "old favorites." (If you prepare song sheets and use copyrighted material, be sure to include your church license number on these sheets. Check with your choir director or organist for this information.) This is also a good time to check in with the group and see how the retreat is going. Are there any problems? Any discoveries?

DINNER   (6:00 p.m.–7:00 p.m.)

Form a circle and say or sing the blessing. Then enjoy more community-building time as you share food and fellowship.

SESSION 5: SERVICE   (7:00 p.m.–9:00 p.m.)

Open   (5 minutes)

Play the selection "The Very Best Gift," included on Colleen Haley's CD From the Heart, *or choose another appropriate song. Sing along together, if you like.* ♪

Talk   (5 minutes)

Read this section several times until you can paraphrase and present it in your own speaking style. Listen to these words from the author of this retreat.

Time, only time
God's great gift of time
How will I spend my share of time?

I want time . . .
Time to dream, to laugh, to love, to pray
I want time . . .
Time to share, to lead, to wonder, to give

Who will teach the children?
Who will feed to hungry?
Who will clothe the naked?
Who will tell the story?

It only takes time . . .
Time, only time . . .
God's great gift of time . . .

My prayer, O Master of my heart, is simple:
  May my time be worthy of eternity.
  Amen.

This weekend we've been examining the simple path. We've seen that the fruit of silence is prayer, the fruit of prayer is faith, and the fruit of faith is love. What, then, is the fruit of love? Service.

Service yields the freedom to do *something*—not to do *everything*. We are called to perform an act of service, but we are not called to do every service that the community might need. Mother Teresa once said, "I picked up one person—maybe if I didn't pick up that one person I wouldn't have picked up 42,000."[12] I am sure that by the time of her death in 1997, Mother Teresa had picked up many, many more sick, hungry, and needy individuals. If each one of us shared what we have to give, wouldn't there be enough for all the world? Isn't that what God intended?

The problems of this world continue. The work of God is constant. The point is to do *something*. What can *you* do? Can you read stories to children? Can you mentor, bake for a neighbor, take someone to the doctor, take an elderly person shopping? Each of us is called to do something.

Explore (15 minutes)

Listen as I read aloud the story of the woman with the jar of costly perfume. *Read aloud Mark 14:3-9.* 🕐

This woman did what she could for Jesus. She gave all that she had. She anointed him. She spread his fragrance. We too are called to spread the fragrance of Jesus. Do you do that? In what ways? *Encourage participants to respond briefly; allow approximately five minutes.* 🕐

Now listen to these words from scripture. *Read aloud Matthew 20:25-28 and John 13:14-15.* How do these verses speak of service? What do they say to you? *Encourage participants to respond briefly; allow approximately five minutes.* 🕐

Journal   (10 minutes)

John Melton said, "They also serve who only stand and wait." What does that mean to you? Write your response in your journal. We'll allow about three minutes. 🕐   Now, silently "brainstorm" as many characteristics of true service as you can. Record them in your journal. We'll allow another three minutes for this. 🕐

Does your list include any of the following?

True service . . .
• comes from the heart,
• is patient,
• does not expect anything in return,
• is not concerned with a projected goal.

Keeping these and your own attributes in mind, journal in response to these questions: When have I truly been in service? Do I know anyone who lives a life of true service? We'll allow about three minutes for this. 🕐

Talk   (3 minutes)

Read this section aloud.

There are times when service happens almost accidentally. Listen to this story told by the author of this retreat:

I remember one day a number of years ago when my daughter was undergoing some extensive testing at Texas Children's Hospital. We ducked into a nearby restroom between appointments and met a mother who was holding her young child. The child was about a year and a half old and obviously could not walk, stand, or sit. The mother was simply holding the child across her arms, and she seemed to be trying to figure out what to do with the child while she used the restroom. When I offered to hold her baby, she said, "Can I trust you?" She looked at me—no, *through* me. I don't believe anyone had ever looked at me that way before—or ever has since! She was evaluating me to determine if she could trust her most precious possession—her greatest love—to me. She eventually did. I have never forgotten what it felt like to hold her baby, her cherished gift from God, and to have been of some small service in her very difficult life.

As God's people, we must look for ways to deny ourselves and serve others in the name of Christ.

Scripture Surf   (20 minutes)

Write the following scripture references on a chalkboard or a dry erase board; or instruct the participants to write them in their journals as you read them aloud.

In silence, "scripture surf" the following verses:

Romans 12:4-8
Matthew 5:14-16
1 Peter 2:9-10
Ephesians 4:11-13

Galatians 6:9-10

2 Corinthians 5:14

Read each passage silently. Meditate on the words. Then journal as God's Great Spirit leads you. You have fifteen to twenty minutes to do this. ⏰

Explore (10 minutes)

Let's divide into small groups of three to five. ⏰ Now, each person is to tell about someone she knows who has a missionary heart. Here's the catch: Each of you can use only one sentence to describe the person's commitment to service. Take time to think before you speak, choosing your words carefully. We'll come back together in about seven minutes. ⏰

Journal (6–8 minutes)

What sentence might a friend of yours use to describe *your* commitment to service? What would you *like* your friend to be able to say? After responding to these questions in your journal, write an attainable goal for yourself and highlight it in some way—circle it, put a star beside it, and so forth. We'll allow five to seven minutes for this. ⏰

Talk   (2 minutes)

Read this section several times until you can paraphrase and present it in your own speaking style.

True service is not a burden. Mother Teresa did not consider the people of the world to be a burden. She saw every person as if he or she were Jesus. She helped them—one person at a time. To be able to serve in this manner, you must put yourself into the hands of God. You must become an instrument of God's desires and creativity. Remember that God's strength is perfect; our strength is only a hindrance to what we do.

Sometimes our service is purely physical, such as painting a house, repairing a fence, or collecting socks for needy children. Other times our service is both physical and spiritual, such as helping a single mom organize her bills and checking account while sharing our personal faith in Jesus Christ. However you choose to serve, it is the service you give as a "work of love" that will bring you closer to God.

Journal (15 minutes)

During the next fifteen minutes, you will have three journaling assignments to complete. Take notes in your journal now as I share some instructions.

1. As you think about the ways you currently serve others, make a list of the "have to" versus the "want to." What does your list tell you about yourself?

2. On a scale of one to ten, with one being the lowest and ten being the highest, rank your eagerness to serve God. Do you serve out of duty? Do you feel inadequate to serve? Whom do you consider to be your neighbor?

3. One of the closing lines from the movie *Dances with Wolves* reveals great wisdom: "There is one path that is singularly important—it is the path of becoming a true human." What does this statement mean to you? One of the ways we can experience the process of "becoming truly human" is to give of ourselves to others completely—with no reservation. As the Velveteen Rabbit says in Margaret Williams's book by the same name: "In loving this way we become real." How would you describe those times in your own life when you have given of yourself completely? ⏰

Explore (10 minutes)

Note: You might want to dim the lights and play some meditative instrumental music in the background during the following guided imagery exercise. It is important not to rush through the exercise; wait in silence at least twenty to thirty seconds whenever a pause is indicated. This form of prayer is often very emotional for some participants. Whenever using guided imagery in a group setting, be sure that someone is available to listen to participants after the experience.

Let's participate in a guided imagery exercise now. First, place any objects you are holding on the floor and get comfortable in your seat. *Pause.* Take several deep, cleansing breaths. *Pause.* Close your eyes and become aware of your own breathing. *Pause.* Imagine yourself walking along the beach. *Pause.* Feel the warmth of the sand as you walk; the sand covers your feet with each step. *Pause.* You feel the warmth of the sun's heat and light on your head. *Pause.* Each part of your skin feels the warmth of the sun and reflects it. You feel very alive. *Pause.* You continue walking along until you meet the water's edge. *Pause.* You are alone; no one is in sight. *Pause.* You stop and look at the horizon. *Pause.* What do you see? . . . smell? . . . hear? *Pause.* You contine to walk. *Pause.* You are joined by someone; it is Jesus. He is looking at you; it is as if he is asking you a question without speaking aloud. What does Jesus ask of you? *Pause.* After a few moments, you continue your walk filled with deep peace. *Pause.* When you are ready, become aware of your breathing. *Pause.* Then open your eyes and become aware of your surroundings. *Sit in silence until all the participants have opened their eyes.*

Journal   (12 minutes)

Take a few minutes to write in your journal about what you experienced during the guided imagery exercise. We'll come back together in about five minutes. 🕐

Read aloud John 21:15-19. 🕐

In this dialogue between Jesus and Peter, Peter is given the responsibility of caring for the people of Jesus. We, too, are called to care for Jesus' people. How have you responded in the past? How would you like to respond in the future? *Pause momentarily so that participants may reflect silently; then continue.*

When determining what form our service will take, we sometimes need to let go of other activities that have cluttered our hearts' desires. Are there responsibilities you have assumed that are not a match for your gifts or for the places God is calling you to serve? In your journal, make a list of these distracting responsibilities and consider how you can bring closure to your work so that you may serve God more effectively in other ways. We'll allow about five minutes for this. 🕐

Close   (5 minutes)

Read the following poem aloud:

Feeding Sheep

He said, "Feed my sheep."
There were no conditions:
Least of all, Feed my sheep if they deserve it.
Feed my sheep if you feel like it.
Feed my sheep if you have any leftovers.
Feed my sheep if the mood strikes you.
if the economy's OK . . .
if you're not too busy . . .

No conditions . . . just, "Feed my sheep."
Could it be that God's Kingdom will come
when each lamb is fed?
We who have agreed to keep covenant
are called to feed sheep
even when it means the grazing will be done
on our own front lawns.[13]

Play the selection "The Lord Will Provide," included on Colleen Haley's CD From the Heart, *or choose another appropriate song. Sing along, if you like.* 🎼

FREE TIME   **(9:00 P.M.–9:15 P.M.)**

During this time, participants may stretch, take restroom breaks, visit with one another, and prepare for Evening Worship (remind them to grab blankets if worship is to be held outside) while you and members of the design team set up for worship.

EVENING WORSHIP   **(9:15 P.M.–10:00 P.M.)**

Gathering

Quietly sing or hum a familiar hymn or worship song as you gather together for worship.

Scripture Reading

Have someone read aloud Matthew 18:3.

Special Music/Worship Song

Play the selection "Put Your Life in His Hands," included on Colleen Haley's CD From the Heart, or choose another appropriate song. Sing along together, if you like.

Invitation to Meditation and Prayer

Have you ever wanted to change someone? Have you ever hoped that perhaps someone in your life could be blessed with some new "seeds" that would bring about a change you deem necessary? Anthony De Mello wrote: "To a disciple who was forever complaining about others the Master said, 'If it is peace you want, seek to change yourself, not other people. For it is easier to protect your feet with slippers than to carpet the whole of the earth.'"[14]

What is it about yourself that needs to be changed? How can the necessary "seeds" be planted? Reflect on this in a moment of silent meditation and prayer. *Pause for approximately two minutes; then move into corporate prayer as instructed below.*

Prayers of the People of God

After leading the group into prayer, invite the participants to share their prayers aloud "popcorn style." When all who wish to pray have done so, close the prayer time.

Communion or Love Feast

A Love Feast is symbolic of a traditional communion service. You will need grape juice or water and a loaf of bread. Place the juice or water in a chalice. As you give each member of the community a piece of bread and she dips it into the juice or water, remind her of the sacrifice made on her behalf though Jesus Christ. Simply say, "This is because Jesus loves you no matter what."

Benediction

Go into the night as God's beautiful creations, full of many seeds—seeds to sow and seeds to reap. Amen.

Day 3

BREAKFAST   **(8:00 A.M.–9:00 A.M.)**

Again, have the coffee ready for the early risers. By this time, you will note that the group has "jelled" and most are interacting as family. Enjoy this breakfast together after a group blessing.

MORNING WATCH   **(9:00 A.M.–9:45 A.M.)**

Reproduce the material on page 186 and distribute to all participants as they leave breakfast and find a place apart for their Morning Watch. Remind them that Session 6 will begin at 9:45.

SESSION 6: PEACE   (9:45 A.M.–11:00 A.M.)

Open   (5–7 minutes)

Read the children's book Old Turtle *by Douglas Wood (Duluth, Minn.: Pheifer-Hamilton, 1992), or choose another appropriate reading.* 🕐

Talk   (3 minutes)

Read this section several times until you can paraphrase and present it in your own speaking style.

Let's review God's simple path. God's simple path makes a circle as the words lead one to another. Can you picture it?

> Silence leads to prayer
>   Prayer leads to faith
>   Faith leads to love
>   Love leads to service
>   Service leads to peace
>   Peace leads to prayer. . . .

There is an often-told story of two painters. Each was challenged to paint a picture to illustrate his conception of peace. The first chose for his painting a quiet, still lake in the midst of mountains. The second artist threw on his canvas a thundering waterfall, with a fragile tree bending over the foam of the water; and in one of the branches sat a robin on its nest. Which picture illustrated *true* peace? The second one, for in the midst of the storm, we can find moments of peace.

Peace—the final step of the simple path. It is God's supreme gift. Peace is greater than any emotion. Peace is beyond joy or suffering, and can exist through both. Peace is the rerooting of ourselves in God, so that the feeling of being separated from God does not exist. It is the tranquil order of everything. It is experiencing God through the senses. Peace is every value together in simplicity and unity. Peace can be the present moment regardless of its content. We trick ourselves into waiting for peace until the bills are paid, or school is finished, or the babies are out of diapers, or the project is finished, or we are well. The truth is, peace can be found in the midst of all these things.

Explore (5 minutes)

Turn to a neighbor and describe *your* picture of true peace. We'll come back together in five minutes. 🕐

Journal (5 minutes)

Thomas à Kempis, a German spiritual writer and monk of the fourteenth century, suggested there are four things we can do that will bring peace: (1) Place the will of others before our own; (2) have few worldly riches; (3) seek to be under others rather than above them; (4) pray that the will of God will be done in you. How are you doing in terms of peace? Do you have fleeting moments of peace? None at all? Do you possess a peaceful undercurrent in your soul? Which one of the four steps to peace suggested by Thomas à Kempis needs your attention? Write a related goal in your journal and circle it. Then make a conscious decision to achieve this goal. Take about three to four minutes to reflect and write your goal. 🕐

Talk (3 minutes)

Read this section aloud.

Peace literally means "to bind together." Peace binds and weaves us into wholeness. It is the realization that God is in control of the present and the future, and that God forgives the past. Anne Frank knew what it meant to have true peace. She wrote these words in her diary while she and her family were in hiding from the Nazis during World War II:

I keep [my ideals] because in spite of everything I still believe that people are really good at heart. I simply can't build up my hopes on a foundation consisting of confusion, misery, and death. . . . I can feel the sufferings of millions and yet, if I look up into the heavens, I think that it will all come right, that this cruelty too will end, and that peace and tranquility will return again.[19]

The twenty-third psalm has been called the "psalm of peace." Visualize the words as I read the psalm aloud now. ⊕

Scripture Surf (15–20 minutes)

Write the following scripture references on an easel board, chalkboard, or dry erase board; or instruct participants to write them in their journals as you read the references aloud.

In silence, "scripture surf" three to four of the following verses.

John 14:27; 16:33
Philippians 4:6-7
Romans 12:18; 5:1
Colossians 3:15
1 Corinthians 7:15
Isaiah 9:6-7; 26:3-4
Luke 2:8-9; 2:13-14; 19:37-38

Read each passage silently. Meditate on the words. Then journal as God's Great Spirit leads you. You have fifteen to twenty minutes to do this. ⊕

Journal (10 minutes)

Remember that peace is not the absence of strife. As you reflect on this statement, take time to write about your most peaceful moment. We'll come back together in ten minutes. ⊕

Talk (3–5 minutes)

Read this section aloud.

Peace is a virtue, a state of mind—not necessarily a physical state, but a disposition. Your "surface" may be disturbed, but it is your "depth" that counts. In other words, outwardly you may be experiencing trials, but inwardly—within your soul—you still can be at peace. Listen to this poem by the author of this retreat:

Sharon Gave Me Lilies

Have you ever watched a lily?
I mean, have you ever *really* watched a lily?
As it blooms?
Such a glorious sight!
It begins so small . . . a seed planted deep in the soil,
Nurtured with the warmth of the light and dampness of the water of Life.
Then a bud appears
And grows
And changes
And becomes.

Then as if music were to make it dance,
The lily opens.
Full of beauty
Full of fragrance
Full of possibility
Full of grace
Becoming all its Creator intended!

Glorious!

Sharon gave me lilies.
I wonder, are we like lilies?

Journal   (10–12 minutes)

As we near the end of our retreat and you embark on your own simple path, reread the entries you have made in your journal and note the learnings that have influenced you. Write about this now. We'll come back together in ten to twelve minutes. 🕐

Close   (5 minutes)

Sing together the hymn "It Is Well with My Soul." 🎵

CLOSING WORSHIP   (11:00 A.M.–12:00 P.M.)

Note: In advance of the service, the leader should ask six participants to be prepared to share and/or read an excerpt from their journals related to one of the following key words: silence, prayer, faith, love, service, and peace.

Call to Worship

Read aloud Psalm 121. 🕐

A Time of Remembering

Invite three of the volunteers to share and/or read from their journal entries at this time. 🕐

Special Music

Play the selection "The Seed Becomes a Prayer," included on Colleen Haley's CD From the Heart, *or choose another appropriate song.* 🎵

A Time of Remembering

Invite the remaining three volunteers to share and/or read from their journal entries at this time. 🕐

An Invitation to Share

Invite all participants to respond freely to the following questions:
What else needs to be said?
What difference will this retreat make in your life? 🕐

Closing Prayer

Have the participants stand in a circle and hold hands. Remind them that they will never be "one" like this again. This time has been sacred and set apart. Begin an open-ended prayer, allowing group members to take turns praying aloud in "popcorn" fashion. Make sure everyone knows it is OK to pass. Close with this line: "And all God's women said, 'Amen.'"

RETURN HOME   (12:00 P.M. until . . .)

Thank each person for her participation in the retreat and make any necessary closing remarks. 🕐 *Now it is time for the design team to clean, pack up, and evaluate the retreat; or, if you prefer, the team may save the evaluation for a later time.*

Power for Living

◆

OVERVIEW

This retreat is based on the books *Do What You Have the Power to Do* by Helen Bruch Pearson (Nashville: Upper Room Books, 1992) and *Inner Healing for Broken Vessels: Seven Steps to a Woman's Way of Healing* by Linda Hollies (Nashville: Upper Room Books, 1992). Participants study several biblical women face-to-face and heart-to-heart. The inner strength of the individual is identified as a tool for nurturing personal spiritual growth.

PREPARING FOR THE RETREAT
- Review "How to Use This Book: Planning and Preparing for Retreats" (pp. 11-15).
- Assemble the design team.
- Read through the retreat; make revisions and additions as appropriate for your group or situation.
- Pray for the retreat.
- Advertise; invite and recruit participants.
- Send correspondence noting details of the retreat. (Be sure to let participants know what items they are to bring.)
- Gather the supplies.

SUPPLIES AND MATERIALS
To be brought by the leader
- nametags
- cassette/CD player
- cassettes/CDs, including meditative music
- hymnals or other songbooks (see suggested hymns and songs throughout the retreat)
- newsprint and marker, chalkboard and chalk, or dry erase board and marker
- white pillar candle and matches or lighter
- paper, pens, pencils
- a journal for each participant (Note: For large groups, ask participants to bring their own.)
- medium-size basket
- *Inner Healing for Broken Vessels* by Linda Hollies
- *Do What You Have the Power to Do* by Helen Bruch Pearson (Note: If possible, have multiple copies available for participants to share during a journaling exercise in Session 2 and/or encourage participants to bring their own copies.)
- angel postcards, one for each participant (see Session 2)
- worksheet based on pp. 64-67 of Pearson's *Do What You Have the Power to Do*, one for each participant (see Session 3)
- *Opening to God* by Carolyn Stahl (optional, see Session 3)
- *Knots on a Counting Rope* by Bill Martin (see Evening Worship, Day 2)
- a short piece of rope (six to twelve inches) for each participant (see Evening Worship, Day 2)
- *Let the Celebrations Begin* by Margaret Wild and Julie Vivas (optional, see Session 4)
- *It Was on Fire When I Lay Down on It* by Robert Fulgum (see Closing Worship)
- small reflective craft mirrors, one for each participant (see Closing Worship)
- anointing oil (see Closing Worship)
- Morning Watch handouts for Days 2 and 3, one for each participant (see pp. 189)

To be brought by each participant

- Bible
- quilt or blanket
- pen or pencil

The Retreat **Day 1**

ARRIVAL   (3:00 P.M.–6:00 P.M.)

Have nametags ready for the participants as they arrive. Designate one or more greeters to personally escort each participant to her room and invite her to relax by resting, sleeping, reading, walking, hiking, talking with others, and so forth.

DINNER   (6:00 P.M.–7:00 P.M.)

This is the first group activity. If space allows, form a large circle and say or sing the blessing. As leader, wait to be served last so that you may walk around the room and welcome everyone. Encourage the participants to sit with others whom they do not already know. Look for those who seem lost or who are alone. Assign persons from the design team to keep an eye on these participants and see that connections with others begin to take place.

GROUP ANNOUNCEMENTS/GET-TO-KNOW-YOU ACTIVITIES   (7:00 P.M.–7:30 P.M.)

After dinner, formally welcome everyone and make any necessary group announcements—such as telling the location of bathrooms, telephones, and first-aid kits, and reviewing the retreat schedule. Then begin a get-acquainted game or activity. 🕐

SESSION 1: RECOGNITION   (7:30 A.M.–9:00 A.M.)

Open   (2 minutes)

"How precious life is!"
"If only I'd realized that when I was younger."
"It's later than you think."

Have you ever found yourself saying those words? It *is* later than we think. With each moment, life continues to whirl past us. Moments are lost—the only ones we will ever have. Now listen to these words:

The shepherd calls his sheep by name and leads them out. . . . They follow the shepherd because they know his voice. (John 3*b*-4, paraphrase)

I am the good shepherd. The good shepherd lays down his life for his sheep. (John 10:11, paraphrase)

I know my sheep and my sheep know me. (John 14*b*, paraphrase)

For it is time to seek the lord, until he comes and showers righteousness on you. (Hosea 10:12)

Taste and see that the lord is good. (Psalm 34:18)

We have to be willing to discover and then appreciate the authentic moments of happiness available to all of us every day. —Sarah Ban Breathnach

Talk   (5–7 minutes)

Read this section several times until you can paraphrase and present it in your own speaking style.
The purpose of this retreat is to help us focus on our unique relationship with God and celebrate our gifts as we become community. In each session we will look at the lives of two biblical women and take an intense look within our own lives.

What comes to mind when you hear the word *women*? Let us brainstorm some words and phrases now. *Allow a couple of minutes for participants to suggest words and phrases; write them on newsprint, a chalkboard, or a dry erase board. Examples: worker, people of God, female, in God's image, mother, aunt, sister, daughter, organizer, teacher, instrument.* 🕐 Because we have many shared realities as women, we have an inner connection that needs no articulation. Listen to these words from the author of this retreat:

> When I think about the birth of my first child, I remember the intense feeling of being connected to all women who had ever given birth. I remember seeing total strangers and feeling connected to them because they were mothers and had probably traveled the same path as I. I also experienced a new connectedness with my own mother—a new sense of understanding and camaraderie. Even those women who are not mothers themselves possess within a maternal instinct, a unique ability to love and nurture others. This is one of the many unique responsibilities, rights, and privileges we have been given by God. We are cocreators with God, bringing forth new life, new images, new ideas, new things. As we express our creativity, we often serve as "midwives" to one another—encouraging new growth and helping to meet one another's needs. Regardless of the roles we may play, we are all God's daughters.

In Hebrews 2:7 we read: "You are made a little lower than the angels; crowned with glory and honor" (paraphrase). Each one of us is a precious daughter of God, crowned with glory and honor. From now on, whenever you hear the word *women,* think of our heads and the crowns we are privileged to wear as God's precious children. Remember that our names are engraved in God's hand, and we never will be forgotten. Then think of our feet and all the places they have been. Our feet tell the story of many diverse yet similar travels. We do not journey through this life alone; we are bound together in community. As God's daughters, we all long for unity, wholeness, and peace, which nothing can repress or deny.

Journal   (20 minutes)

Silently read chapter one from the book of Esther. Then journal about this world-changing incident. Include the facts as well as your feelings. We'll allow ten minutes for this. When I indicate that time is up, find a partner and share your thoughts. We'll allow another ten minutes for sharing. 🕐

Talk   (2 minutes)

Read this section aloud.

In the first chapter of the book of Esther, Queen Vashti changes the course of history. In her book *Inner Healing for Broken Vessels: Seven Steps to a Woman's Way of Healing,* Linda Hollies writes:

Now we must understand that he [the King, Vashti's husband] was not calling the queen to have her address her loyal subjects. She was not sent for in order to allow her to be seen as his equal, co-monarch. But, she was "fetched" in order that the men in the kingdom could view her as an object, a thing the king owned, a possession. Truly a beautiful thing, but a thing nevertheless. The king sent seven eunuchs into her courts to escort her to his palace. While she was busy entertaining their wives, her guests, these men entered her quarters and declared that they had been told to bring her to the king. On this day, she said no.[1]

Queen Vashti had finally had enough. By refusing to follow the King's order, Queen Vashti gave up her security. She took what was likely to be the biggest risk of her life. What do you think she was searching for? What are you searching for?

Explore   (15 minutes)

Write the following excerpts on newsprint, a chalkboard, or a dry erase board; then say the following aloud.

Let's probe a little deeper by responding to some excerpts from *Inner Healing for Broken Vessels* by Linda Hollies, and *Do What You Have the Power to Do* by Helen Bruch Pearson. I'll read each excerpt aloud and I invite you to briefly share your thoughts with the group. We'll allow about fifteen minutes. 🕐

From *Inner Healing for Broken Vessels* by Linda Hollies:

"Scripture does not detail exactly what [Vashti] experienced, but each one of us has our own story to tell of that particular day when something switched on, and we changed and became different inside" (p. 20).

"Vashti paid a high price for her recognition of her selfhood" (p. 21).

"Giving up security is difficult" (p. 22).

From *Do What You Have the Power to Do* by Helen Bruch Pearson:

"Through discipline and commitment, empowerment can assist those who choose to experience and realize the power to do what they can do" (p. 37).

Then, with the empowerment of the Holy Spirit, we can do it.

Talk   (3 minutes)

Read this section several times until you can paraphrase and present it in your own speaking style.
Now let us consider the story of another woman, the woman who anointed Jesus. It is interesting that this story is recorded in all four Gospels, yet the stories aren't identical. In Mark, the woman's name is never mentioned—only her action. Nor does Mark tell us how she earned her living. We learn from the other Gospels that she was called a prostitute. This fact didn't seem to matter to Mark. He does tell us, however, that the incident took place in the city of Bethany at the house of Simon the leper. In each Gospel we see that the woman was bold enough to approach Jesus without asking permission, and she was affirmed and defended by Jesus. We also know that she was treated rudely by the other guests at the dinner, including the disciples.

This woman blessed Jesus. He revealed yet a third time to the disciples that he was going to die, and they just did not get it. But *she* got it! She was filled with love and tenderness and compassion. In Pearson's words, "She, alone, behaved as though she understood."[2] She was a servant to Jesus. She offered all that she had and all that she was. She simply did what she could do. She didn't do it to receive anything in return. In fact, her action was a huge risk on her part. Yet she did it bravely and openly. She anointed Jesus; she prepared him; she gave him her support as he faced certain death. She seemingly was the only one who gave Jesus the appropriate honor and response.

Explore   (5–7 minutes)

Have the participants break into pairs and give the following instructions.
Read aloud Mark 14:3-9 and briefly discuss this question: What do you think is the most significant thing this woman did? We'll come back together in about five to seven minutes. 🕐

Journal   (15 minutes)

Write the following excerpts from Do What You Have the Power to Do *by Helen Bruch Pearson, and the accompanying questions, on newsprint, a chalkboard, or a dry erase board; then provide the following instructions.* In silence, read and reflect on these excerpts from *Do What You Have the Power to Do* by Helen Bruch Pearson. When you have finished, respond in your journal to the questions and then write a prayer of thanksgiving for the woman who anointed Jesus. We'll allow fifteen minutes for this. 🕐

"It was the woman, not Simon or the male guests and disciples, who was doing, acting, caring, touching, anointing, giving, and risking. And Jesus accepted her silent acts of intimacy and devotion with profound respect and reverent silence" (p. 47).

"Disciples must have an appreciation for the beauty of God—for those fine and beautiful things that God has so extravagantly given us. Song, dance, poetry, painting, sculpture, art, movement, gesture—these are not luxuries. These are essentials to the Christian experience, for as we return to them, they take us to God's heartbeat and the rhythms of all life" (p. 49).

Questions for Reflection and Journaling:
• What beautiful things have been done for you?
• What beautiful things have you done for others?
• What beautiful things will you do for others? for yourself?
• What similarities, if any, do you see between you and the woman who anointed Jesus?

Journal   (15 minutes)

We need to recognize that we are women who are called to be disciples of an extravagant God; we are called to be recognized as followers of Christ.

Let us enter again into a time of silent reflection and journaling. List ten women, living or dead, who have significantly influenced and shaped your life. Perhaps there have been some important women in your life who have been less than positive influences, yet through these negative relationships you nevertheless were empowered in some way. Do not forget them. What can you remember about these influential women? In her book book *Do What You Have the Power to Do*, Helen Bruch Pearson offers these helpful questions: "Were they all 'anointers'? How did they help empower you to do what you have the power to do? Through positive or negative examples? What values did they hold that have become your values? Is it important to pass these values on to future generations? Why? Why not? How many of the women on your list are well known or world famous?"[3] We'll come back together in fifteen minutes. ⏰

Close   (4 minutes)

Play the selection "Put Your Life in His Hands," included on Colleen Haley's CD From the Heart, *or choose another appropriate song. Sing along, if you like.* ♪

EVENING WORSHIP   (9:00 P.M.–9:45 P.M.)

Gathering

As everyone gathers, play instrumental music in the background—either from a cassette or CD or a musician in the group.

Scripture Reading

Paraphrase Psalm 139, or ask participants to read selected verses only. ⏰

A Time of Sharing

Have the participants break into small groups of three to five and take turns answering the following questions: How is it with your soul tonight? What do you hope/pray that this retreat will bring for you? ⏰

Prayer

Offer the following prayer on behalf of all: Lord, we know you are holy. With you, all things are possible. We lift all these holy conversations up to you. Bless them, hold them, answer them. In your name we pray. Amen.

Homily

Once upon a time, a long time ago, there was a church in the Southwest. The city and surrounding county had experienced a long and thorough drought. The members of the church thought that they should gather together to pray for rain. When the minister of the church arrived, she was delighted to see so many gathered together for prayer. Out of the corner of her eye, she saw a child in the first pew holding an umbrella in her hand. Many had come for prayer. The child had come expecting a miracle! Are you expecting a miracle during your time here?

Worship Song

Sing together the hymn "It Is Well with My Soul." ♪

Benediction

Go now with the knowledge and peace that God is in control of all things. May your soul rest well until morning's light.

Day 2

Note: Minor revisions have been made in the afternoon schedule to allow for a role-playing activity before dinner.

BREAKFAST (8:00 A.M.–9:00 A.M.)

Have coffee ready for the early risers. Remember that this meal is an act of the total community. Join together in a large circle to greet the morning and to give thanks to God for the night's rest and for the food that is to be received. Encourage the women to sit beside new faces during breakfast.

MORNING WATCH (9:00 A.M.–9:45 A.M.)

Reproduce the material on page 187 and distribute to all participants as they leave breakfast and find a place apart for their Morning Watch. Remind them that Session 2 will begin at 9:45.

SESSION 2: SHARING (9:45 A.M.–11:45 A.M.)

Open   (5 minutes)

If possible, invite someone in advance who knows American Sign Language—perhaps someone in your group—to present a song interpretation of a contemporary worship song at this time ("Shine, Jesus, Shine" is a great song for the morning). A song interpretation is made by making the appropriate American Sign Language motions for the key words in the music. If this is not possible, plan an appropriate worship song and/or sing along. ♪

Talk   (5 minutes)

Read this section several times until you can paraphrase and present it in your own speaking style. Begin by having someone read aloud the Gospel story found in John 4:1-30, 39-42. 🕐

Jesus established some new patterns and behaviors with the women of his time. In this particular instance, Jesus initiated the conversation; he sought out the woman at the well. Why this woman? Why had the disciples gone for food in the hottest part of the day? Weren't the markets closed because of the heat? Why did John, the beloved disciple of Jesus, record this story? Why did the woman linger and converse with Jesus? Was this meeting purely accidental? Jesus went out of his way to be with those who were and are at the end of their rope—such as this woman at the well, the widow whose daughter died, and the woman with the flow of blood.

It is important to note that Jesus never condemned the woman at the well. Instead, he reached out to her and offered her living water. None of the disciples ever would have thought that Jesus would reveal his Messiahship to this woman. But, nonetheless, he choose her. He choose *her.* He initiated the encounter! He revealed himself to her, a sinner.

Journal   (30 minutes)

If possible, have multiple copies of Do What You Have the Power to Do *available for the women to take turns using during this exercise, and/or encourage participants in advance of the retreat to bring their own copies with them.*

First, write about a time when you felt unworthy, but God used you anyway. Then, in silence, read "Encounter" from *Do What You Have the Power To Do* (pp. 155-61) and journal your thoughts. We'll allow thirty minutes for both exercises. I'll tell you when there are fifteen minutes remaining. 🕐

Explore   (25–30 minutes)

In advance, purchase a book of angel postcards; most large bookstores carry these. Invite each participant to choose an angel postcard. Then provide the following instructions.

Spend a moment looking at the angel postcard you chose. *Pause for thirty to sixty seconds; then continue.* Now, divide into groups of three and take turns telling why you chose this angel. Make up a story with the others in your group. Share your story. What does this angel have to do with the women we have discussed? Is there a connection? Is there a connection with your life? We'll come back together in fifteen to twenty minutes. 🕐

When everyone has come back to the large group, sing together the hymn "Lord, You Have Come to the Lakeshore." 🎵

Say aloud to the group: Jesus comes to all of us. Are you prepared to look at him fully and follow him? *Pause momentarily for silent reflection; then continue.*

Sharing—what does that word mean to you? Perhaps it means to own our portions, to divide, to be reasonable, or just to enjoy, to endure, to receive, to use. Look at your angel postcard again. *Pause momentarily; then continue.* Now give away your angel to someone else in the group. *Pause until everyone has given away her angel; then proceed.* 🕐

Talk   (15–20 minutes)

Read this section several times until you can paraphrase and present it in your own speaking style. Have someone read aloud Luke 1:26-56. 🕐

Mary—she is perhaps the most famous and most portrayed of all biblical women. At the time of Christ's birth, she probably was only a teenager. We often forget that part, don't we? Where was her mother during all this? Mary was smart enough to question the angel, but then she consulted no one. When most of us make a big decision, we usually consult a few people. But Mary didn't ask her mother or Joseph or anyone. What a risk taker! It is interesting that she turned to her cousin Elizabeth, who recognized Mary's child as "special" while Mary was still pregnant! I wonder if Mary's mother could have done that? But then, don't we often turn first to a peer for comfort during crisis?

Mary was God's "favored one," yet she did not receive a trouble-free, pain-free life; she did, however, receive fame—but only after her own life had ended. What does this say to us today? *Encourage participants to respond freely; then continue.* 🕐

Journal   (20 minutes)

Write the following excerpts from Inner Healing for Broken Vessels *by Linda Hollies, and the accompanying questions, on newsprint, a chalkboard, or a dry erase board; then say the following aloud.*

Read these excerpts from *Inner Healing for Broken Vessels* by Linda Hollies, and respond in your journal to the accompanying questions. We'll allow about twenty minutes. 🕐

"Mary found herself in a crisis. Her immediate response had to be fear. For the angel continued, saying, 'Do not be afraid. . . .'" (p. 35).

Do you think Mary was a passive woman? . . . a strong woman? What can you speculate about her faith and her personality? How do you respond in a crisis?

"The *why* question has never been answered in the biblical record. The *how* question only gives assent and asks for clarification. God responds by giving good directions. For the work of the Holy Spirit is to lead and to guide. . . . While we are busy, running around, trying to get God to do things our way, it is the power of the Holy Spirit to put a yes to God's way deep down in the inside of our soul. . . . As we yield our lives to the leading of the Holy Spirit, our *why* questions will become 'How?'" (p. 36).

"It is a great moment in our lives when we can cease to wrestle with our present state and learn to cultivate passivity and watch God work on our behalf" (p. 37).

When was the last time you yielded to the leading of the Holy Spirit and allowed God to work on your behalf? What happened?

Talk   (5 minutes)

Read this section several times until you can paraphrase and present it in your own speaking style.

Mary's story is about yielding to God; it also is about sharing the load—about being a friend. Mary went to Elizabeth, but she didn't go there to hide out. She went there to build up her courage and stamina. Sometimes we, too, have to go away in order to think and refuel and get prepared to handle life. Listen to this story told by the author of this retreat:

On a retreat I led several years ago, I met a woman who looked distant and aloof. She kept mostly to herself and to one special friend. I couldn't read how she was assimilating the retreat and its activities. I later learned that her husband, a healthy, athletic father of three, had recently been diagnosed with a very progressive case of Lou Gehrig's disease. He was already in a wheelchair. She was preparing herself for what lay ahead. She went away with a friend, she studied God's Word, and she was embraced by forty-five other women who essentially let her be while they prayed for her. It was a beautiful thing. As we said our goodbyes, she thanked me and told me that she felt better prepared to face the things she must face. She didn't run away by going on retreat—although running away probably sounded like a good idea. She went away to build herself up in Christ.

There are times in each of our lives when perhaps the most important thing we can do is fill ourselves with Christian love and build up our resources within the Body of Christ. When we do, we have renewed focus, energy, and peace.

Close   (5 minutes)

Sing together a couple of favorite hymns or contemporary worship songs. 🎵

BREAK   (11:45 A.M.–12:00 P.M.)

LUNCH   (12:00 P.M.–1:00 P.M.)

This is another time for building community. Gather again in a large circle, give thanks, and encourage the women to sit beside some new faces.

FREE TIME   (1:00 P.M.–4:30 P.M.)

This time is provided for sleeping, walking, crafting, sharing, playing games, or simply relaxing. If everyone is not comfortable with this amount of free time, feel free to adjust the schedule accordingly. Make sure that each woman finds something she wants to do.

SINGING   (4:30 P.M.–5:30 P.M.)

Singing unites our spirits! Perhaps one or more individuals in your group are singers who may take turns leading the group in singing—and may even sing a few solos themselves. You may want to prepare one or more song sheets, use hymnals, or sing "old favorites." (If you prepare song sheets and use copyrighted material, be sure to include your church license number on these sheets. Check with your choir director or organist for this information.) This also is a good time to check in with the group and see how the retreat is going. Are there any problems? Any discoveries?

SHARING   (5:30 P.M.–6:00 P.M.)

Have the women divide into groups of three to four, reread the story of the woman at the well (John 4), and then role-play it. Ask each group to create a list of "I wonder" questions that relate to the story.

DINNER   (6:00 P.M.–7:00 P.M.)

Form a circle and say or sing the blessing. Then enjoy more community-building time as you share food and fellowship.

SESSION 3: RECONCILIATION (7:00 P.M.–8:00 P.M.)

Open (10 minutes)

Have a time of group singing. Allow participants to suggest hymns or songs, if you like. 𝄞

Talk (8–10 minutes)

Read this section several times until you can paraphrase and present it in your own speaking style—with the exception of the book excerpts, which are to be read aloud.

Have someone read aloud Luke 13:10-17, the story of the bent-over woman.

This woman was named; she was called. Jesus spoke to her, and she could no longer be ignored. He stopped in the middle of everything and healed her. She didn't ask him to heal her. Yet he spoke to her and healed her. There were no words and no explanation. And what did she do? She immediately praised God. (I wonder if that is what I would have done?) The others there were blessed by this action—except for the synagogue ruler!

In her book *Do What You Have the Power to Do*, Helen Pearson writes, "The bent-over woman, now standing upright and free in the midst of the gathered congregation, was both the subject and the object of Jesus' healing and teaching ministries. . . . Jesus felt no need to justify healing. . . . Instead Jesus was compelled to confront an unjust situation.[4] This is a story with justice issues. Pearson continues:

Those of us who call ourselves disciples must also be willing to let our hands be an extension of our commitment to do away with unjust and unfair traditions and laws. We must be personally involved in helping those who suffer and in challenging the structures of our society that keep so many bent over. We must call out in public places and in public ways. . . . Jesus challenges us to make their struggle our struggle. His life and death instruct us that it is not two different struggles; it is one common struggle. . . . As long as anyone remains bent over, no one stands fully upright. When one is lifted, we are all lifted—and we all rejoice at the glorious things Jesus has done. When one is empowered, we are all empowered. Then what is left to do? We praise God![5]

When and how have you lifted someone up? When and how have you been an extension of God's hands?

Journal (15 minutes)

Prepare in advance a worksheet on the "Encounter" in Pearson's book Do What You Have the Power to Do, *including the essence of "A Letter from Jonella" (pp. 64-67). Distribute copies now and have each participant work through this silently.* 🕐

Explore (15–20 minutes)

Lead the group in the guided imagery exercise "Ruth" found on page 55 of Opening to God *by Carolyn Stahl (Nashville: Upper Room Books, 1977), or you may choose to write your own guided imagery exercise. For our purposes, a guided meditation is simply an imaginary story that requires participants to picture themselves in a place where they may come into contact with God. Using a lot of descriptive words, describe a beach or mountain scene; then ask a "wondering" question, such as, "What/Where is God calling you to do? . . . to be? . . . to go?" Afterward, instruct participants to journal in response to this question: Do you see any similarities between this story and our welfare system? Allow fifteen to twenty minutes for the entire exercise. (Note: This form of prayer is often very emotional for some participants. Whenever using guided imagery in a group setting, be sure that someone is available to listen to participants after the experience.)* 🕐

Close (5 minutes)

Read the following "storyteller's creed."

I believe that imagination is stronger than knowledge.
That myth is more potent than history.
I believe that dreams are more powerful than facts.
That hope always triumphs over experience.

That laughter is the only cure for grief.
And I believe that love is stronger than death.[6]

FREE TIME   (8:00 P.M–9:00 P.M.)

During this time, participants may stretch, take restroom breaks, visit with one another, and pre-pare for Evening Worship (remind them to grab blankets if worship is to be held outside) while you and members of the design team set up for worship.

EVENING WORSHIP   (9:00 P.M.–9:45 P.M.)

Worship Song

Sing together the hymn "I Have Decided to Follow Jesus."

Scripture Reading

Have someone read aloud 1 Corinthians 3:16.

Prayers of the People of God

Say the following aloud: In preparation for prayer, let's spend a few minutes calling the names of the women who have gone before us in faith. They may be biblical women, women in your family, or even women you do not know personally.
When all are silent, offer a prayer of thanks for all the women who have been named.

Meditation

Read or simply retell the children's story Knots on a Counting Rope *by Bill Martin (New York: Henry Holt, 1987).*
At the conclusion of the story, give each woman a piece of rope and instruct her to share her own story with another. After she has told her story, she may tie a knot on the counting rope.

Closing Prayer

O God, Giver of all stories, bless our sharing—and those whose names we have spoken this night. May our names be spoken for having shared your story with one another. We love you, Lord. Amen.

Day 3

BREAKFAST   (8:00 A.M.–9:00 A.M.)

Again, have the coffee ready for the early risers. By this time, you will note that the group has "jelled" and most are interacting as family. Enjoy this breakfast together after a group blessing.

MORNING WATCH   (9:00 A.M.–9:45 A.M.)

Reproduce the material on page 187 and distribute to all participants as they leave breakfast and find a place apart for their Morning Watch. Remind them that Session 4 will begin at 9:45.

SESSION 4   (9:45 A.M.–11:00 A.M.)

Open   (5–8 minutes)

Read aloud the children's book Let the Celebrations Begin *by Margaret Wild and Julie Vivas (New York: Orchard Books, 1991), or choose another appropriate story or reading.*

Journal   (15 minutes)

Choose one of the characters from the story and write in your journal how she spoke to your soul, what inner strength the character possessed, what you recognized in her, and what you want to weave through your own experience. Also, respond to this question: How is our spiritual growth nurtured through experiences that are out of our control? We'll come back together in about fifteen minutes. 🕐

Explore   (10 minutes)

Find a partner and discuss the following: What do you have the power to do? What can enable you? What do you need? What don't you need? Share your thoughts for about five minutes each. Remember, it sometimes is more important to listen than to speak. 🕐

Talk   (15 minutes)

Read this section several times until you can paraphrase and present it in your own speaking style.

For this session, our text is John 7:53–8:11. It is the story of the woman caught in adultery—caught, but not condemned. What can we learn from this woman? *Pause.* What discoveries can we make for ourselves? *Pause.* Did this woman have the power to choose? *Pause.* Let's take a look at the scripture.

Ask a volunteer to read the text aloud. 🕐

Here is what we seem to know:

- The woman appeared guilty and, by law, could be put to death.
- Jesus did not react to the situation; he was thoughtful.
- The law had been disregarded, for the man was not present.
- It was an obvious trap for Jesus—a no-win situation. If he did not advocate for the woman to be stoned, he would be violating the Law of Moses. If he urged her execution, he would be reported to the Romans, for the Jews were not allowed to carry out their own executions.
- Jesus did not condone her actions or ignore her sin.
- Jesus did not forgive her (in the story).
- Jesus challenged her to live a life free from sin.

What can we learn from the woman caught in adultery?

- If you reprove others, you should be without reproach yourself.
- Not one of us is without sin; we all have need of forgiveness and liberation.
- We always have a choice. The accusers had a choice: to throw the first stone or to walk away. The woman had a choice at the conclusion of the story: to go and sin no more or to return to her old life.

We all have places, habits, situations, and opportunities that bring us to the point of decision. What matters most is not the past, but how we choose to move forward from this point. Of course, we don't know what happened to the people involved in this story. We don't know what happened to the woman as she lived out her life, nor do we know what happened to the accusers. I wonder, did they, too, "go and sin no more"? What do you think? *Pause momentarily for silent reflection; then proceed with the journaling exercise.*

Journal   (15 minutes)

Jesus gave the woman a promise and a blessing. First, the promise: "Neither do I condemn you" (John 8:11 NRSV). In her book *Do What You Have the Power to Do*, Helen Bruch Pearson suggests that we have a tendency to hear these words with our heads but not our hearts. It is extremely difficult to believe that Jesus would not blame this woman—or any of us.

If you believe this promise that Jesus made long ago and still makes today, how can this change your life? The blessing Jesus gave was "Go your way, and from now on do not sin again" (John 8:11 NRSV).

We all have been caught in sin; we all have need of forgiveness. For the next ten minutes, journal your response to these questions: What is Jesus telling you to walk away from? Are you willing to take Jesus at his word and to avoid that sin? 🕐

Explore   (5–10 minutes)

Both of the resources we have used this weekend are excellent and deserve to be read in their entirety. I hope this retreat has tempted you to do just that. Now, as we close this session, I invite you to respond in "popcorn" fashion to the following questions as you are comfortable: How have the biblical women we have been reading about and studying this weekend challenged or affected you? What will you do about it? In the interest of time, please try to limit your response to one or two sentences. *Encourage all participants to share as they are comfortable; then proceed with the closing.* 🕐

Close   (1–2 minutes)

Read the following litany, adapted from Galatians 6:2, from Pearson's Do What You Have the Power to Do *as a responsive reading, with the participants echoing each line after you:*

Bear someone's burdens (participants repeat each line)
Whose?
Yours?
Mine?
Ours?
Theirs?
Bear each other's burdens
Lift
Carry
Share
Free one another
You Me
Us
Them
And so fulfill
Fulfill the law
The law of Christ.[7]

CLOSING WORSHIP (11:00 A.M.–12:00 P.M.)

Gathering

As everyone gathers, play instrumental music in the background—either from a cassette or CD or a musician in the group.

Worship Songs

Sing favorite songs from the weekend. If possible, play the selection "The Lord Will Provide," included on Colleen Haley's CD From the Heart. 🎵

Scripture Reading

Have someone read aloud the following verses, or ask a different person to read each verse:

Genesis 1:3
2 Corinthians 4:6
Matthew 5:16
John 8:12
🕐

Meditation

Pass out the small reflective craft mirrors, giving one to each woman. 🕐
Now read aloud the story found on page 173 of Robert Fulgum's book It Was on Fire When I Lay Down on It *(New York: Random House, 1988). In the story, Dr. Alexander Papaderos answers a student's question about the meaning of life. He tells of finding a small piece of shattered glass during*

World World II, and explains that he has carried that piece of glass in his wallet since that time as a reminder to shine light into dark places. 🕐 *At the conclusion of the story, invite the participants to look into their mirrors; then say the following aloud:* The theme of this story is shining light into dark places. Our call as women of God is to shine light into the dark places that we find. Prepare to come forward one at a time and be anointed, remembering that you are God's chosen women.

Anointing

Prior to the retreat, purchase some anointing oil from a Christian bookstore or church supplier. As the participants come forward one at a time, anoint them with oil on the forehead or hand, making the sign of the cross. As you anoint each woman, you may say these or similar words: Remember that God has chosen* you.* Amen. 🕐

A Final Question

Invite the participants to respond freely to this question: Is there anything we have left unsaid? 🕐

Closing Prayer

Lord God, you anoint us with your love every day in countless love. May we become the anointers of your love in all the places we go. Amen.

RETURN HOME (12:00 P.M. until . . .)

Thank each person for her participation in the retreat and make any necessary closing remarks. 🕐 *Now it is time for the design team to clean, pack up, and evaluate the retreat; or, if you prefer, the team may save the evaluation for a later time.*

If Only I Had More Time!

◆

OVERVIEW

This retreat model is a compilation of my reflections and journal writings after reading *Ordering Your Private World* by Gordon MacDonald. Participants will find it helpful to read the book either before or after this retreat. Methods of prioritizing one's own life in order to find deeper meaning and a closer walk with God are outlined.

PREPARING FOR THE RETREAT

- Review "How to Use This Book: Planning and Preparing for Retreats" (pp. 11-15).
- Assemble the design team.
- Read through the retreat; make revisions and additions as appropriate for your group or situation.
- Pray for the retreat.
- Advertise; invite and recruit participants.
- Send correspondence noting details of the retreat. (Be sure to let participants know what items they are to bring.)
- Gather the supplies.

SUPPLIES AND MATERIALS

To be brought by the leader

- nametags
- cassette/CD player
- cassettes/CDs, including meditative music
- hymnals or other songbooks (see suggested hymns and songs throughout the retreat)
- newsprint and marker, chalkboard and chalk, or dry erase board and marker
- white pillar candle (and additional candles for worship, if desired)
- matches or lighter
- paper, pens, pencils
- a journal for each participant (Note: For larger groups, ask participants to bring their own.)
- medium-size basket
- *Ordering Your Private World* by Gordon MacDonald
- handouts for journaling exercises in Session 2 (optional)
- handout summarizing the chapter "Moon Shell" from Anne Morrow Lindbergh's book *Gift from the Sea* (see Session 3)
- handout for journaling exercise in Session 4 (optional)
- chalice of juice and loaf of bread (see Closing Worship)
- Morning Watch handouts for Days 2 and 3, one for each participant (see Appendix)

To be brought by each participant

- Bible
- quilt or blanket
- pen or pencil

The Retreat   Day 1

ARRIVAL   (3:00 P.M.–6:00 P.M.)

Have nametags ready for the participants as they arrive. Designate one or more greeters to personally escort each participant to her room and invite her to relax by resting, sleeping, reading, walking, hiking, talking with others, and so forth.

DINNER   (6:00 P.M.–7:00 P.M.)

This is the first group activity. If space allows, form a large circle and say or sing the blessing. As leader, wait to be served last so that you may walk around the room and welcome everyone. Encourage the participants to sit with others whom they do not already know. Look for those who seem lost or who are alone. Assign persons from the design team to keep an eye on these participants and see that connections with others begin to take place.

GROUP ANNOUNCEMENTS/GET-TO-KNOW-YOU ACTIVITIES   (7:00 P.M.–7:30 P.M.)

After dinner, formally welcome everyone and make any necessary group announcements—such as telling the location of bathrooms, telephones, and first-aid kits, and reviewing the retreat schedule. Then begin a get-acquainted game or activity. 🕐

SESSION 1   (7:30 P.M.–9:00 P.M.)

Open   (5 minutes)

Read the following aloud:

> I heard a story about three bowls.
> The first bowl is inverted, upside down, so that nothing can go into it. Anything poured into this bowl spills off.
> The second bowl is right-side up, but stained and cracked and filled with debris. Anything put into this bowl gets polluted by the residue or leaks through the cracks.
> The third bowl is clean. Without cracks or holes, this bowl represents a state of mind ready to receive and hold whatever is poured into it.
> Sometimes I am that first bowl, being so "productive" that I don't notice when the very thing I want presents itself. Sometimes I am the second bowl, with such a fierce judging voice that focuses on what's *not* working that I'm unable to see or appreciate all the things that are going well.
> And sometimes, wonderful times, I am the third bowl, able to be present and absorbed in what I am doing, whatever it is.[1]
>
> May you be the third bowl during this time set apart for learning and growth. May you be in a state of mind to receive and hold what will gracefully be poured into your life.

Listen to the selection "The Lord Will Provide," included on Colleen Haley's CD From the Heart *(see p. 15), or play another appropriate song.* 🎼

Talk   (3 minutes)

Read this section several times until you can paraphrase and present it in your own speaking style.
There was a time when people took time for one another. They talked face-to-face. They sat on porches at night, chatting and watching fireflies. They celebrated with one another. They mourned with one another. Now it seems that we always are chasing—chasing things rather than chasing God.
Finish this sentence: If only I had more _____. *Pause momentarily; then continue.* Time is the universal answer for most of us. Very few of us seem to have enough of it. We put off so many things, thinking that we'll have more time "one day."

Is your private world very different from your public world? Where can you be real? What are your priorities? These are some of the questions we'll be exploring during this retreat.

Explore   (5–7 minutes)

Listen to these words from the author of this retreat:

> On my bedside table I have a purple glass doorknob that my friend Marlys and I bought while on retreat in Nacogdoches. It is a sort of icon for me. You see, as a child, I moved approximately twelve times. There were a lot of different doors to open and close. I opened doors to new cities, new homes, new schools, and new friends; and I closed doors to old cities, old homes, old schools, and old friends. But everywhere I went, there were also a lot of churches that had doors—and those doors were already open. There was Santa Monica's First Church, where I sang in the children's choir; St. John's in Santa Fe, where I learned the Golden Rule while looking out the windows at the mountain; the church on St. Simons Island, where I became a baptized Christian; the chapel at Epworth, where I spent many youth retreats; Mulberry Street United Methodist Church, where I spent much of my youth; First United Methodist Church of Bryan, where I was a college student and newlywed; Bear Creek United Methodist, where I was a young mother and church employee; and St. Luke's United Methodist, where my call to ministry came. Inside those doors I found people, friends, love, trust, and most of all, Christ. My purple glass doorknob reminds me that whatever door I open, wherever it is, I can find Christ.

Think of an object that helps define who you are. Then find a partner and tell her about it. You don't need to have the object with you now; simply describe it so that your partner can visualize it. We'll come back together in about five minutes. 🕐

Talk   (3 minutes)

Read this section several times until you can paraphrase and present it in your own speaking style.

Ours is a driven society. We value accomplishments, status, anything that is "bigger and better," the deception of ourselves and others, projects (more than people), competition, anger, busyness, and so forth. Listen to these words from the author of this retreat:

> I once attended a meeting where I was asked to bring my Bible and my calendar. I was struck during the meeting that my calendar was larger than my Bible—in more ways than one! I use my calendar multiple times throughout the day. I take it with me on vacation. I take it with me when I make hospital calls. I can't say the same about my Bible. Ouch!
>
> After my friend Beth got a speeding ticket, she praised God for it. She said that she had gotten herself into a routine of rushing to the many places that she had to go to in her day, but because of this ticket, she intentionally slowed down. How about you? How many times have you said, "I am busy; I am spinning out of control"?

Journal   (12 minutes)

Does this description of our driven society hit a little too close to home? What are the parallels in your own life? Where is the rub? What is it that makes you driven? Before you respond to these questions in a time of silent journaling, listen as the author of this retreat shares a personal confession:

> The parallels between our driven society and my life leap off the page at me. Busy, busy, busy. I am challenging myself not to say that word—not to say it when people ask me how I am; not to say it at all. I used to be very accomplishment oriented; now, however, I value peace. It has softened my edges. I also struggle not to let projects become more important than people—and yet, as I write this book, my family is playing without me. I strive for balance.

Take time now to reflect on your own tendency to live a driven life. Record your thoughts in your journal. We'll allow ten minutes for this. 🕐

Talk   (5 minutes)

Read this section several times until you can paraphrase and present it in your own speaking style—with the exception of the author's words, which are meant to be read aloud.

We are not meant to live driven lives. As women who are called by God, we are meant to be wise stewards of what God has given us, including our time. We are meant to know ourselves, to have a sense of purpose, and to be committed servants of Jesus Christ. We are called to be fully present with those whom we meet on life's journey. There is a place of knowing deep within us that calls for us to seek space and silence and stillness. There is a longing to catch up with our souls. This knowing cannot come if we are racing about at ninety miles an hour.

Listen as the author of this retreat gives expression to her own identity as a servant of Christ:

I am not Twiggy. I am not "Susie Homemaker." I do not live a relaxed pace of life. I am not a "homeroom mother." I am enthusiastic, creative, warm, motherly, loving. My weakest link is being too busy and letting projects take over my time. My primary purpose as a servant is living to enable others to come to faith, to provide avenues that help place people in positions to know God, and to have a strong relationship with the living Christ.

There is a place within us that is homesick for God. We yearn for this connection. We yearn to be still enough to hear the voice of God calling to us. Our private world is our soul, our eternal connection to the Holy One. It is our roots—who we are; where we are safe. It is essential that we order our world in terms of our priorities and our relationship with the Living God. We can begin to know ourselves when we listen through journaling. Often it is through this experience of self-expression that we begin to be aware of our strengths and our weaknesses, our lessons and our hungers. Journaling is one of the most important steps in beginning to order your world.

Journal   (15 minutes)

Reflect on your own identity as a woman called by God—a servant of Christ. Complete the following self-defining statements in your journal.

What I am not . . .
What I am . . .
My weakest link is . . .
My primary purpose is . . .

We'll come back togther in fifteen minutes. 🕐

Talk   (5 minutes)

Read this section several times until you can paraphrase and present it in your own speaking style—with the exception of the author's words, which are meant to be read aloud.

As we explore the discipline of journaling, we are led into communion with God. Communion with God is God revealing God's self to us—by teaching us, affirming us, rebuking us, directing us, and guiding us. We listen and learn about our life with Christ through our time together. This relationship, this life of glorifying God, cannot take place unless we spend time with God; time—and lots of it; regular time; time that is freely given—not a minute here or there, but large chunks of our days and nights given to the One who knows us better than we even know ourselves. Listen as the author of this retreat tells about an experience of communion with God—a time when God provided direction for her life:

> While I was writing this book, I took a two-day prayer retreat to seek God's guidance about pursuing another degree. I had been invited by a university to participate in their advanced degree program and I wanted to do just that. However, I knew that it would be quite expensive and that I soon would have three children in college. Because I do not live in the city where the university is located, I would have to commute while juggling a full-time job. Besides the fact that the application was far too involved, I decided that the program didn't fulfill my passion. What I really wanted was to learn about becoming a spiritual director. Well, to my surprise, I learned that the very center where I was staying is a center for training spiritual directors. God is so cool!

A two-day retreat is a marvelous thing, but you don't have to take a two-day retreat to encounter God. Instead, you can simply and regularly spend time with God in "listening prayer."

Journal   (10 minutes)

Journal about a recent experience when God revealed God's self to you. We'll allow ten minutes for this. 🕐

Scripture Surf   (20 minutes)

Write the following scripture references on newsprint, a chalkboard, or dry erase board; or instruct participants to write them in their journals as you read the references aloud.

Genesis 1:1
Genesis 2:7
Acts 2:2
Psalm 23:2-3*a*
Matthew 7:24
Psalm 100
Ephesians 1:3-14
Revelation 21:6

Read each passage silently. Meditate on the words. Then journal as God's Great Spirit leads you. You have fifteen to twenty minutes to do this. 🕐

Close   (5 minutes)

Share the following thought:

As the sun is full of light,
The ocean is full of water,
Heaven is full of glory,
So may my heart be full of thee.
—A Puritan prayer

Sing together the hymn "Here I Am, Lord." 𝄞

EVENING WORSHIP   (9:00 P.M.–9:45 P.M.)

Note: Hold this worship experience outside, if possible; otherwise, dim the lights and fill the room with lighted candles.

Call to Worship

Let us be silent so that we may hear the divine whispers of our own hearts. Come, Holy Spirit.

Worship Songs

Sing together "Jesus, Remember Me" and "Precious Lord, Take My Hand." (Note: You may want to have a soloist sing the verses while the participants sing only the refrain.) 𝄞

Meditation

Mother Teresa once said that we do not do great things; we do only "little things with great love."[2]

I like projects. I like to finish projects, and then I like to just look at them. I like being able to say, "Hey, this is great! Look at what I made!" I wonder, does the Holy One feel that way about me and you? Does the Creator hold us in his hands and marvel at the creation? Does God ever look at us and make an exclamation of joy and pride?

Every day of our lives we are surrounded by miracles, holy moments, snatches of the ordinary made holy—sunrises, sunsets, the voice of a child, a smile, a warm embrace, the presence of someone we need, the feeling of being needed. Silently name the miracles you have seen this day. *Pause for thirty to sixty seconds; then continue.*

Can we, at the end of the day, imagine the Creator saying, "This one is fine—this woman is just right!"?

Prayer

Lord God, we pray that you are happy with your creations. May we be more aware of the tiny miracles that surround our lives. Amen.

Day 2

BREAKFAST (8:00 A.M.–9:00 A.M.)

Have coffee ready for the early risers. Remember that this meal is an act of the total community. Join together in a large circle to greet the morning and to give thanks to God for the night's rest and for the food that is to be received. Encourage the women to sit beside new faces during breakfast.

MORNING WATCH (9:00 A.M.–9:45 A.M.)

Reproduce the material on page 188 and distribute to all participants as they leave breakfast and find a place apart for their Morning Watch. Remind them that Session 2 will begin at 9:45.

SESSION 2 (9:45 A.M.–11:45 A.M.)

Open (1 minute)

Read aloud Ecclesiastes 3:1-13.

Talk (5 minutes)

Read this section several times until you can paraphrase and present it in your own speaking style. How do you sleep? When you first wake up, are your fists clenched? Are your hands tucked together under your chin? Are you in the fetal position? Do you sleep on your back? Is your body language "open" or "closed"? *Invite participants to respond briefly; then continue.* 🕐

Henri Nouwen encourages us to live with open hands. When our hands are open, we can live as better stewards. A steward is someone who cares for something or someone until the owner returns. We belong to God. God has trusted us to be stewards with our lives, our talents, our service, our money, and our time. As women, it seems there are times when we spend a lot of energy being stewards of others who share our lives. We place ourselves on the bottom of the "caring list." Yet this is not what God calls us to be or to do. Rather, as we lovingly become good stewards of ourselves, we can then help take care of the significant other, the children, the pets, the friends, and the extended family who have been placed in our lives.

Journal (10 minutes)

As a steward of time, how do you rate? Good or bad? How do you spend your time? Respond in your journal. We'll come back in about ten minutes. 🕐

Explore   (20 minutes)

Have the participants divide into small groups of three to five. Then choose one of the following three options: (1) Give the following instructions verbally, asking participants to record the scripture references in their journal; (2) Write the material (and the author's sample response, if you choose) on newsprint, a chalkboard, or a dry erase board; or (3) Prepare a handout in advance of the retreat and distribute copies now. Announce that you will come back together as a full group in about twenty minutes. 🕐

Read aloud these verses from the book of Luke and remember how Jesus spent his time:

4:16
4:42-44
5:27
6:12
9:51
18:16
19:5

Share your responses to the following questions with the others in your group.

How is the way you spend time similar to the way Jesus did?
How is the way you spend time different from the way Jesus did?

Author's response: My time is similar in that often I am filled with childlike wonder. My time is different because I do not have enough prayer time or enough time away. Also, Jesus set his face to the cross and did not turn back. I turn back a lot.

Journal   (30 minutes)

Choose one of the following three options: (1) Give the following instructions verbally, asking participants to record the scripture references in their journals; (2) Write the following questions (and the author's sample responses, if you choose) on newsprint, a chalkboard, or a dry erase board; or (3) Prepare a handout in advance of the retreat and distribute copies now.

Reflect seriously on these questions regarding your time, and record your responses in your journal. We'll come back together in about thirty minutes. 🕐

1. When and where do I take time away from it all—time to be alone?

Author's response: One year my New Year's resolution was to take a mini retreat on the day closest to my birthday each month. During that time I would ask myself what kind of steward I was being with the time, talents, and people God had placed in my life. I would journal. I would listen. I would try to be fully present with God.

2. When and how do I spend time training someone for the future?

Author's reponse: I spend time developing and equipping my children for the world. I hope that I also am helping prepare the children of my church and my community for the future. I certainly am providing opportunities for the biblical story to be heard, but I fall short in many ways; there is so much more that could and should be done for children in this city and in the world.

3. Where is my unseized time?

Author's response: I don't do well at having "unseized time." I am either "cooking" or not! Television can be a real time-waster.

4. How can I recapture or gain time in my schedule?

Author's response: By knowing my rhythms of sleep, emotional debts, pressures, and stresses, I can be more productive with my time. For the past nineteen years my husband and I have taken a nap on Sunday afternoon. It began when our children were little and would take naps themselves. They have outgrown their naps, but we have not! (It is interesting that as our children approach adulthood, they are returning to the Sunday nap tradition.) It is a time of refueling. If I miss my Sunday nap, my body knows it! It is essential rest for me. In a similar way, I know the things that rob me of energy and add stress to my life. I have learned to be constantly aware of my "spiritual lifestyle" so that my time is well spent.

5. When am I most effective? (This is good criteria for choosing time; for planning when to do certain activities.)

Author's response: Through the years, I have become a morning person. I can get an incredible amount of work accomplished in the hours before noon. I am also a late-night person. I can get into high gear after 10:00 at night and be very productive for several hours. I have learned that early morning and late afternoon are not the times for me to start an intense project. My rhythms are not at their best. What about you?

Talk   (3 minutes)

Read this section several times until you can paraphrase and present it in your own speaking style.
Sometimes being a good steward of time is simply a matter of knowing when to say no and when to say yes. Here's a good rule of thumb: Say no to good things and yes to the best things. What are the criteria for determining what the best things are? *Invite participants to take notes as you read the following aloud.*

1. What is God calling you to do?
2. Does it allow for family time?
3. Does it provide a stretch? (For example, will it allow you to grow in some way?)
4. Is it worthwhile?
5. Will it be fulfilling?
6. Will it help someone?

Learn to budget your time as well as your money. Plan your time as far ahead on your calendar as possible—just be sure those things that get penciled in are the best things! Learn to leave open space in your days—time to wonder, time to breathe deeply, time to enjoy a cold glass of water. There are days when I find that my calendar is as crammed full as it can possibly get. It looks efficient, but there is no time to inhale deeply, no time to step outside and look at the clouds. We all are given twenty-four hours each day. As stewards of our time, we simply must choose how to spend it.

Journal   (1 minute)

Respond in your journal to this question: What difference has the discussion of this session made for you? We'll allow about five minutes. 🕐

Close   (1 minute)

Read the following aloud:

It's only when we truly know and understand that we have a limited time on earth—and that we have no way of knowing when our time is up—that we begin to live each day to the fullest, as if it was the only one we had. —Elisabeth Kubler-Ross

Spend your free time this afternoon in silence, reflecting on your Morning Watch and our first two sessions. Journaling is an excellent way to capture your learning during this time of silence.

BREAK (11:45 A.M.–12:00 P.M.)

LUNCH (12:00 P.M.–1:00 P.M.)

This is another time for building community. Gather again in a large circle, give thanks, and encourage the women to sit beside some new faces.

FREE TIME (1:00 P.M.–5:00 P.M.)

This time is provided for sleeping, walking, crafting, sharing, playing games, or simply relaxing. If everyone is not comfortable with this amount of free time, feel free to adjust the schedule accordingly. Make sure that each woman finds something she wants to do.

SINGING AND SHARING (5:00 P.M.–6:00 P.M.)

Singing unites our spirits! Perhaps one or more individuals in your group are singers who may take turns leading the group in singing—and may even sing a few solos themselves. You may want to prepare one or more song sheets, use hymnals, or sing "old favorites." (If you prepare song sheets and use copyrighted material, be sure to include your church license number on these sheets. Check with your choir director or organist for this information.) This is also a good time to check in with the group and see how the retreat is going. Are there any problems? Any discoveries?

DINNER (6:00 P.M.–7:00 P.M.)

Form a circle and say or sing the blessing. Then enjoy more community-building time as you share food and fellowship.

SESSION 3 (7:00 P.M.–8:00 P.M.)

Note: Participants are to complete this session individually. Prepare a handout that summarizes the chapter "Moon Shell" from Anne Morrow Lindbergh's book Gift from the Sea *(New York: Pantheon Books, 1955). After distributing copies of the handout, instruct the participants to find a place apart, read the handout, listen to their hearts, and journal about whatever may be awakened in them through this reading. Tell the women that they may stop after an hour and have free time until Evening Worship at 9:00 P.M.; or, if they prefer, they may use the free time to continue their reflection and journaling.* 🕐

FREE TIME (8:00 P.M.–9:00 P.M.)

During this free time, participants may stretch, take restroom breaks, visit with one another, and prepare for Evening Worship (remind them to grab blankets if worship is to be held outside) while you and members of the design team set up for worship.

EVENING WORSHIP (9:00 P.M.–9:45 P.M.)

Gathering

As everyone gathers, play instrumental music in the background—either from a cassette or CD or from a musician in the group.

Call to Worship

Let us be silent so that we may hear the divine whispers of our hearts.

Scripture Reading

Have someone read aloud Isaiah 43:1, 4a. 🕐

Worship Songs

Sing together some favorite hymns. Ask participants to make suggestions, if you like. 🎵

Meditation

There is an old story told of a water bearer in India. He had two large pots that he carried each day to be filled with water. One of the pots had a crack in it; the other pot was perfect. By the time the water bearer had filled the pots with water and walked to his master's house, the pot with the crack was only half full. That cracked pot was ashamed of its imperfection and inability to perform the function it was made to perform. After many years, the pot complained about its brokenness to its owner. The water bearer loved his pot and told it to watch for beautiful flowers on the way to the master's house. As the owner and his pots traveled toward the master's house with the daily water, the cracked pot noticed the flowers that were only on its side of the path. When the pot asked the owner about them, he explained that because the pot was cracked, it had watered the path and provided the beautiful flowers for all in the master's house to enjoy.

What is the point of this story? Each of us is an imperfect being. Each of us has flaws. But God can use our flaws and make something beautiful out of them. As you are called into God's service, do not be afraid because of your mistakes or your flaws or your brokenness. God can use us all. In fact, we are God's bouquet!

Prayer

Living weaver, create a blanket of love around us.
May its colors remind us of your creation;
its pattern be a call to an ordered life.
May it wrap us in the warmth of your presence and circle us in peace and security for all our tomorrows. Amen.

Day 3

BREAKFAST   (8:00 A.M.–9:00 A.M.)

Again, have the coffee ready for the early risers. By this time, you will note that the group has "jelled" and most are interacting as family. Enjoy this breakfast together after a group blessing.

MORNING WATCH   (9:00 A.M.–9:45 A.M.)

Reproduce the material on page 188 and distribute to all participants as they leave breakfast and find a place apart for their Morning Watch. Remind them that Session 4 will begin at 9:45.

SESSION 4   (9:45 A.M.–11:00 A.M.)

Open   (3–5 minutes)

Say the following aloud:

There are voices which we hear in solitude, but they grow faint and inaudible as we enter the world. —Ralph Waldo Emerson

Sing together the hymn "Spirit of the Living God." Add motions as you sing it a second and third time.

Talk   (5 minutes)

Read this section several times until you can paraphrase and present it in you own speaking style.

Are you disorganized?
Do you spend time on unproductive tasks?
Is your "to do" list a mile long?
Have you overscheduled your time?
Are your personal papers a mess?
Do you have a lack of intimacy with God?
Are you dissatisfied with yourself, your job, your world?

If you answered yes to even one of these questions, then you need to order your private world! Take time to get your priorities in order—the priorities of your daily activities. This process involves getting your mind, spirit, and body in shape. During this session, we will consider each one individually.

1. Get your mind in shape.

In other words, be in a growth mode. Begin to think creatively. Try to see the old in new ways. Ask yourself: What are the ways creation speaks to me? Seek information that can serve the world, not just yourself. Prepare your mind to grow by listening, asking questions, reading, practicing self-discipline, and studying God's Word as well as various disciplines that interest you. Spend time browsing in a bookstore or a craft store or a museum. Look for opportunities to think. Listen to the words from the author of this retreat:

> I once had the opportunity to attend an Impressionist show at a local museum. That exhibit did much for my soul! I found that as I stood in front of those larger-than-life paintings, I was often moved to tears. That exhibit stretched my mind. As I learned about the lives of the painters, their passion for what they did, and their absolute giftedness, I couldn't help but think about myself and my life. What is it that I am called to create? How am I allowing God to work in my life? How am I responding to God?

Journal (10 minutes)

How do you keep your mind in shape? What are some ways that you receive mental stimulation? Respond in your journal. We'll come back in about ten minutes. 🕐

Talk (5 minutes)

Read this section several times until you can paraphrase and present it in your own speaking style. In addition to getting your mind in shape, you need to . . .

2. Get your spirit in shape.

John Wesley's Rule puts it this way:

Do all the good you can
By all the means you can,
In all the ways you can,
In all the places you can,
At all the times you can,
To all the people you can,
As long as ever you can.

Do you ever hear God whispering in a still, small voice, or have you soundproofed your heart so well that nothing but the loud noises of life seem to penetrate it? Open your heart to the peaceful sounds of nature and music. Look at art and contemplate its beauty. Listen for God's voice. Reflect, journal, meditate, and pray. Be open to resting in prayer; you'll find that the results are real. Have no agenda. Align yourself with God. Surrender.

Listen to the words from the author of this retreat:

> I find that as I surrender to God, I hear God's direction in new and fresh ways. I have learned to be open to God—to allow God to speak to my heart and soul in the quiet. When was the last time you were really quiet and listened for God?

Journal (10 minutes)

How do you keep your spirit in shape? What are some of the ways you open yourself to God? Respond in your journal. We'll come back together in about ten minutes. 🕐

Talk (5–10 minutes)

Read this section several times until you can paraphrase and present it in your own speaking style.
We've addressed the mind and spirit; now we come to the body. Although proper nutrition and regular exercise are important to physical fitnesss and good health, we're not going to talk about those things today. There is another requirement for a sound body that also contributes significantly to one's mental and spiritual health: rest.

3. Get your body in shape with rest.

Rest doesn't necessarily mean less work. Sometimes less work means a restless person. Have you ever found this to be true in your own life? *Pause momentarily; then continue.* Find the balance or rhythm of work and rest that works for you. It's OK to substitute amusement and leisure for rest at times, as long as you take time to rest—really rest—on a regular basis. Rest is deeper than leisure. Rest frees us from burnout.

Observe the Sabbath each week. Give yourself permission to take a Sunday nap—in a hammock under some tall trees would be nice, wouldn't it? Regardless of where or when you can find some time to rest, "just do it," as the popular slogan goes. Sabbath rest:

- closes the loop on the week. God saw that it was good! If God needed it, don't you?
- defines your mission and purpose. Rest allows you to clear your mind so that your life and activity are in sync.
- helps you return to eternal truths, standards, and values. When you are rested, it is easier to think about and know what you believe and to be committed to those beliefs. When you are rested, you can challenge your own thoughts and those of others.

We need Sabbath rest because our hearts can be deceitful. Our hearts can encourage us to say yes to things that sound like fun and may need to be done, but that don't fit into our day. How often we women add to our duties out of guilt. When and why do we release our Sabbath time for others? When a child or spouse or friend needs or wants some of our time, we often will supply the need rather than schedule it for another time. Of course, there always will be emergencies that change our priorities. That is a part of life. However, if we are giving up our own priorities for those of others, we are not being good stewards.

Some find that true Sabbath comes on a day other than Sunday. Those who care for young children or elderly parents find it much more difficult to find Sabbath. We must learn to rest when they rest. Take "mini Sabbath" experiences. It may also help to remember that there are many seasons in our lives as women, and each season lasts for a while. It will pass. It will be replaced by another.

Journal (20 minutes)

Write the following questions and statements on newsprint, a chalkboard, or a dry erase board, and instruct participants to write their responses in their journals; or, prepare a handout in advance and distribute copies now. Tell the participants they will have twenty minutes for journaling. 🕐

Close (5 minutes)

Read aloud the following paraphrase of Psalm 72:

May you rule from sea to sea,
from one end of the earth to the other.

May you shine as long as the sun does,
as long as the moon, from age to age.
May you be like the rain in the meadows,
like the soft showers watering the earth.

May your justice flower in the land,
and profound peace reside

until there is no more sun or moon.

Listen to the selection "The Seed Becomes a Prayer," included on Colleen Haley's CD From the Heart, *or choose another appropriate song.* ♩

Close with this statement: Remember, only when your private world is ordered can your public world also be ordered.

CLOSING WORSHIP (11:00 A.M.–12:00 P.M.)

Note: You may want to have this worship service outside or in a quiet, secluded setting. Make sure there is comfortable seating for everyone.

Gathering

As everyone gathers, play instrumental music in the background—either from a cassette or CD or from a musician in the group.

Worship Songs

Sing together the hymns, "Be Still, My Soul" and "Pass It On." Then play the selection "Listen to the Words of Jesus," included on Colleen Haley's CD From the Heart, *or choose another appropriate song.* ♩

Scripture Reading

Read aloud Hosea 10:12b: "For it is time to seek the LORD."

A Time of Sharing

I invite you to share a memory of a time in which God was a strength to you. Take turns completing these sentences: "God was a strength to me when . . ." And then, "I will praise you, God, for . . ." *Allow participants to respond "popcorn" style. Remind them that they may pass if they do not wish to share.* 🕐

Holy Communion

Lead the participants in a simple communion ritual, sharing the bread and the cup. You may want to begin by reading the account of the Last Supper found in Mark 14:12-16. 🕐

Prayers of the People of God

Who are the people in need of our prayers this evening? Let us call their names aloud and, if we choose, make a request on their behalf. After each name is called and each request is spoken, may the people say, "Lord, hear our prayer." *When all are silent, close the time of prayer.*

A Time of Sharing

Invite each participant to respond to this question: What truth will you take back to weave into your life as a result of our time together? *Be sure to remind the participants that they may pass if they do not wish to share.* 🕐

Closing Hymn

Sing together the hymn "'Tis So Sweet to Trust in Jesus." (Note: You might have a soloist sing the verses while the participants sing only the chorus.) ♩

RETURN HOME   (12:00 P.M. until . . .)

Thank each person for her participation in the retreat and make any necessary closing remarks.
🕐 *Now it is time for the design team to clean, pack up, and evaluate the retreat; or, if you prefer, the team may save the evaluation for a later time.*

Joyful Heart— Dancing Spirit

◆

OVERVIEW

This can be an intergenerational women's retreat. Based on Maria Harris's book *Dance of the Spirit,* the retreat helps participants step back and take a deep, penetrating look at their spiritual lives. At its conclusion, every woman will learn to embrace her own unique spirituality.

PREPARING FOR THE RETREAT
- Review "How to Use This Book: Planning and Preparing for Retreats" (pp. 11-15).
- Assemble the design team.
- Read through the retreat; make revisions and additions as appropriate for your group.
- Pray for the retreat.
- Advertise; invite and recruit participants.
- Send correspondence noting details of the retreat. (Be sure to let participants know what items they are to bring.)
- Gather the supplies.

SUPPLIES AND MATERIALS
To be brought by the leader
- nametags
- cassette/CD player
- hymnals or other songbooks (see suggested hymns and songs throughout the retreat)
- newsprint and marker, chalkboard and chalk, or dry erase board and marker
- white pillar candle and additional candles of various sizes for worship
- matches or lighter
- paper, pens, pencils
- a journal for each participant (Note: For large groups, ask participants to bring their own.)
- medium-size basket
- *Dance of the Spirit* by Maria Harris (for reference; see also guided meditation exercise in Session 3)
- handout for get-to-know-you activity
- construction paper in a variety of colors (see Session 1)
- *Searching for Shalom* by Ann Weems (see Session 2; Evening Worship, Day 2; and Closing Worship)
- copies of the handout "Naming Your False Selves" found on p. 20 in *When the Heart Waits: Leader's Guide,* by Sue Monk Kidd (see Session 2)
- instructions for holding a Love Feast (see p. 581 in *The United Methodist Book of Worship,* or use another source available to you; see Evening Worship, Day 2)
- *Just a Sister Away* (San Diego: LuraMedia, 1988); optional, see Closing Worship
- Morning Watch handouts for Days 2 and 3, one for each participant (see Appendix)

To be brought by each participant
- Bible
- quilt or blanket
- pen or pencil
- special candle and holder for worship use

The Retreat   Day 1

ARRIVAL   **(3:00 P.M.–6:00 P.M.)**

Have nametags ready for the participants as they arrive. Designate one or more greeters to personally escort each participant to her room and invite her to relax by resting, sleeping, reading, walking, hiking, talking with others, and so forth.

DINNER   **(6:00 P.M.–7:00 P.M.)**

This is the first group activity. If space allows, form a large circle and say or sing the blessing. As leader, wait to be served last so that you may walk around the room and welcome everyone. Encourage the participants to sit with others whom they do not already know. Look for those who seem lost or who are alone. Assign persons from the design team to keep an eye on these participants and see that connections with others begin to take place.

GROUP ANNOUNCEMENTS/GET-TO-KNOW-YOU ACTIVITIES (7:00 P.M.–7:30 P.M.)

After dinner, formally welcome everyone and make any necessary group announcements—such as telling the location of the bathrooms, telephones, and first-aid kits, and reviewing the retreat schedule. Then begin a get-acquainted game. Before the retreat, copy the following instructions onto a sheet of paper (one for each person attending the retreat). If your group is small, you can let the participants mingle, instructing them to write the names of those who fit each criterion in the space provided. If your group is large, lead the participants through the activity one line at a time. 🕐

Find persons whose:
Birthday is the same as yours
Zip code is the same as yours
Shoe size is the same as yours
Favorite color is the same as yours
Immediate family is the same size as yours
Birthplace was in the same state as yours

After the get-acquainted game, have the participants divide into two groups: those who have been on a retreat before, and those who have not. Explain that each person is to find a partner from the other group. (Note: If all or most of your group have not been on a retreat before, simply ask each person to find a partner for this conversation.) Once everyone has a partner, instruct them to talk about their hopes, dreams, and fears for this retreat during the remaining time. 🕐

SESSION 1:   WAITING AND TRANSFORMATION (7:30 P.M.–9:00 P.M.)

Open   (5–7 minutes)

In your own words, present the goals of this retreat:

- Increased confidence in your relationship with God
- Spiritual renewal
- Time for centering, prayer, peace, and guidance

Sing together the hymn "Spirit of the Living God." 🎼

Talk   (5 minutes)

Read this section several times until you can paraphrase and present it in your own speaking style.
In the midst of change, beautiful things can happen. Think for a moment about autumn leaves. Once-green leaves change radically, displaying brilliant colors, and then fall to the ground as if making a magnificent carpet. Think of the caterpillar—fuzzy, greenish-brown, and

crawling on the ground—who wraps itself inside a warm silk bed to sleep and awakens as a beautiful butterfly that can soar across rivers and fields. Beautiful things can happen in the midst of change.

Change: some of us thrive on it. Others of us are made uncomfortable by the sound of the word. Change: to make radically different; to replace with another; to switch or exchange. Change takes us out of our comfort zone. Change is unpredictable. Change will come.

Briefly share with the group your own thoughts about change, perhaps describing a time of change in your life. 🕐

Journal   (15 minutes)

In your journal write these questions (*pause after reading each question so that participants may write*):

- Am I searching for something deeper in my life?
- Is it peace? Perspective? Self-control? A deeper prayer life? A truer self that is lost in the world? Something else?
- How deeply am I searching?

Spend about fifteen minutes journaling your thoughts, prayers, and petitions. 🕐

Explore   (7–10 minutes)

Just as the seasons are not static, so also our relationships and our spirituality are not static. Growth is the sacred intent of life. We grow physically from childhood into adulthood, yet often we do not stretch ourselves in terms of our spiritual life.

As women, we play many roles. Sue Monk Kidd wrote that we women celebrate the "Trinity of the Three P's: the Pleaser, the Performer, the Perfectionist."[1] Turn to your neighbor now, offer a smile, and share with her which of the three P's you most identify with and why. We'll come back together in about five to seven minutes. 🕐

Journal   (10 minutes)

To discover your true self, you must realize your false self. Journal in response to this question. When have I felt an aching in my soul? We'll allow about ten minutes for this. 🕐

Talk   (5–6 minutes)

Read this section several times until you can paraphrase and present it in your own speaking style.

As women, we identify ourselves by our relationships to others. Who are you? A daughter, wife, friend, sister, aunt, employee . . . Is there someone else who is waiting to get loose within? Do you sense a change? A new passage? For change to occur, we must be able to let go of the false images that we hold. But change takes time.

We live in a fast-paced society. We look for the quickest, cheapest deals we can find. Some have called it a "quickaholic society," where we look only for the shortcut answers. The truth is: *real is slow, and slow takes time.*

We have been able to wait for change. Just as the caterpillar waited to become the beautiful butterfly, so also we must acknowledge the rhythm between waiting and doing. Between the waiting and the doing is the place where change takes place. It is both passive and passionate. We can't rush it.

The ministry of Jesus was a balance of waiting and doing. Jesus lived aware of the rhythm of life. He took time apart with God and he spent time with his friends. He spent time resting and time confronting political and religious leaders of the day. We must try to be more like Jesus, balancing our being with our doing; balancing our time apart with our activity; balancing our "to do" list with our "heart's desire" list.

Sometime during this retreat, read the fourth chapter of Luke. Look for interruptions that Jesus faced, and look for the work he accomplished. Ask yourself this question: In his humanness, how was Jesus able to keep his focus and priority?

Explore   (15 minutes)

Turn to your neighbor again, offer a smile, and wrestle together with these questions:

Am I tired of the roles I play?
Who does God want me to be?

We'll come back together in about fifteen minutes. 🕐

Journal   (10–12 minutes)

God is not found in the erasing of a problem, but in the embracing of the pain. When have you been so busy that you avoided the pain and/or the problems in your life? Are you walking in slow motion, zooming on a train, or living somewhere in between? Take about five minutes to reflect and respond in your journal. 🕐

Now hear these familiar words from Psalm 46:10 "Be still, and know that I am God." What implications does this verse have for your life? Take another five minutes to journal your thoughts. 🕐

Close   (7–10 minutes)

One at a time, come forward and choose a piece of construction paper of any color. 🕐 Now, tear the paper into a shape that is symbolic of your life. 🕐

In groups of two or three, take turns telling about your symbols and then place them on your worship table. 🕐

EVENING WORSHIP   (9:00 P.M.–9:45 P.M.)

Note: If possible, have this worship time in a candlelit setting.

Worship Songs

Sing songs such as "Kum Ba Yah," "Alleluia," and other familiar, quiet praise songs. 🎵

Scripture Reading

Before reading the scripture, invite the participants to become aware of their breathing. Ask them to become aware of inhaling and exhaling—of feeling the body relax as breath flows in and out. Encourage them to continue being aware of their breathing as they listen to the reading of the Holy Scriptures. Then read passages about breath and how God touches life through breath (for example, Ezekiel 37:1-5 and John 20:19-23). Tell them to think about God entering their lives as they inhale. Invite them to feel life as God touches them in significant ways. 🕐

Prayers of the People of God

Invite the participants to share one-sentence prayers in "popcorn" fashion. When all are silent, close the prayer time. 🕐

Closing Hymn

Sing together the hymn "Breathe on Me, Breath of God." 🎵

Day 2

BREAKFAST   (8:00 A.M.–9:00 A.M.)

Have coffee ready for the early risers. Remember that this meal is an act of the total community. Join together in a large circle to greet the morning and to give thanks to God for the night's rest and for the food that is to be received. Encourage the women to sit beside new faces during breakfast.

MORNING WATCH (9:00 A.M.–9:45 A.M.)

Reproduce the material on page 189 and distribute to all participants as they leave breakfast and find a place apart for their Morning Watch. Remind them that Session 2 will begin at 9:45.

SESSION 2: FROM FALSE SELF TO TRUE SELF (9:45 A.M.–11:45 A.M.)

Open (10 minutes)

Begin with joyful singing! Suggestions: "Morning Has Broken"; "Rise, Shine, Give God the Glory"; "This Is the Day."

Explore (15 minutes)

Nudge your neighbor and talk for a minute about your Morning Watch experience. What happened? How did you feel? We'll come back together in about fifteen minutes.

Talk (5 minutes)

Read aloud "The Messiah" from Searching for Shalom *by Ann Weems (p.83). Or, prior to the retreat, ask a participant to do the reading and give her the book so that she has time to become familiar with the material.*

Journal (15 minutes)

It has been said that a journal is a portable altar. A journal provides a chronicled life. When we journal, we begin to understand and to learn, and we stop repeating ourselves.

Journal in response to these questions:

Who have been the mentors (spiritual mothers) in my life?
What did these mentors offer me?
Why are role models important to my spiritual life?

We'll come back in about fifteen minutes.

Explore (10–15 minutes)

Would anyone like to share a significant "aha" she discovered while journaling? *Allow time for participants to share as they are comfortable.*

Talk (3–5 minutes)

Read this section several times until you can paraphrase and present it in your own speaking style—with the exception of the book excerpt, which is to be read aloud.
Sue Monk Kidd writes in her book *When the Heart Waits:*

Over and over again God calls you and me to the gardening of our own divine depths . . . to our truest nature—the God-image or True Self. . . . In the process of spiritual transformation there's a bulb of truth buried in the human soul that's "only God." . . . Throughout our lives we create patterns of living that obscure this identity.[2]

Just as a whittler discards the useless pieces of a carving, so also the art of soulmaking is taking our lives in our hands and with all the love and discernment we can muster gently whittling away the parts that don't resemble the True Self.

Meister Eckhart wrote that the important thing is not saving the soul, but entering it, greening it, developing the divine seed that awaits realization, and then intertwining with other souls in love and reconciliation. Wait a minute; does that mean we are to devote time to our own souls? Absolutely! We must spend time developing, growing, stretching, and knowing our own souls. What are some of the ways you have found to do just that? Invite a few participants to respond briefly; then continue.

Explore (10 minutes)

Prior to the retreat, make copies of the handout "Naming Your False Selves" found on p. 20 in Sue Monk Kidd's When the Heart Waits: Leader's Guide *(San Francisco: HarperSanFrancisco, 1991).*

Distribute copies of the handout now and provide the following instructions. Circle the masks that you identify as part of yourself. Then, find a partner and share how you have used those masks in your life. We'll come back together in about ten minutes. 🕐

Explore (15–20 minutes)

The Word of God helps us grow our souls. We also grow our souls with other pilgrims. In small groups of three to five, read and discuss Ephesians 4:11-16. Discuss these questions together:

- What does it mean to say that we are to grow in every way into Christ?
- Can all of you be a part of the whole body that Christ has created you to become?
- What strength can you offer to others?

We'll come back together in fifteen to twenty minutes. 🕐

Journal (5 minutes)

Change—think of the change that occurs from bulb to flower, from seed to tree. We are called to be the "gardeners" of our True Selves. There is something in the soul that is only God! Imagine!

The soul is like a garden from which we must root out weeds, thorns, and briars in order to reveal God's image glistening in the soil.

Journal in response to this question: What must be rooted out of your soul? We'll allow about five minutes. 🕐

Close (15–20 minutes)

Lead the group in the following guided imagery excerise. Remember to speak slowly and allow a lot of silence, pausing as indicated. It is sometimes helpful to play instrumental music softly in the background during the exercise. It is always useful to journal afterward. Allow fifteen to twenty minutes for the entire exercise. (Note: this form of prayer is often very emotional for some participants. Whenever using guided imagery in a group setting, be sure that someone is available to listen to participants after the experience.)

Let us close this session with a guided imagery experience. Get comfortable. Sit in a relaxed position with your arms and legs unfolded; or, if the room allows, lie down on the floor. *Pause.* Close your eyes. *Pause.* Take a deep breath. *Pause.* Exhale. *Pause.* Take another deep breath. *Pause.* Now exhale. *Pause.* Take one more deep breath and imagine all tensions and pain leaving you body. *Pause.* Become aware of the breathing of your body. *Pause.* Imagine yourself in a place where you are the most comfortable. *Pause.* You are your True Self here. *Pause.* What are you feeling? *Pause.* Are there people present, or are you alone? *Pause.* What changes have been made in this place? *Pause.* What do you hear? *Pause.* What things do you see in this place? *Pause.* Look around as if you want to remember every detail. *Pause.* Now bring one thing back with you to remember this place. What will it be? *Pause.* When you are ready, become aware of your breathing. *Pause.* Become aware of your surroundings. *Pause.* When you are ready, journal your thoughts and feelings for the time remaining in this session. I'll let you know when time is up. 🕐

BREAK (11:45 A.M.–12:00 P.M.)

LUNCH (12:00 P.M.–1:00 P.M.)

This is another time for building community. Gather again in a large circle, give thanks, and encourage the women to sit beside some new faces.

FREE TIME (1:00 P.M.–5:00 P.M.)

This time is provided for sleeping, walking, crafting, sharing, playing games, or simply relaxing. If everyone is not comfortable with this amount of free time, feel free to adjust the schedule accordingly. Make sure that each woman finds something she wants to do.

SINGING AND SHARING (5:00 P.M.–6:00 P.M.)

Singing unites our spirits! Perhaps one or more individuals in your group are singers who may take turns leading the group in singing—and may even sing a few solos themselves. You may want to prepare one or more song sheets, use hymnals, or sing "old favorites." (If you prepare song sheets and use copyrighted material, be sure to include you church license number on these sheets. Check with your choir director or organist for this information.) This is also a good time to check in with the group and see how the retreat is going. Are there any problems? Any discoveries?

DINNER (6:00 P.M.–7:00 P.M.)

Form a circle and say or sing the blessing. Then enjoy more community-building time as you share food and fellowship.

SESSION 3: CONCENTRATED STILLNESS (7:00 P.M.–8:30 P.M.)

Note: This session has been expanded to ninety minutes, resulting in a shorter break prior to the Evening Worship.

Open (5 minutes)

Sing together the hymn "Lord, You Have Come to the Lakeshore." 𝄞

Explore (10 minutes)

If you had free time earlier this afternoon, ask each participant to find a partner and talk about how each of them spent the afternoon. If they happened to do the same thing during free time (for example, sleep, pray, journal, etc.), they must look for different partners. Ask each pair to also talk about this question: Where did I find God this afternoon? *Tell them they will have about ten minutes for sharing. If for some reason your group did not have free time, move on to the next Explore exercise.* 🕐

Explore (15 minutes)

In advance, write the following spiritual disciplines and definitions on newsprint, a chalkboard, or a dry erase board; or instruct the participants to make notes as you read them aloud.

It has been said that the only thing predictable in life is change. Yet even in the midst of change, we can let our spirits dance. A part of our role as pilgrims of faith is to prepare ourselves for change. How have you prepared yourself? Have you woven spiritual disciplines into your life? Spiritual disciplines include the following:

- prayer (communion with God)
- Scripture (reading God's Word with the mind and heart)
- fasting (going without food for a prescribed period of time for holy purposes)
- solitude (spending time *listening* for God)
- meditation (spending time focusing on scripture or praise)
- journaling (writing your innermost thoughts)
- Sabbath keeping (keeping one day for soul work—focusing on God)
- service (performing some duty for others)
- confession (admitting to God the times you have fallen short)

Practicing spiritual disciplines nourishes your spirituality by clarifying your focus on God. Richard Foster's *Celebration of Discipline* is an excellent resource for more information on spiritual disciplines.

Find a partner—someone other than your previous partner—and briefly share which discipline is especially challenging for you. Or, if there are several disciplines that you have never practiced, tell which one you are most reluctant to try and why. We'll come back together in about five to seven minutes. 🕐

Journal   (5 minutes)

Journal in response to these questions: Do you pray? Regularly? For what? We'll come back together in about five minutes. 🕐

Talk

Read this section several times until you can paraphrase and present it in your own speaking style.
Why is it that we try to propel people on to the next stage of faith as quickly as possible? Why do we do this? Perhaps it is the "quickaholic" syndrome. We don't have to rush after faith. Faith is present—we merely need to make ourselves present to the face of God. Give your faith a chance to make itself known to you. When you return to your daily life after this retreat, try one of these challenges to feed and enrich yourself spiritually. *Encourage the participants to write each of the following suggestions in their journals as you read them aloud.*

- Each day observe twenty minutes of prayer, meditation, contemplation, or silent stillness.
- One day each week, don't use your car.
- One day each week, go without a meal.
- One day each week, give three to four hours of service to others.
- Keep a journal for one week.
- Each week set aside one day as a genuine Sabbath.[3]

Explore   (10 minutes)

As we whittle away the unwanted parts of ourselves, let us read Galatians 2:20 and 5:19-23. *Have someone read each passage aloud; then continue.* 🕐
It is our task to dig our hands in the soil and begin to name ourselves. Find a partner and briefly share what insights you can glean from the scriptures. We'll come back together in about five minutes. 🕐

Journal   (10 minutes)

When we speak of spirituality, we assume that God is always active in the world. My task is not to get God to do what I think needs to be done, but to become aware of what God is doing so that I can become involved in it.
Journal in response to the following:

- What can you do to heighten the awareness of God's action in your life?
- We sometimes achieve our deepest progress being still. How has this been true for you? When are you still?

We'll come back together in about ten minutes. 🕐

Talk   (10 minutes)

Read this section several times until you can paraphrase and present it in your own speaking style.

Be patient with yourself.
Live the questions that reside within your heart.
Do not search for answers,
Rather live into your life
as a journey of waiting . . .
of listening . . .
Be patient.

Spiritual growth comes from living the questions, from waiting and watching and learning. Along the way, times of concentrated stillness play an important part in the process.
A mentor or spiritual mother can lead you into the spiritual discipline of solitude or concentrated stillness. She is one who can assist you in your waiting and in your learning. A

spiritual mother is someone with whom you can be honest; someone who is a good listener and who can articulate the faith; someone who is truthful, nonjudgmental, open, focused, and peace-filled. A spiritual mother does not necessarily give advice; rather, she is a reflective listener and a poser of questions. The relationship can be intentional or unintentional.

Let us spend a few minutes listing any other qualities of a spiritual mentor. *As the participants name qualities, list them on newsprint, a chalkboard, or a dry erase board.* 🕐 Which characteristics do you most want to develop? *Allow the participants to respond briefly.* 🕐

Close   (10–20 minutes)

Note: The following centering prayer exercise can last anywhere from ten to twenty minutes, depending on your group's experience with centering prayer.

We will close this session with a centering prayer based on Psalm 63. Listen and follow along in your Bibles as I read aloud Psalm 63:1-8. 🕐

Now, as I read the Psalm again, listen for a verse that especially touches your heart. 🕐 Sitting quietly, repeat this verse over and over to yourself either silently or aloud. *Pause for thirty to sixty seconds; then continue.* 🕐

Let us close our prayer time by saying the Lord's Prayer in unison. 🕐

Now journal your experience. We'll allow about five minutes for this. 🕐

FREE TIME   (8:30 P.M.–9:00 P.M.)

During this time, participants may stretch, take restroom breaks, visit with one another, and prepare for Evening Worship (remind them to grab blankets if worship is to be held outside) while you and members of the design team set up for worship.

EVENING WORSHIP   (9:00 P.M.–9:45 P.M.)

Note: If possible, hold this worship service outside. Sit on quilts or blankets in a large circle, with participants holding lighted candles of all shapes and sizes to provide light for the gathering.

Worship Song

Sing together "Sweet, Sweet Spirit" and "Spirit of the Living God." 🎵

Prayers of the People of God

Explain the following prayer exercise. You will announce four topics, one at a time. Persons are invited to pray aloud or silently during each section or category. The sections are adoration (praise), confession, thanksgiving, and supplication (requests). Close by saying the Lord's Prayer in unison. 🕐

Love Feast

In advance: Prepare for the Love feast according to the instructions on page 581 in The United Methodist Book of Worship, *or use another source available to you. If possible, use the poems "Communion" (p.42) and "Bread and Wine" (p. 82) in the book* Searching for Shalom *by Ann Weems.*

Invite participants to share this "meal" in remembrance of the body and blood of Christ, who died for our sins. You may want to use a chalice of grape juice and a loaf of bread. The whole loaf symbolizes that we, though many individuals, are one in Christ. Invite each participant to take a piece of bread, dip it into the juice, and remember the gift of everlasting life that was given for her. 🕐

Worship Song

Sing together "Amazing Grace." 🎵

Closing Prayer

Say a closing prayer on behalf of the group. 🕐

Day 3

BREAKFAST   (8:00 A.M.–9:00 A.M.)

Again, have the coffee ready for the early risers. By this time, you will note that the group has "jelled" and most are interacting as family. Enjoy the breakfast together after a group blessing.

MORNING WATCH   (9:00 A.M.–9:45 A.M.)

Reproduce the material on page 189 and distribute to all participants as they leave breakfast and find a place apart for their Morning Watch. Remind them that Session 4 will begin at 9:45.

SESSION 4: EMERGENCE   (9:45 A.M.–11:15 A.M.)

Note: this session has been extended fifteen minutes, for a total of ninety minutes.

Open   (5 minutes)

Sing together "Here I Am, Lord" and "Something Beautiful."

Explore   (10 minutes)

Chose a partner—someone you haven't spent much time with—and talk about this question: How is it with your soul? You also might share what happened during today's Morning Watch. We'll come back together in about ten minutes.

Explore   (15–20 minutes)

Lead the participants in the following guided meditation adapted from Dance of the Spirit *(p. 145). Or, if you prefer, write your own guided meditation. For our purposes, a guided meditation is simply an imaginary story that requires participants to picture themselves in a place where they may come into contact with God. Using a lot of descriptive words, describe a beach or mountain scene; then ask a "wondering" question, such as, "What/Where is God calling you to do? . . . to be? . . . to go?" Afterward, instruct participants to write about the experience in their journals. Allow fifteen to twenty minutes for the entire exercise. (Note: This form of prayer is often very emotional for some participants. Whenever using guided imagery in a group setting, be sure that someone is available to listen to participants after the experience.)*

Let us begin by being still. *Pause.* Sit back in your spirit; do this by sitting back in your body. *Pause.* Breathe gently, slowly, and easily. *Pause.* As I read aloud several questions, let your own reflections on how spirituality has been handed—or "traditioned"—to you emerge from your inner self. Take time, do not hurry, and try to spend a few moments pondering each question. Do the same with each of your responses. *Pause.*

- Is spirituality something that makes you feel comfortable? *Pause.*
- Has it always been that way? *Pause.*
- Have you ever felt that the spirituality you were offered or taught needed something more in order to fit you as a woman? *Pause.*
- Were there older women who assisted you, as a child, to develop a spiritual life? *Pause.* If so, can you remember what they did? *Pause.*
- Do you find yourself doing some of those things now, with the next generation?
- Are there women in your adult life who model spirituality for you? Women you would like to imitate? Women about whom you say, "I want to be like her when I grow up"? *Pause.* If so, can you pinpoint what about them or their lives is a lure for you? *Pause.*
- Are there men in your life who also model spirituality for you? Men you would like to imitate? *Pause.* If so, what about their spirituality appeals to you? Is it something in yourself they mirror?

When you are ready, you may journal your thoughts. I will let you know when time is up.

Scipture Surf   (10 minutes)

Write the following scripture references on an easel board, chalkboard, or dry erase board; or instruct participants to write them in their journals as you read them aloud.
"Scripture surf" three or four of the following verses:

Judges 9:15
Psalm 17:8; 36:7; 57:1; 63:1; 91:1
Isaiah 49:2

Silently read each passage you have chosen. Meditate on the words. Then consider this statement: The shadow of your influence is powerful; more powerful still is the shadow of God. What impact does this statement have on your spirituality? Journal as God's Great Spirit leads you. You have about ten minutes to do this. 🕐

Journal   (10 minutes)

List people you know who refelct a vibrant spirituality. Write two or three sentences describing these persons. Think about these persons in terms of their energy to keep going—how they cope with daily life. Have you ever seen them weary? Have they confessed to being worn out? Do you suppose they recognize that there is a limit to what they can offer? Do *you* realize this? Offer a prayer of thanksgiving for their lives. We'll allow about ten minutes for this. 🕐

Talk   (5 minutes)

Read this section several times until you can paraphrase and present it in your own speaking style. Encourage participants to take notes in their journals as you speak.

As you grow spiritually and change, you may meet resistance—from yourself or from those you are closest to. How will you hold fast to your spiritual growth despite resistance? *Pause momentarily; then continue.* One way is to explore *lectio divina* as a method of continued spiritual growth. *Lectio divina* is the Latin word for *holy reading* of the Scriptures. It includes:

Lectio = reading
Meditatio = reflection/meditation
Oratio = prayer
Contemplatio = comtemplation with God

It is best to begin this practice with a Gospel reading. Read with a listening heart until a verse "moves your heart." Once you have identified this verse, simply dissolve yourself into the verse. This may take several minutes. Then move to the the third step, prayer, focusing on what you share with God. The final step is simply resting in God—resting in silence and in God's love.

Reading the Scripture this way not only will result in your continued spiritual growth; it also will equip you to share your spirituality with the rest of God's creation.

Explore   (15 minutes)

By this time, most participants will be sharing at a deeper level. Try to allow ample time for them to wrestle with the questions.

How does your spirituality connect with the way you treat the earth? What is the connection between solitary and communal spirituality? Can you think of a time that your life and God's time intersected? Share your insights with someone near you. We'll come back together in about fifteen minutes. 🕐

Journal   (5 minutes)

There is an old Hassidic tale that goes something like this: A rabbi named Zusya died and went to stand before the judgment seat of God. As he waited for God to appear, he grew nervous thinking about his life and how little he had done. He began to imagine that God was going to ask him, "Why weren't you Moses or why weren't you Solomon or why weren't you David?"

But when God appeared, the rabbi was surprised. God simply asked, "Why weren't you Zusya?"

Write a one-sentence answer to the question "Who am I?" We'll allow about three to five minutes for this. 🕐

Close   (10 minutes)

Prior to this session, fill a basket with envelopes and paper hearts—one for each particpant.

As we close our time together, please take an envelope and a paper heart from the basket. Then spend a few minutes reflecting silently on these questions:

- What gift of the heart did God give me during this retreat?
- What difference will this gift make in my life?
- How will I sustain this change in my life in the coming weeks and months?

When you have answered each question, write the gift you have been given on the paper heart, place it in the envelope, seal the envelope, and address it to yourself. You will receive this envelope in the mail within the next six weeks. 🕐

As we close this session and prepare for closing worship, please remain in quiet reflection. *Note: Be sure to mail the envelopes to the participants one month from the date of the retreat.*

CLOSING WORSHIP   (11:15 A.M.–12:00 P.M.)

Note: Hold this worship outdoors in an open space, if possible. Instruct the participants to gather in silence.

A Time of Silence

Invite the participants to sit in silence for several minutes. 🕐

A Time of Reflection

Read aloud "An April Place," found on page 27 in Searching for Shalom.

Worship Song

Sing together the hymn "Alleluia." 🎼

A Time of Affirmation

Invite participants to affirm those who have had an impact on their spiritual journey by simply calling the names aloud. 🕐

A Time of Prayer

"Pass the peace" (see Romans 15:33). Explain that you will begin by giving the woman next to you a warm embrace, saying: The peace of God be with you. *She is to respond:* And also with you. *Then she is to "pass the peace" to the woman next to her. Continue in this manner, having the last woman "pass the peace" to you.* 🕐

Meditation

Tell the story of Martha and Mary in your own words or see p. 39 in Just a Sister Away *(San Diego: Luramedia, 1988).* 🕐

Closing Prayer

Say the Lord's Prayer aloud in unison. 🕐

RETURN HOME   (12:00 P.M. until . . .)

Thank each person for her participation in the retreat and make any necessary closing remarks. 🕐 *Now it is time for the design team to clean, pack up, and evaluate the retreat; or, if you prefer, the team may save the evaluation for a later time.*

Appendix

Getting First Things First— and Keeping Them There!

Day 2: Morning Watch

> Be still, and know that I am God. (Psalm 46:10)

• Read the following paragraphs as a prayer, adding your own personal conclusion:

Time for myself . . . Why do I find it so difficult to take time for myself, Lord? Time to be, rather than time to do. Time to think, to talk to you, and most of all, to be silent in your presence while you speak to me.

You know how it is, Lord. Teach me the art of creating islands of stillness in which I can absorb the beauty of everyday things: clouds, trees, a snatch of music. Prompt me to lift up my heart to you in a moment of thankfulness. Impress upon my mind that there is more to life than packing every moment with activity. Help me fence in some part of my day with quietness. And please talk to me and help me listen, so that I take your peace, rather than my confusion, back with me into the hurly-burly of a hurting world.

• Read Luke 1:5–2:19. What can you learn from the silence/solitude of Zacharias, his wife, Elizabeth, and Mary, the mother of Jesus?

• What are some of the ways God breaks through into your everyday life?

• Reflect on some of the noisy intrusions in your life that rob you of your silence and solitude. List them here, if you like.

• Read Psalm 27. What did David gain from his communion with God? What can you gain from your communion with God?

• Close your morning watch by reading aloud these words from Psalm 18.

> I love you, O lord, my strength.
> The lord is my rock, my fortress and my deliverer;
> my God is my rock, in whom I take refuge. . . .
> To the faithful you show yourself faithful. . . .
> to the pure you show yourself pure. . . .
> You, O lord, keep my lamp burning;
> my God turns my darkness into light. (Psalm 18:1-2, 25*a*, 26, 28)

Day 3: Morning Watch

> Then God said, "Let us make humankind in our image,
>   according to our likeness." (Genesis 1:26 NRSV)

• Read Genesis 1–2:3. Read slowly, savoring the rhythm. Imagine that you are reading aloud with the congregation during a worship service.

• Now read the passage again, using your imagination. Hear the swarms of birds flying and calling, the whales breaching, the lions and elephants trumpeting newness. Smell spring, with flowers bursting open, and salt air.

• Read the following paragraphs and then journal as God's Great Spirit leads you:

On the sixth day, God created male and female in his image. We are reflections of all that happened before. God's creativity is immense, and because we are made in his image, our spirits have no limit. Nothing can exhaust our spiritual potential—not death, not divorce, not financial setbacks, not layoffs.

Think about the apostle Paul's journeys and shipwrecks; about the angry mobs, the beatings, and the times he was imprisoned (see Romans 1; 1 Corinthians 2, 10; and 2 Corinthians 10). Nothing—not chains, not even success—limited him. If I had been shipwrecked and beaten, you can be sure I would have stopped traveling upon finding a loving congregation! But Paul journeyed on, leaving his footprints on many countries, communities, and generations of people.

We are each called as a distinctive part of God's creative world. I remember one spring when God's call directed us to leave family, friends, and a loving church. All that we knew—all that was familiar—was suddenly removed from out daily routine. We journeyed on.

One day, during our first fall in Georgia, the Lord blessed us with his creativity! We found ourselves traveling with a group of confirmands to a rural retreat center along the coast. It was a dear place from my childhood where I first heard God calling my name. Here I was, thirty years later, telling eighty or so seventh graders how God's creative hand had been a part of my life! Now, how creative is that? Later that afternoon, after a rain storm, as I walked a section of beach by myself, I reflected on the Genesis passage. There were dolphins dancing in the surf, the air was thick with salt, and beautiful shells filled with living creatures rested on the beach, and it was good!

Come to the Well

Day 2: Morning Watch

> Jesus said to her, "Everyone who drinks of this water will be thirsty again, but those who drink of the water that I will give them will never be thirsty." (John 4:13 NRSV)

You have come to the well, and Jesus is here. Face-to-face, like the Samaritan woman, he stands before you and offers you the Living Water. He knows your needs, your desires, your fears, your potential—your *thirst*. As only he can, he welcomes you to drink.

• Read John 4:1-26. Take several minutes to reflect on the story.

• Spend some time quietly listening for God. Hear the message for you this morning. Then write a letter from your Lord to you in the space that follows. What are God's words for you? When you are through writing your letter, place it in the envelope you were given and address it to yourself. When you return to the gathering place, place the envelope in the basket you will find there.

Day 3: Morning Watch

> But we have this treasure in jars of clay to show that this all-surpassing power is from God and not from us. (2 Corinthians 4:7)

• Sit quietly with the "dough" of your life—or take it for a slow, reflective walk. Be attentive! This is a *holy hour!*

• Make a list—mental or written—of all the ways you feel frail, powerless, empty, little, and so forth.

• Ponder all the masks you wear to keep your frailty hidden.

• Now look at these pieces of frailty and ask yourself this question: In what way could each of these pieces of frailty be a gift for my ministry?

• Prayerfully consider the following scripture readings:

2 Corinthians 4:1-8
2 Corinthians 12:1-10
Matthew 18:1-4

There are times in each of our lives when we feel, and therefore are, frail—frail, fragile, about to break. We have forgotten whose we are. We are out of touch with our Maker.

When that happens to me, I have learned to do something about it by being with those who are childlike.

• I take my children and we visit those shut in homes or nursing homes. I love to watch my children as they comfortably talk, tease, and care for the elderly. They encourage me! They are brave!

• I enjoy teaching a class of mentally challenged adults on Sundays from time to time. Each time they hear the stories of Jesus, they are filled with wonder, awe, and faith.

• I visit with persons who need me:
  a young mother with a newborn baby

a widow
someone hurt, lonely, or dying

• I do something nice for someone completely anonymously.

When I do these things, I remember . . .
God made me
God made all of us
God loves us
God looks after us

Journal as you are moved.

Windows of Prayer

Day 2: Morning Watch

I want their hearts to be encouraged and united in love, so that they may have all the riches of assured understanding and have the knowledge of God's mystery, that is, Christ himself, in whom are hidden all the treasures of wisdom and knowledge. (Colossians 2:2-3 NRSV)

• Who first guided you into the paths of the knowledge of faith? Write about that person in the space that follows.

• Read: Exodus 3:3-7. Now read the poem below. Just like Moses, we are on a spiritual journey, attracted to the mystery of faith. We seek a vision of God. Where or what was your most recent "burning bush"? Are you allowing yourself to be led? Should you be led? Are you frightened of the journey? Record your thoughts in your journal.

A burning bush?
No, not me.
I did smell your faithfulness
forest of giant redwoods.
I did feel your presence
in the wind.
I heard your voice
in the music.
I saw your hand in
the sunset.
You are all around me!

• Reflect on these words and their meaning for you in this moment:
It is in the moment of contemplation, of openness to the sacred, that we meet Christ. In the mystery of the union with God, we are asked to confront and to comprehend. The gift of an encounter with Christ leads us to respond; that is our responsibility.

• Pause to look at the many green things that are a part of the earth. If you can find flowers or buds, touch them; smell them. Let them speak to you of the mystery of faith.

• Look at the inner garden of your life. Where do the waters of life flow freely? Where do you see signs of growth, life, birth, hope, change, and nurturing? How is God coaxing life *out* of you? What is being raised to life *in* you?

Day 3: Morning Watch

"I tell you this, any good thing you do for one of the least of these, my brothers and sisters, however humble, you do it for me." (Matthew 25:40 NCV)

When renowned writer Martin Buber was asked "Where is God?", he made a fascinating response. He did not give the cliché answer "God is everywhere." Rather, he said, "God is found in relationships." When you and I relate to one another in an authentic way, that is sacred; and God is there. This is what Jesus meant in Matthew 25 when he said: "I tell you this—any good thing you do for one of the least of these, my brothers and sisters, however humble, you do it for me" (NCV).

Nothing pleases God more than to see us loving and caring for one another; and nothing hurts God more than to see us harming one another.

In his book *When All You've Ever Wanted Isn't Enough* (New York: Summit Books, 1986), Rabbi Harold Kushner tells about sitting on a beach one summer day and watching a little boy and girl building a sand castle by the water's edge. It was an elaborate sand castle with gates and towers and moats and windows. Just when they had nearly finished their project, a big wave came and knocked it down, reducing it to a heap of wet sand. Rabbi Kushner said he expected the children to burst into tears, devastated by what had happened to all their hard work; but instead of crying, they laughed and laughed and ran up the shore, holding hands, and then sat down to build another castle. Rabbi Kushner then wrote that those two children had taught him an important lesson; that all the things in our lives, all the complicated structures we spend so much time and energy creating, are built on sand. It is only our relationships with other people that endure. Sooner or later, the waves may come along and knock down what we have worked so hard to build up. When that happens, we will be able to laugh only if we have somebody's hand to hold.

There's no doubt about it: Relationships are extremely important.

- Where are you in your relationship with yourself? Do you feel good about yourself—about who you are and where you are going?

- Where are you in your relationships with your family? Have you been neglecting your family? Do you need to spend more time with your children/spouse/parents?

- Where are you in your relationships with other people?

- Where are you in your relationship to God? Are you really listening? Are you hearing God's call?

- Close your Morning Watch with prayer—silent, spoken, or written.

Becoming: A Journey of Spirituality for Women

Day 2: Morning Watch

> For it was you who formed my inward parts;
> you knit me together in my mother's womb.
> I praise you, for I am fearfully and wonderfully made.
> Wonderful are your works; that I know very well. (Psalm 139:13-14 NRSV)

Come and listen with the One who held you in his hand and formed your very being.

> When I was young, one of my favorite television shows was *The Invisible Man*. Do you remember it? Have you ever felt invisible? Just try being new! I remember when our oldest son went to a new junior high school. I knew how he felt the moment he stepped off the bus. My heart ached for him. He said, "Mom, I just felt invisible all day."

There is One with whom we are never invisible. There is One who loves us no matter what. There is One who inspires love within us. There is One with which we are always "at home."

• When was a time you felt as if you were "home"?

• What alleviates "homesickness" in your life?

• How can you become more filled with God's love?

Day 3: Morning Watch

> I have called you by name, you are mine. When you pass through the waters, I will be with you; and through the rivers, they shall not overwhelm you; when you walk through fire you shall not be burned, and the flame shall not consume you. For I am the lord your God, the Holy One of Israel, your Savior. . . . Because you are precious in my sight, and honored, and I love you. . . . Do not fear, for I am with you. (Isaiah 43:1-5 NRSV)

• Can you imagine there is no place you can go where God is not? Do you believe that? God holds you in the palm of his hand. What trials have you experienced? What fires have you experienced? How have you grown in the midst of them?

• Spend the remainder of your Morning Watch meditating on what the above verses from Isaiah mean for you. Summarize your thoughts.

God's Simple Path

Day 2: Morning Watch

Good Morning! As you awake this morning, PRAISE GOD for the gift of rest!

Does music move your heart and soul? What are the hymns of your childhood? Are there melodies that carry you to people? . . . to places? . . . to churches? . . . to moments suspended in time? How many synonymous names for Jesus can you list?

Do you feel the presence of Jesus? Do you visually see our sweet Savior? This morning, spend some time meditating on the name of Jesus. Listen for God to speak to you about his wonderful Son.

• Read John 14:13-14; 15:16; 16:23-24. Praying in the name of Jesus is our privilege by way of the cross.

BE OPEN TODAY TO THE MESSAGE OF JESUS!
HAVE A GREAT DAY OF FELLOWSHIP!

Day 3: Morning Watch

In the morning, O LORD, you hear my voice. (Psalm 5:3*a*)

• Start your morning watch by stilling your mind. If you have trouble doing this, meditate on these words:

In the morning, O LORD, you hear my voice;
in the morning I lay my requests before you
and wait in expectation.
(Psalm 5:3)

Be still and cool in thy own mind and spirit.—George Fox (1624–91)

• Psalm 46 has a heading of "Alamoth." Some scholars believe that this word is a technical term for *women's voices*. Read this psalm in first person singular rather than first person plural, as it is written. "God is *my* refuge and strength. . . ." Can you hear women chanting these verses?

• In her book *A Simple Path,* Mother Teresa said we all must take the time to be silent and to contemplate, especially those who live in cities where everything moves so fast. In her own life, she began every prayer in silence. It was her belief that God speaks in the silence of the heart. She said that God is the friend of silence. We need to listen to God, because it's not what we say but what God says to us and through us that matters. Mother Teresa's faith was based on the fact that prayer feeds the soul. As blood is to the body, so prayer is to the soul. It gives us a clean and pure heart. A clean heart can feel, see, and respond to the love of God in others. Begin a time of prayer in silence now. Listen for God in the silence of your heart.

• Prayer is a journey in which you meet God. Remember the story of Jonah? He began a journey to get away from God and, instead, he ran into him. The sea is a wonderful image. It is full of mystery, uncertainty, and life. In his book *Care of the Soul,* Thomas Moore writes: "To set out on the sea is to risk security, yet that risky path may be the only way to the Father." What does this statement mean to you at this point in your life?

• Journal as the Spirit leads you in response to the following quote:

Work of sight is done. Now do heart work on the pictures within you. —Rainer Maria Rilke

Power for Living

Day 2: Morning Watch

• Read the following words from the author of this retreat:

> I remember a vacation we took one summer in New Mexico. The children were small and it was easy to drive at night while they slept. The night sky was just unbelievable. I have never seen anything like it! The stars appeared to be very close to us, and there were so many of them. It was a beautiful sight. Then I remembered this phrase from the book of Philippians: " . . . in which you shine like stars in the world" (2:15 NRSV). I began to wonder: Do I shine like a star? What makes me shine?

I remember a vacation we took one summer in New Mexico. The children were small and it was easy to drive at night while they slept. The night sky was just unbelievable. I have never seen anything like it! The stars appeared to be very close to us, and there were so many of them. It was a beautiful sight. Then I remembered this phrase from the book of Philippians: " . . .in which you shine like stars in the world" (2:15 NRSV). I began to wonder: Do I shine like a star? What makes me shine?

What makes you shine like a star?

• Read the following passage and reflect on its meaning for your life. What changes do you need to make?

Do all things without murmuring or arguing, so that you may be blameless and innocent, children of God . . . in which you shine like stars in the world. (Philippians 2:14-15 NRSV)

Day 3: Morning Watch

Morning has broken like the first morning!
Praise for the singing! Praise for the morning!
> —from "Morning Has Broken"

• Consider Lamentations 3:21-26. It is good to be silent and to wait upon the Lord. This is a sacred time. Wait for God.

Alone
All-one
Alone with God
All one with God
Being alone with God
Being all one with God
All one
Alone.

This morning, spend time being "all one" with God. May your soul be filled!

If Only I Had More Time!

Day 2: Morning Watch

For it is time to seek the LORD. (Hosea 10:12)

- This morning you are to take a "parable walk." Weather permitting, walk outside until something of nature or the world catches your attention. (In the event of inclement weather, walk throughout the building where you are meeting, or in a particular room, until some object catches your attention.) Then meditate on the significance of this object.
- Reflect on these questions and record your thoughts in your journal:

Why did this particular object catch your attention?
What significance does this object hold in your life?
What Bible verse, if any, comes to mind?
What effect does thinking about this object have on you?

Day 3: Morning Watch

Your throne, O God, will last forever and ever. (Psalm 45:6)

Sometimes I consider myself as a blank canvas just waiting to be painted.
Sometimes I consider myself as quilt that is yet to be designed.
Sometimes I consider myself as a piece of music that is yet to be written.

This morning, meditate and imagine that you are in front of the Lord God. What parts are added? What parts are cut away? What is your perfect image? Is it the same as God's? Why or why not? What does this have to do with time? Journal about these things.

Joyful Heart— Dancing Spirit

Day 2: Morning Watch

I know your works. Look, I have set before you an open door, which no one is able to shut. I know that you have but little power, and yet you have kept my word and have not denied my name. (Revelation 3:8)

• Read Revelation 3:8 silently. Ask yourself: What does this say to my life?

• List three barriers that keep you from being completely open to God.

1.
2.
3.

• How can you break these barriers and open yourself to God?

• Read and reflect on Psalm 46:10.

• Write your closing prayer.

Day 3: Morning Watch

Write Psalm 151 in the space below. (This is *not* a typo!) True, there is no Psalm 151 in the Bible. You are to write an *original* psalm! Allow yourself to enjoy this powerful learning and devotional exercise.)

Notes

◆

Seeking Growth

1. Oswald Chambers, *My Utmost for His Highest* (Grand Rapids: Discovery House, 1935), 213.
2. Richard Foster, *Prayer: Finding the Heart's True Home* (San Francisco: HarperSanFrancisco, 1992), 174.
3. Charles Ewing Brown, *The Meaning of Salvation* (Anderson, Ind.: Gospel Trumpet Company, 1944), 192-93.

The Tapestry

1. See the song "Tapestry" by Carole King (New York: Screen Gems-Columbia Music, 1971).
2. Anne Morrow Lindbergh, *Gift from the Sea* (New York: Pantheon Press, 1955), 25-28.
3. Anne Ortlund, *Disciplines of the Beautiful Woman* (Waco, Tex.: Word Publishing, 1977), 129.

Discovering My Spiritual Gifts

1. Macrina Wiederkehr, *Tree Full of Angels* (New York: Harper & Row, 1988), 27.

Getting First Things First—And Keeping Them There!

1. Oswald Chambers, *My Utmost for His Highest* (Grand Rapids: Discovery House, 1935), 9.
2. Anne Morrow Lindbergh, *Gift from the Sea* (New York: Pantheon Press, 1955), 29.
3. Deena Metzger, *Writing for Your Life: A Guide and Companion to the Inner Worlds* (San Francisco: HarperSanFrancico, 1992), 254-55.

Come to the Well

1. Robert A. Raines, "My Frail Raft" in *Living the Questions* (Waco, Tex.: Word Publishing, 1976), 74-75.
2. Macrina Wiederkehr, *The Song of the Seed: A Monastic Way of Tending the Soul* (San Francisco: HarperSanFrancisco, 1995), 36.

Windows of Prayer

1. See Macrina Wiederkehr, *Song of the Seed: A Monastic Way of Tending the Soul* (San Francisco: HarperSanFrancisco, 1995), 10-20.
2. David Keirsey and Marilyn Bates, *Please Understand Me* (Del Mar, Calif.: Prometheus Nemesis Books, 1978), 5-10.
3. Ibid., 11.
4. Dag Hammerskjold, "Prayer for a New Heart" in *Markings* (New York: Alfred A. Knopf, 1964), 214.
5. Christina G. Rossetti, "For Illumination" in *The United Methodist Hymnal* (Nashville: The United Methodist Publishing House, 1989), 477.

Becoming: A Journey of Spirituality for Women

1. Dietrich Bonhoffer, *Life Together* (New York: HarperCollins, 1954), 85.
2. Anthony De Mello, *Wellsprings: A Book of Spiritual Exercises* (Garden City, N.Y.: Doubleday, 1984), 25.
3. Mother Teresa, *A Simple Path* (New York: Ballentine, 1995), 25.

God's Simple Path

1. Sister Wendy Beckett, *Meditations on Silence* (London: Dorling Kindersley, 1995), 8.

2. Mother Teresa, *A Simple Path* (New York: Ballentine, 1995) , 7.

3. Macrina Wiederkehr, *Song of the Seed: A Monastic Way of Tending the Soul* (San Francisco: HarperSanFrancisco, 1995), xv.

4. Henri Nouwen, *With Open Hands* (Notre Dame, Ind.: Ave Maria Press, 1972), 36, 44.

5. Richard Foster, *Prayer: Finding the Heart's True Home* (San Francisco: HarperSanFrancisco, 1992), 123.

6. Sue Monk Kidd, *All Things Are Possible* (Norwalk, Conn.: C. R. Gibson, 1979), 23.

7. Mother Teresa, *A Simple Path,* 79.

8. Bennet Cerf, "The Gift" in *Chicken Soup for the Soul: 101 Stories to Open the Heart and Rekindle the Spirit,* ed. Jack Canfield and Mark Victor Hansen (Deerfield Beach, Fla.: Health Communications, 1993), 24.

9. Mother Teresa, *A Simple Path,* 93.

10. Ibid.

11. Sue Monk Kidd, *All Things Are Possible,* 23.

12. Mother Teresa, *Words to Love By* (New York: Phoenix Press, 1984), 76.

13. Ann Weems, "Feeding Sheep" in *Searching for Shalom: Resources for Creative Worship* (Louisville: Westminster John Knox Press, 1991), 47.

14. Anthony De Mello, *One Minute Wisdom* (New York: Doubleday, 1986), 38.

15. Anne Frank, *Anne Frank: The Diary of a Young Girl* (New York: Random House, 1952), 278.

Power for Living

1. Linda Hollies, *Inner Healing for Broken Vessels: Seven Steps to a Woman's Way of Healing* (Nashville: Upper Room Books, 1992), 20.

2. Helen Bruch Pearson, *Do What You Have the Power to Do: Studies of Six New Testament Women* (Nashville: Upper Room Books, 1992), 40.

3. Ibid., 51.

4. Ibid., 57.

5. Ibid., 59-60.

6. The Storyteller's Creed (Anonymous).

7. Helen Bruch Pearson, *Do What You Have the Power to Do,* 73.

If Only I Had More Time!

1. Sue Bender, *Everyday Sacred: A Woman's Journey Home* (San Francisco: HarperSanFrancisco, 1995), 12-13.

2. Mother Teresa, *A Simple Path* (New York: Ballentine, 1995), xxxii.

Joyful Heart—Dancing Spirit

1. Sue Monk Kidd, *When the Heart Waits: Spiritual Direction for Life's Sacred Questions* (San Francisco: HarperSanFrancisco, 1990), 6.

2. Ibid., 47.

3. Adapted from Maria Harris, *Dance of the Spirit* (New York: Bantam, 1989), 115.

Additional Resources

Books

Delbene, Ron. *Alone with God: A Guide for Personal Retreats*. Nashville: Upper Room Books, 1992.

Foster, Richard. *Devotional Classics*. San Francisco: HarperSanFrancisco, 1993.

_____. *Prayer: Finding the Heart's True Home*. San Francisco: HarperSanFrancisco, 1992.

Gire, Ken. *The Reflective Life: Becoming More Spiritually Sensitive to the Everyday Moments of Life*. Colorado Springs, Colo.: Chariot Victor Publishing, 1998.

Hollies, Linda. *Inner Healing for Broken Vessels: Seven Steps to a Woman's Way of Healing*. Nashville: Upper Room Books, 1992.

Job, Rueben. *A Guide to Retreat for All God's Shepherds*. Nashville: Abingdon Press, 1994.

_____. *Spiritual Life in the Congregation: A Guide for Retreats*. Nashville: Upper Room Books, 1997.

Keating, Thomas. *Reawakenings*. New York: Crossroad, 1992.

Kidd, Sue Monk. *God's Joyful Surprise*. San Francisco: HarperSanFrancisco, 1989.

Klug, Lyn. *Soul Weavings: A Gathering of Women's Prayers*. Minneapolis: Augsburg Fortress, 1996.

Pearson, Helen Bruch. *Do What You Have the Power To Do: Studies of Six New Testament Women*. Nashville: Upper Room Books, 1992.

Rupp, Joyce. *Fresh Bread and Other Gifts of Spiritual Nourishment*. Notre Dame, Ind.: Ave Maria Press, 1985.

Watson, Lillian. *Light from Many Lamps: A Treasury of Inspiration*. New York: Fireside, 1988.

Weems, Renita. *Just a Sister Away*. San Diego: LuraMedia, 1988.

Wiederkehr, Macrina. *Seasons of Your Heart: Prayers and Reflections*. San Francisco: HarperSanFrancisco, 1991.

Periodicals

Two periodicals that may be helpful are *Alive Now: Strengthening the Faith Life of Groups and Individuals,* and *Weavings,* both published by The Upper Room, Nashville, Tenn.

Music

Clawson, Cynthia. *Prayer and Plainsong*. Calla Lilly Productions, 1995.

Haley, Colleen. *From the Heart*. Seed Productions, 1999.

Jones, Michael. Narada Productions:
After the Rain, 1988.
Pianoscapes, 1985.
Seascapes, 1984.

Lanz, David. Narada Productions:
Beloved, 1995.
Heartsounds, 1983.
Nightfall, 1985.
Sacred Road, 1996.

Winston, George. Windham Hill:
December, 1984.
Forest, 1994